Memoirs of a Yukon Priest

Segundo Llorente, S.J., 1906–1989
Ordained June, 1934

Memoirs of a Yukon Priest

Segundo Llorente, S.J.

Georgetown University Press
Washington, D.C.

10 9 8 7 6 5 4 3 2

Library of Congress Cataloging-in-Publication Data

Llorente, Segundo.
    Memoirs of a Yukon priest / Segundo Llorente
        p.   cm.
    ISBN 0-87840-494-5 : $17.95
    1. Llorente, Segundo.   2. Eskimos--Yukon Territory--Missions.
  3. Jesuits--Missions--Yukon Territory.   4. Catholic Church-
  -Missions--Yukon Territory.   5. Missionaries--Yukon Territory-
  -Biography.   I. Title.
  -E99.E7L565   1990
  266' .2'092--dc20   89-27434
  [B]

Contents

Foreword   ix

Preface   xiii

1   The Beginning   1

2   The Inside Passage   6

3   The Alaska Railroad   13

4   The Yukon River   21

5   Traveling Down River   30

6   Welcome to the Akulurak Mission   37

7   Akulurak Stories   47

8   Crossing the Line: Kotzebue   59

9   Kotzebue and Beyond   70

10   Bury Me Next to Fr. Jette   82

11   The Winter Trail   91

12   Quiet Nunakhock   108

13   Summer in Akulurak   117

14   Bethel and Beyond   121

15   Holy Cross and McGrath   133

16   Starting Over   147

17   Alakanuk   160

18   Emmonak   168

19   Eskimo Life and Lore   177

20   Kwiguk and Saint Marys   193

21   The Alaska State Legislature   201

22   Nome   211

Epilogue: More Missionaries   224

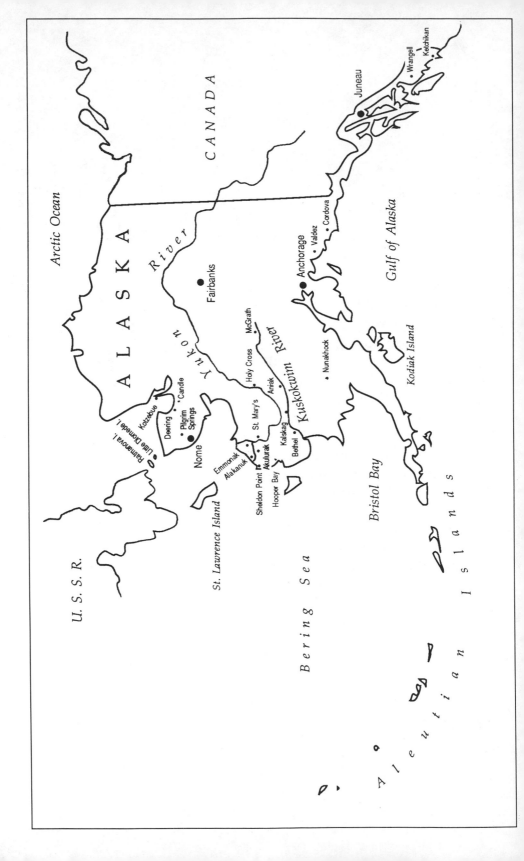

Chronology

November 18, 1906	Born near León, Spain
1917–1918	Attended pre-seminary school
1919–1923	Attended seminary of the Diocese of León
1924–1925	Trained at Jesuit novitiate at Carrion de los Condes in Castile
1926–1930	Studied Latin and philosophy at Salamanca and Granada
1930–1931	Studied English and taught Spanish at Gonzaga University, Spokane, Washington
1931–1934	Studied theology at St. Mary's, Kansas
June, 1934	Ordained Jesuit priest
1934–1935	Completed theology studies at Alma College, Los Gatos, California, then left for Alaska
1935–1937	Served at the Akulurak mission
1938–1941	Served at the Kotzebue mission; said Mass and gave retreats in Candle, Deering and Pilgrim Springs
1941–1948	Served at the Akulurak mission again, with trips to Hooper Bay and Nunakhock
1948–1951	Served at the Bethel mission on the Kuskokwim River, with visits to Holy Cross, Kalskag, Aniak and McGrath
1951–1963	Served at the Akulurak mission and district headquarters at Alakanuk, on the other side of the Yukon
1956	Became a U.S. citizen in Nome
November, 1960	Elected by write-in vote to serve in Alaska's newly formed House of Representatives
1961–1964	Served two terms in the state legislature in Juneau
1964–1966	Served as pastor in Nome
1966–1967	Served as pastor in Fairbanks
1967–1970	Served as pastor in Cordova
1970–1975	Served as pastor in Anchorage
1975–1981	Left Alaska, worked with Hispanics at Our Lady of Fatima Parish in Moses Lake, Washington
1981–1984	Served as assistant pastor at St. Joseph's Church, Pocatello, Idaho
1984–1989	Served as hospital chaplain in Lewiston, Idaho
January 26, 1989	Died at Jesuit House, Gonzaga University, Spokane, Washington

Foreword

The first Jesuit priests arrived in northern Alaska in 1887. At the time
Alaska was a raw, undeveloped territory purchased from Russia only
two decades earlier. Means of travel were what they had been for
countless generations. Communications systems were primitive at
best. By the time Father Segundo Llorente came to northern Alaska,
in 1935, many changes, many improvements had taken place. Still, he
was not too late to get a generous taste of what the early pioneers, the
first missionaries had gone through.

In 1935 sternwheelers still plied the major rivers in the summer
and dog sleds the trackless snows in the winter. Snowmachines, bush
planes, and modern jets were still wonders of the future—as were
radio, telephone, and telecommunications.

Llorente regarded himself as a link between the old and the new.
He entered the land of the Indians and Eskimos on river boats; he left
Alaska for the last time on a jet. He knew an isolation that bordered
on the absolute; he lived to see Alaskan communities joined together
by reliable telephone systems, radio and television. He personally
knew some of the founding fathers of the Catholic Eskimo and Indian
missions of northern Alaska; he was to be exercised by many of the
changes occasioned by the Second Vatican Council.

Moreover, he saw the Territory of Alaska become the forty-ninth
state of the Union. The Alaska he first entered was a Vicariate
Apostolic under the jurisdiction of one bishop. The Alaska he left
forty years later was an Ecclesiastical Province with the Archdiocese
of Anchorage and Dioceses of Juneau and Fairbanks. Where he found
80,000 people in 1935, he left behind close to half a million in 1975.
In his *Memoirs,* Llorente sweeps the reader along with him as he, the
church in Alaska, and the Territory of Alaska cross a great threshold.

"I was encouraged by my friends," we read in Llorente's preface
to his *Memoirs,* "to write these memories (and to tell it as it

was) . . . "Along with Oregon Province archivists at the time, Clifford A. Carroll, S.J., and Richard J. Sisk, S.J., I was one of those privileged friends who, in my voluminous correspondence and in various conversations with Llorente, repeatedly urged him to tell in writing his life's story for the general public. Only an autobiography would do in his case. His singular personality and experiences could be captured and communicated only by the man himself. At the time, however, he no longer had much desire to do writing of any kind.

From Moses Lake, Washington, he wrote to me in 1979: "Concerning my translating into Spanish your life of Fr. Lafortune, please take notice . . . that typing tires me. I have done so much during my lifetime that my whole body rebels, especially the fingers. If I could have a secretary that would type Spanish correctly, then I would take your book, sit in a comfy chair, and while my eyes would look at your prose, my lips would utter refined Spanish sentences between sips of orange juice. But, as it is, typing has become a heavy cross for me. . . . Writing is an all-consuming activity, an exhausting one. Reading is a pleasure. Readers should bear this in mind."

Nevertheless, in spite of his reluctance to write, Llorente, yielding to the entreaties of his friends, did produce an autobiographical sketch of a kind. "I typed," he wrote me in June 1981, "what I saw and heard in my many years in Alaska. I have no idea what may become of said manuscript." The manuscript was a considerable disappointment to us. It recounted mostly objective facts. It was flat, uninspired and uninspiring. It lacked the colorful, witty, sparkling, yet broad and deep, personality that we knew to be Father Segundo Llorente. The manuscript was filed in the Province Archives at Gonzaga University, Spokane, Washington. That seemed to be the end of the matter.

Great, then, was my surprise when in October 1989, John B. Breslin, S.J., of Georgetown University Press asked me if I would consider writing a foreword to the *Memoirs*. I was not sure what we were talking about and asked to see a copy of said *Memoirs*. Great, again—and very pleasant—was my surprise when I read what was a wholly new manuscript, written in the genuine, inimitable Llorente style: an oral style, an outpour, a torrent of words rich in concrete, vivid detail, saturated with personal opinions, reflections, observations. When Llorente did the talking, it was always a pleasure to do the listening.

From Llorente's religious superior in Lewiston, Idaho, John J. Morse, S.J., I learned that Llorente had spent long hours at the typewriter during the final months of his life. Who inspired him, what inspired him, drove him to produce a new, a lengthy account of his forty years in Alaska, we will never know. His own brother, Father Amando Llorente, S.J., to whom he handed the finished manuscript in the summer of 1988, does not know. It was Father Amando who brought it to the attention of Georgetown University Press. The published *Memoirs* are sure to inform, entertain, edify many.

When death overtook Father Segundo Llorente, it did not do so unexpectedly, or as an unwelcome spectre. Ten years before he died, he wrote to me: "In the meantime we grow older and come closer to the Pearly Gates where Saint Peter will turn his magnifying glass on our poor trembling souls. But it won't be that old renegade Pete who will judge us, but our Lord Himself in person aided by our blessed Mother who will stand there also to put in a good word for us, priests of her Son the High Priest. And the Lord will be kind to us and will take us to Himself and bury us in His divine Heart. May you and I enter that place and be immersed in God to live His divine life forever. Amen." Six years later in 1985, he wrote: "I have begun my 51st year as a priest and my 62nd in the Society. How much longer? It can't be far away now. May our dear Lord temper His justice with mercy. Amen."

In mid-November 1988, in Lewiston, Idaho, where Father Llorente was still active as chaplain at St. Joseph's Hospital, he collapsed after struggling through Mass. He was found to have cancer of the lymph glands. Told that it was treatable, he said: "No; I'm eighty-three years old. I want to meet St. Ignatius and his first companions." This he did, at Jesuit House, Gonzaga University, Spokane, Washington, on January 26, 1989.

The passing of this exuberant, joyous, modern-day mystic from sunny Spain was noted in high places. In Alaska's capital, Juneau, where Llorente had served two terms in the state legislature, he was honored by the Sixteenth Alaska Legislature with a special *In Memoriam* document. This states that "he served with distinction and was loved by all who worked with him." He is cited, too, for being "a perceptive and knowledgeable legislator who gave outstanding service during his term."

In the nation's captital, Llorente's close friend and admirer,

Senator Ernest Gruening, after pointing out that Llorente had made history inasmuch as he was the first Roman Catholic priest to hold elected office in a U.S. state, asked that the lengthy article that appeared in *Time* magazine when Llorente was elected unanimously to the House of Representatives of Alaska as a write-in candidate, be printed in the *Congressional Record*. There being no objections, the article was ordered to be printed in the *Record*.

Louis L. Renner, S.J.
Editor, *Alaskan Shepherd*

Preface

This book is a modest attempt to keep alive the missionary work done in northern Alaska from 1887 when the first Jesuit priests arrived till the Second World War and thereafter. The Alaska of today is a far cry from the Alaska the first missionaries saw. Alaska today is the forty-ninth state of the Union with two senators and one representative in Washington who see to it that the formerly so-called "ice box" and "penal colony" is treated with the respect and dignity granted by the U.S. Constitution. Add to this the discovery of huge deposits of oil and you have the ingredients for an Alaska modernized and with tremendous potentials. Yet, regardless of all improvements, the long Alaska winters remain as cold as ever.

I was encouraged by my friends to write these memories (and to tell it as it was) because I had the privilege of living with the early men as well as with the recent ones in the forty years I spent in Alaska (1935–75), thus being a link between the old and the new. Nobody else seemed to want to write, so I agreed to do it.

I read many diaries and wrote many myself covering the doings in those remote and largely isolated areas with their small settlements. I talked with priests and sisters and brothers and discussed the pros and cons of the then prevailing policies. Alaska became like my mother, I must say.

This book is written by memory. Here I tell what I saw and what I heard and what I did and what I read about the Land of the Midnight Sun on those long winter nights when a book can save a man from going temporarily insane.

The reader will get an idea of the conditions under which the missionaries on those Arctic regions had to live in their efforts to implant the faith by walking in the steps of the Master.

Segundo Llorente, S.J.

1

The Beginning

I was born on November 18, 1906, near León, a city in northwestern Spain. It was Sunday, I was told, and on Thursday I was baptized. My parents celebrated the event by treating the invited guests to a turkey dinner with all the trimmings washed down with glasses of sparkling *tinto* wine from the family vineyards. I was followed by six brothers and two sisters. Those were times when families in an environment markedly Catholic were large and healthy.

When I was ten (yes, ten), I was sent to a preseminary school under a young bulky priest who made his living teaching Latin to youngsters who might later apply to the major seminary of the Diocese of León. We were about thirty boys spread out over four years. The main academic fare was Latin eight hours a day for eight months of the year for four years. To break the Latin monotony we had also geography, history, and Spanish literature.

The priest was my father's cousin. He adhered strongly to the belief that "learning has a bloody entrance," so he thoroughly enjoyed beating us daily and mercilessly. May the good Lord have mercy on his soul.

My father was sure that what the priest was doing was good for us, so he delivered me to his cousin with these very words: "Here is the kid. If you kill him, give me the hide." I stood there helpless, like a lamb led to the slaughterhouse.

Four years later I entered the major seminary. From October 1 to June 1, I wore a black cassock and a biretta. We were sent home for the summer. Toward the end of my second year in the seminary, a fellow seminarian confided to me that he was thinking of going to the Jesuits and to please keep it under my hat. Who were those Jesuits? I had never heard of them, yet two months later I was received in the Jesuit novitiate at Carrion de los Condes in the heart of Castile.

Here there was no nonsense. Up at five every day; lights out at ten every night. We were forty-six novices, but soon the numbers went up to sixty. My spiritual journey in the Society of Jesus began with a thirty-day retreat in total silence given by an experienced master, a holy Jesuit in his late forties.

Every day we had four meditations of one hour each, plus one lengthy lecture on the matters being proposed for those meditations. I was, then, submitted to a grand total of 150 meditations within that prodigious month.

In the middle of it I became a sweet seventeen, with wavy hair and all. The purpose of the retreat was to wash with ardent tears the crimes of my youth, to reflect on the life, passion, death, and resurrection of Christ, and thereby to fall desperately in love with Him. *Desperately* meant to develop a spiritual climate in the soul that fostered a fascination, a real infatuation, with Christ, and to be ready to be sent anywhere on earth to preach the gospel and to die a martyr's death if God would grant such an undeserved favor.

One novice was so carried away by religious fervor that he shouted out, asking where could he die for Christ. The master answered that here, right here within these very portals, we kill for Christ, but that we kill with pins and needles, that is, the attrition of an ascetic daily life.

On the walls of the corridor of our novitiate hung huge paintings of heroic Jesuits of past ages. I recall one depicting the three Jesuits martyred in Nagasaki in 1597 together with twenty-three other religious and lay people. It showed a long row of crosses. On each cross there was a Christian, tied securely and looking up to heaven. The executioners (Japanese men with pigtails) held long sharp lances. Some three or four lances were already entering through the chests and coming out through the backs of the crucified ones. To make it really ghastly, the executioners were smiling as though they were enjoying it. I must admit that that painting almost killed my vocation. Passing through that corridor I used to feel my ribs instinctively to make sure that there was no lance around.

In the two years of the novitiate several young men left and went home. I went on to take my vows and to move on in the regular studies: to Salamanca one year for more Latin, to Granada for three years of philosophy and sciences.

In those years as a Jesuit in Spain I came to the conclusion that God was calling me to be a missionary in northern Alaska. Since Spain already had enough priests, I had to go beyond the seas to help where priests were scarce.

Africa was much too hot. China had impossible characters. Japan was out of the question. The lepers of Culion in the Philippines were fine for elderly priests who had not many years to live anyway. The Indians of the Amazon River were all right, but there were boas so big that they swallowed crocodiles, and I was allergic to poisonous snakes, constrictor snakes, and all manner of snakes. The many islands of Micronesia had some attraction, but one had to be constantly in canoes between islands and I would be forever seasick. I preferred to move on solid ground instead of dancing at the mercy of the waves.

Why not India? Well, I had read about the Brahmans, their Sanskrit, their philosophical subtleties, and I had also seen pictures of fakirs sleeping or trying to sleep on metal beds with sharp spikes sticking out several inches. That definitely was not for me.

So by way of elimination I came to the Alaska missions. They appealed to me. It was almost love at first sight. I fancied being found frozen somewhere on the trail. Now that was a clean death, a painless death buried under a clean mantle of pure snow falling from heaven. That was it! And it was also a martyr's death, naturally. And Alaska had no native priests, so I was needed there instantly.

Or so I figured. The more I dwelt on the subject, the more convinced I was that God was calling me to the Arctic. I figured that it would be twenty-five years of active ministry that would wear me to a frazzle, and then I would just die. My mouth actually watered at the very thought.

I was twenty when I began to press my superiors in earnest to allow me to go to Alaska. Now, at twenty-three, I was told to go ahead with my plans. My plans could not be more simple: to study theology in America and be ordained there, then to go to the Land of the Midnight Sun.

I arrived in Spokane, Washington, on October 1, 1930, and was told that I was to spend one year in Gonzaga University learning English and helping in the classes of Spanish. It was a very difficult year for me. Here I was, full of energy, with a perfect command of Spanish and Latin which did not help me one bit because I did not know any English. My confreres at recreation were having a good time cracking jokes and laughing while I stood there with a silly grin, looking like a perfect idiot.

Then English itself made me very angry. I had tackled other grammars: Spanish, Latin, French, Greek, and even two semesters of Hebrew. Those were grammars—real grammars. But English, by comparison, did not even have a grammar.

Take the word *work*. It is a noun and a verb, an infinitive, a present, and a future. And I work, you work, they work, I will work, I did work, I go to work. Those four letters could be manipulated for practically anything connected with the operation of work.

Then the spelling! Then the pronunciation, where almost every word has to be learned separately! I can teach people to read Spanish in half an hour, once and for all. Not so with English. Take the word *laughter*. But if you put an *s* before it, then you have *slaughter* with an entirely different sound.

Then came the world of slang, a new language altogether and widely used: shake a leg; make tracks; get lost; beat it; scram. Then the jokes! The cartoons! Oh, Lord, this was too much for me.

The only person in the university who knew Spanish was Fr. Julius La Motta, who was a linguist. I would go to his room once a week just to hear myself speak Spanish. He was the type of man who spoke very little.

March came along and I was still unable to communicate intelligently. By nature I had been inclined to monopolize the conversation. Not now. I was living in a vacuum. Since nature abhors vacuums, I had to seek fulfillment somewhere. Not finding it among men, I turned to the Lord, who did not disappoint me. I made it a habit to go to Saint Aloysius Church on the campus, and there I conversed with the Lord in the blessed Sacrament to my heart's content. He knew Spanish better than I did, so we two had a good time. But that implied faith, deep faith, because the Lord never spoke audibly to me (a good thing He didn't!), but the soul hears, and that is enough.

By July my English had improved considerably. We went then to our villa in Hayden Lake, Idaho, where I learned to swim. In August I took the train for Chicago, Kansas City, and Saint Mary's in Kansas, where I was to study theology.

In my class we were fifty-one, and I was the youngest. There were six Mexicans, one German, one from India, and myself from Spain. The rest, as I remember, were all good red-blooded Americans speaking the best English in the land. This enabled me to become proficient in English and at the same time to go out for long walks with the Mexicans and talk and shout and sing in the best Spanish imaginable.

Some people think that Mexicans speak an inferior Spanish. The poor immigrants who cross the Rio Grande and smuggle themselves into the U.S.A. do speak Spanish poorly. But the educated Mexicans speak Spanish like the best-educated Spaniard in Madrid, itself. Not only that, they still keep some beautiful words that are now obsolete in Spain—and Spain is the poorer for that.

In June of 1934 the fifty-one of us were ordained priests and, to my knowledge, no one left the priesthood. It was clearly understood that a priest is forever, and we have acted accordingly. After my ordination I was sent to Lewiston, Idaho, to help during the summer months in a Jesuit parish, and there I was initiated in the administration of the Sacraments.

In September I was sent to California to finish my theology in the recently built Alma College, affiliated with the University of Santa Clara. On June 1, 1935, my studies in the Society came to an end.

Now a full-fledged priest, I was given the go-ahead sign and I began preparations to go by boat to the Alaska of my dreams, the land flowing with ice and seal blubber.

Those were the years of the Depression with a capital *D*. Cash was scarce. I figured that I had to manage to find money for my trip myself, and I did. WIth some retreats and helping pastors here and there, I collected all the money I needed, even to buy a brand-new typewriter with Spanish characters. I did so with due permission. I told my provincial superior that I intended to support myself in Alaska by writing for publication in spare times. When he heard the magic words "support myself," his eyes beamed and he said, "Sure, sure, go ahead then and buy it, and the sooner the merrier."

2

The Inside Passage

I left Seattle for Alaska on August 30, 1935, on the steamer *Alaska*. The ship would follow the so-called Inside Passage. Cruising along the Canadian coast for six hundred miles, the boat entered the narrow straits—several of them—between Dixon Entrance and Juneau, the capital.

If the weather helps—which is not always the case—passengers on this route are treated to magnificent views. Some passages are so narrow that one feels he could jump off the boat and land between trees. It is all part of the Panhandle, dotted with countless islands, and I mean countless.

I was not by any means the first Spaniard to navigate these waters. Between the years 1774 and 1792 the viceroys of Mexico sent no less than six expeditions with gunboats to explore what they called northern California, then part of the Spanish dominions. Those commanders made detailed naval charts of the whole Panhandle plus the coast along Valdez and Cordova, and twice they even visited Kodiak.

We know that on May 13, 1779, the chaplain of one of those ships, Fr. Francisco Juan Riobo, a Spanish Franciscan, said the first Mass ever on land in what is now Alaska proper. It was on what is now called Prince of Wales Island, across from Revillagigedo Island where Ketchikan is located. Spain, France, and England were making great efforts then to discover the legendary Northern Passage, which was supposed to exist connecting this Panhandle with Hudson Bay. While the efforts proved vain, they were profitable in many other ways.

These waters were properly charted and the world discovered that there was much real estate here for grabs. Eventually Russia got the upper hand and added Alaska to her already vast empire.

Our first stop was at Ketchikan, and I walked up to the hospital run by the sisters to say Mass in their chapel. There I met Fr. Filiberto Tornielli, a saintly Jesuit eighty-five years old.

I knew nothing then about him, but later on I discovered that his father had been an Italian count. His mother, who had died when he was still a boy, had been a sister of Pope Gregory XVI. His widowed father had become a priest, and the boy had gone to Padova to study law. When his father had died he'd left his son the title of count, but Filiberto had felt that he had a vocation and had entered the Jesuits at Monaco. He had come to the Rocky Mountains in America, and for twenty years he had worked with the Indians in Washington and Montana. He had gone to Skagway in Alaska in 1898 when that town had become the gate to the Dawson gold mines. The town had been so corrupt that it defied description, according to those who had seen it.

Now in 1935 Fr. Tornielli was still around. He had an obsession that God wanted him in Alaska and nowhere else; one of those second childhood obsessions.

The good sisters gave me a box to be handled with care. In the box was an elaborate cake, but not for me since I did not need it. It was for Fr. Monroe, the pastor of Wrangell, our next stop. At Wrangell it was easy to find the church. I knocked at the rectory door and, sure enough, the old man appeared in person. After greetings and introductions I gave him the cake which he took in a matter-of-fact way and put away quite unceremoniously. He was then eighty, had a number of missing teeth, and spoke with a strong French accent. Immediately he wanted to go to confession. I raised my eyebrows, wondering if I would understand a single word. But God would understand.

Fr. Monroe was then unknown to me, but in due time I heard a lot about him. His brother, or one of them, had been a general in the French army. Fr. Monroe had come to Alaska way back in 1893. A man of steel, he'd gone around building everywhere, and he built as the Romans did—strong, solid, meant to last forever. He built the first Catholic church in Fairbanks, on the left bank of the Chena River. Later he thought that the right bank was better, so he moved it across the river on the ice.

Francis Monroe, S.J., did things on the trail that left old-timers aghast. He would cover long distances on snowshoes and feel totally relaxed at the end of the trail, as though he were ready to start again.

The city of Fairbanks named a street after him and the Catholic high school there was also named after him. Bishop Crimont admired him so much that he would not tolerate any criticism unfavorable to Fr. Monroe. Knowing that both had come from France, people understood. When anyone pointed to some faults of Fr. Monroe, the bishop quickly answered that those were not faults, but virtues carried to extremes. The old story of "my country right or wrong."[1]

From Wrangell we moved on to Juneau, the capital and also the headquarters of the Vicar Apostolic Joseph R. Crimont, S.J. I went immediately to see him. There he was at his desk, pen in hand, seventy-seven years old, very short, very thin, very quiet, and very kindly looking.

According to tradition, when a young student in France he had been sickly and feared that his missionary dreams could not be fulfilled. Saint John Bosco had come through, and Crimont had asked him to give him a blessing so he could become a missionary in North America. Don Bosco had rested his hands on the head of the young man and predicted that he would be a great missionary. And so it happened.

Crimont came to Alaska in 1894 and spent a few years in Nulato and Holy Cross. In 1904 he became prefect apostolic and in 1917 he became bishop with the title of vicar apostolic. It was his habit to visit the north during the summer and spend the winter in the Panhandle.

As I stood before Bishop Crimont, I asked him if I could say Mass. It was now 3:00 P.M. and I had had no breakfast. In those days Mass was not said in the afternoon. He looked me in the eye and said, "Because I also did foolish things like this when I was your age, yes, go ahead, you can say Mass." Fr. Levasseur led me to the sacristy and served my Mass. Then he provided me with a fine Mass-kit or portable altar so I could say Mass anywhere outside of a church. In the Mass-kit were hosts and a small bottle of altar wine.

Fr. Levasseur took me down to the basement to see the famous "Glacier Priest," Fr. Bernard Hubbard, S.J., who was busy unpacking after another one of his many trips to the interior. Fr. Hubbard gave me a fine sleeping bag and taught me how to use it. Then we sat down. I was fortunate not to miss the boat. Father was the most articulate and talkative man I had ever met, but I was watching my wrist watch.

He was glad, indeed, to see a young priest come to Alaska to reinforce the ranks. But he had a warning that brought me clear to the Gospel of Saint Luke, where we read about the visitation of the Holy Family to Jerusalem to present the infant Jesus to the Lord in the temple. That holy old man Simeon took a close look at Mary and prophesied to her: "You yourself shall be pierced with a sword."

Fr. Hubbard told me point blank that I would find myself often in distress. He had tramped all over Alaska and, believe me, he said, it is tough. That talk about the "friendly arctic" was hogwash. Situations arise all of a sudden that make your hair stand on end. One false step and there is death, staring you in the eye.

It can be the weather. It can be the treacherous ice at break-up or freeze-up time. It can be getting lost in no man's land with snow falling or a nasty bite of a mad dog on the trail or a drunk native with a loaded gun. Then there are those misunderstandings among ourselves, differences of opinion on matters that in themselves could be trivial, but in reality assume ridiculous proportions. And so forth.

But cheer up. Others had made it and I could make it also if I had the stuff. In Alaska it is each one for himself. The survival of the fittest. Weaklings don't last. How about the language? Oh, well, yes, language is important, but English is taking over so fast that in one generation it will be all over. It will depend on where you are living. Is there any danger of going hungry? Absolutely not, unless one gets caught on the trail with little food and a storm comes suddenly from nowhere. And so Fr. Hubbard was both cautioning me and cheering me up.

Back at the bishop's office the bishop gave me instructions concerning my destination. I was to go to Holy Cross on the lower Yukon and he told me why. The local superior, Fr. Tomkin, had a bad heart and had to take it easy. Fr. Post was bedridden—actually on his last legs. Fr. Prange was there only for the winter. He was the procurator of the missions and had to leave for the States in April to do the buying. That would keep him busy well into the month of August. So I was to be stationed at Holy Cross to do the work all year around. Holy Cross was the biggest place then in the Alaska mission field. He wrote a note that I was to give to Fr. Tomkin. It was like a telegram, just to tell him to take me as a member of the Holy Cross community.

And so I left Juneau with a Mass-kit, a warm sleeping bag, and a letter of introduction to Fr. Tomkin. The visit had proved very profitable.

Now the boat headed for Cordova. But to get there we had to cross the stormy Gulf of Alaska, and I am always the first passenger to get seasick. It takes thirty good hours to cross it. The minute the boat began to dance, I went to bed and lay flat till the motions of the boat, or the lack of them, told me that we had entered halcyon waters. We were between islands and soon we reached Cordova.

This little town had become important after the turn of the century, due to the construction of the Northwestern and Copper River Railroad connecting this ice-free port with the famous copper mines around McCarthy and Kennicott. The mines closed in the late thirties. Cordova then settled down to the status of a cozy, little fishing port and main supply center for most of the fishing activities in Prince William Sound.

As usual I made a beeline for the church up on the hill where I met Fr. Tim Ryan, an amiable man who showed great delight at seeing another priest. It had been a long time since he had seen one. Before we parted, he wanted to go to confession.

I did not know at the time that thirty years later I would be pastor of Cordova.

From Cordova we proceeded to Valdez. This little town had seen better times. In 1911 it had even had a community of Ursuline Sisters with a school. Valdez had become for all practical purposes the port of entry for the interior. Then the Alaska railroad had been built connecting Seward with Fairbanks. This had just about killed Valdez, though the town kept going.

I walked to the rectory and met the priest, Fr. Leo Dufour, a young-looking cleric with a great deal of charm. He had not seen another priest for a long time, so he wanted to go to confession before he forgot it. Then he showed me around. I could see that the town had more vitality than I had thought, seeing it from the deck of the boat.[2]

The isolation of these diocesan priests made quite an impression on me at the time. We were in Alaska and things were different here. I asked myself how I would like to be so isolated. Could I stand it? Four years later I had to stand it when I was sent to Kotzebue where

I did not see a priest for thirteen months. Someone said that I could not then afford the luxury of committing a mortal sin. It was well put, I thought, except for the word *luxury.*

Now we were headed for Seward, which was the end of the line for the boat. When we arrived at noon, there was some scramble, as the baggage was being taken to the depot. I was expecting to take the train for Fairbanks and hoped that the train would make connections with the boat. Poor me! The train made the trip to Fairbanks twice a week, and it had just left.

I had to wait three days. But my spirit soared when I saw the steeple of the Catholic church where undoubtedly a lovely priest would be happy to show me around and tell me all about Alaska. I knocked and knocked at the door. A lady in the next house came out and informed me that Fr. Sulzman, the pastor, had left quite some time ago to build a church in Palmer in the Matanuska Valley where a new colony was being settled.

She had the key of the rectory and gave it to me. I thanked her and, sure enough, that was the key. What I saw when I went in made me depressed. Silence, abandonment, and a feeling of destitution. The kitchen was bare. I went upstairs and found nothing but emptiness. Downstairs there was a room with a bed. Thank God for that bed! The church had solid, massive pews covered with a film of dust. That was to be my abode till the train arrived. And yet, was not I the most fortunate of men to have all that building for me alone?

I went to the depot to check my trunk. Then I went to a restaurant to take some food. Back in the streets there was so very little to see that I decided to return to my castle. The days were already very short. To the west and north of Seward, a chain of lofty mountains block the sunlight and accelerate darkness. Before I knew it, it was night. The electricity had been cut off, as I recall, so I just went to bed but not to sleep. Sometime during the night the boat blew the ritual three whistles to let everyone know that she was returning to Seattle. I said to myself, *This is it, big boy. Now you are like those conquistadores who landed in Mexico; then Cortés had the boats scuttled so no one could leave. From then on it was sink or swim. This is for keeps.*

Since sleep would not come to my eyes, I let my imagination roam at will. In that darkest of rooms I said my final good-bye to Spain, to the Spanish language, to my folks, and to everything implied therein. The jets flying back and forth across the Atlantic were then far away. I was convinced that I would never go back. I was finally in Alaska. But was *this* Alaska? Yes, it was, and how fortunate I was to be in *my* house and in *my* bed instead of being a roomer in a roadhouse.

---

1. Fr. Monroe died in Spokane on January 9, 1940, at the age of eighty-five. By any standards, he was one of the greatest men who ever lived in Alaska.

2. Valdez was totally destroyed by the awesome earthquake that hit the southcentral area of Alaska on Good Friday of 1964. The destruction was so great that it had to be rebuilt from scratch; this was done a little distance away on a better location. Only God in His great heaven knew at the time that Valdez was destined to become the terminal of the famous pipe line bringing the oil from Prudhoe Bay on the Arctic Ocean.

The Alaska Railroad

As everyone knows, Alaska has been famous for its deposits of the finest gold. At the end of the century for all practical purposes the only paths of communication were the rivers. But the rivers freeze in the winter months. Most of the gold from Dawson (Canada) and from the gold mines along the Yukon River in Alaska was brought to Seattle and San Francisco in boats that had to navigate the whole length of the river. That was an unacceptable distance. Wasn't there a shorter route?

Thus the bright idea of a railroad connecting the interior of Alaska with an ice-free port, say Valdez or Seward, began to take shape. After careful studies it was decided that the line should run from Seward to Fairbanks. America had finished the Panama Canal in 1914, and huge piles of the finest building material were lying idle on its banks. Why not bring that equipment to Seward to help build the tracks? And so it was done.

By 1916 the site of Anchorage had become the main camp for workers. First it was a city of tents. Soon frame buildings sprang up everywhere and, with that efficiency so typically American, a regular town came into existence. In the summer of 1923 the train was already in motion. To give it official blessing, with an appropriate inauguration, speeches, and all the paraphernalia worthy of the occasion, President Harding rode the train with an imposing entourage and at Nenana declared the railroad open for business. The Department of the Interior became the official owner.

The Alaska Railroad has been operating in the red ever since, or so we were told. When Alaska became a sovereign state, the Department of the Interior did its best to persuade the state to take the railroad, but the state said no thanks. The young state had enough trouble making ends meet without adding the burden of a money-losing railroad. The great Alaskan deposits of oil had not been discovered, though it was known that there was oil.

In 1935 Alaska probably had less than eighty thousand people and most were natives scattered in small settlements. The train had relatively few passengers and relatively little cargo, so it had been decided that running it twice a week would be satisfactory—which it was. This much about the train.

Here I was in Seward in an empty house, unknown to everyone, and waiting patiently for the train. Thanks to the Mass-kit I said Mass, and this helped a great deal to kill the monotony of not having anything to do. I did some walking around and found the town cold, aloof, impersonal, though now I realize that that was due mainly to my own timidity. We get what we give. I was giving nothing, so I was getting nothing. If I had made the first move, like greeting people, grinning, and all that, it might have been different. But I found the short streets almost empty of people.

Finally my deliverance came. The train arrived whistling to let everybody know that it was business as usual. Next morning, rather early, we took off. I doubt that we were more than twenty passengers. As we kept chugging along, the scenery became more and more impressive. *This* was Alaska, I said to myself as the tracks ran through breath-taking ranges. So much beauty and so much of it! The poor locomotive, an antique little thing, coughed and coughed as she bravely tried to climb uphill. At moments, I wondered if she could hack it. But hack it she did and by noon we were in Anchorage. We were told that the train would stop three hours. I wondered if this long rest was so the locomotive could get her second breath.

Anchorage then was a little town of 2,600 people. Not one square foot of it was paved. The minute I climbed up from the depot, I saw the steeple of the Catholic church. I knocked at the door of the rectory, and it was opened by Fr. Dermot O'Flanagan, who was washing dishes and treated me to a sandwich and coffee. He was a fine-looking priest in his early thirties, with a dignified Irish brogue. At the International Eucharistic Congress in Dublin he had met Bishop Crimont who had accepted him for Alaska.

Fr. O'Flanagan was pastor of Anchorage for about sixteen years. While there, he built the present cathedral of Holy Family. The magnificent building was all paid up very shortly after it was built. People stopped him in the streets to ask how much he needed to pay off the debt. I knew one man, now deceased, who asked him how much he needed. He needed four thousand dollars. That afternoon he had the money.

In 1951 he became bishop of Juneau. He was an excellent pastor, loved by everyone. His intellectual acumen was well above average. No doubt these good qualities were the reason for his elevation to the episcopate. But we had here a case of the Peter Principle. One can be an excellent general and commander of the army in wartime, as Ulysses Grant was, and yet be a questionable president of the nation, as Grant was. As pastor of Anchorage, Fr. O'Flanagan was good. As bishop he became so timid that everything stood still and no progress was made. One got the impression that he was overwhelmed by the office and the responsibilities that go with it.

It has been said that the medium is the message. How true! Bishop O'Flanagan, in time becoming scared of the office of bishop, would take off to the lower forty-eight states to attend just about everything: consecrations of new bishops, silver jubilees, and golden jubilees of bishops, funerals of bishops, meetings, workshops, etc., etc. He would inform his priests that he was not to be contacted by telephone. If anyone wanted something from him, that person had to send it in writing. He, then, would take a close look at the letter and would answer it also in writing. The answer more often than not was no. This policy alienated not a few. In time he found himself very much alone. Finally in 1968 he resigned, and he became again the jolly, jovial, genial man that he was at heart.

Now in this cold September of 1935 he and I were chatting amiably over a cup of coffee. No, he had not yet seen the interior or Alaska and had no idea how the Eskimos were. He felt that Eskimoland was like a different nation with its own heritage and culture totally alien to ours. Yes, he had heard of the missions the Jesuits had there and knew of them, like Holy Cross, Akulurak, and Pilgrim Springs, but he had not the foggiest idea of how they operated. He was most sympathetic and hoped and prayed that I would do all right in those regions. He accompanied me to the train depot and there we parted. I was to see much of him in years to come.

Back in the train I noticed that we had lost passengers. Soon we were going through the Matanuska Valley, where in time Palmer would become an imposing city. That very summer that area had received the trainload of colonizers, mostly farmers from Minnesota and surrounding states, sent by Roosevelt to develop the valley and provide the Alaskans with lettuce, cabbage, spuds, carrots, radishes, chickens, eggs, milk, and beef—for the not faraway day when a war with Japan might isolate Alaska from the States.

Probably in Washington they thought that Alaska was a little county where everybody knew everybody and where people could go on horseback to buy the necessities of life. It was later said that America did not discover Alaska till the Second World War. Be that as it may, the sending of those colonizers was a stroke of genius, as the farmers throughout the Matanuska Valley developed the land which eventually flowed with milk and vegetables and produced the cities of Palmer and Wasilla.

In the train we cut through the valley and came to a forest of small trees that seemed to have no end. The conductor, a Mr. Hoover of middle age, sat by me, and we became friends immediately. He was a Catholic from Fairbanks, where he was raising a family.

While I wanted to ask him about Alaska, he was rather interested in asking me things that were bothering him. What was the difference between nazism, fascism, socialism, and communism? When I was through giving him my honest point of view, and it took some time, he nodded and said almost triumphantly: "In other words, communism is the worst of the lot. Just as I had suspected all along."

By now we were coming close to Mount McKinley, the highest mountain in North America, and it was totally covered with snow. Suddenly I looked through the window and cried, "Lord, what a mountain!" He asked me if I wanted him to stop the train so I could take a slow look at it. I was paralyzed. I was sure that I had not heard right. Would the train stop just for me, to give me this personal pleasure?

Yes, sir, it would. Just to see that I was not dreaming, I said that I would love to get out of the train and take a slow look. He disappeared and in seconds the train came to a stop. We two went out and took a look—a short one in fact because there was a breeze much too cold to enjoy. Other passengers just looked through the windows. We went in and the train started as though nothing had happened.

I have to admit that this episode endeared Alaska and the

Alaskans to me. Where else on the whole broad earth would a thing like this happen? I was a nobody, yet the train stopped just to give me a passing pleasure.

Or maybe I was somebody. I learned soon that in Alaska a man was the greatest thing. People were few and far between. The country was so vast. Life in the open was exposed to dangers. When you are on the long trail, the best sight is that of a cabin with a smoking chimney. Inside there are people. Maybe there is only a trapper skinning a mink or a muskrat. But that man will take you in like a brother and will accommodate you. He will give you coffee and a bunk to sleep in. Thank God for that man! There is nothing so distressing as traveling long distances without seeing anybody. There are trails in Alaska so long and so empty of life, any life, that the sight of another man is like an oasis in the midst of an infinite Sahara.

Before sunset the train came to a stop in the middle of nowhere. What had happened? Nothing to worry about. We were now in a place called Curry, about half the distance between Seward and Fairbanks. It was not a town. It was a beautiful hotel built there by the Department of the Interior to accommodate the passengers. The old locomotive could not make Fairbanks in one day, so the train stopped here for the night.

The surroundings were lovely. A river flowed very close to the building. Those who wanted could take a bath, not in the river though, for the water was too cold, but in their rooms. We were given individual rooms simply because there were more rooms than passengers. A bell rang, calling us to the dining room where we were treated to a royal repast. We were warned that in the morning there would be two bells: one to get up and have breakfast and the other to board the train. The silence of the place was conducive to a peaceful sleep.

I got up before the first bell rang and said Mass in my room. The peace and silence of the surroundings made me feel pious while saying Mass, which I offered in thanksgiving to God for having brought me that far and also as a petition, begging Him to lead and guide me in the rest of the long trip. That was my first Mass in the very heart of the Alaska Peninsula. I was beginning to feel the remoteness of it all and was much excited about it. The bell rang. Breakfast was served. But what a breakfast! Bacon and eggs, hot cakes, coffee, you name it.

Before leaving the door we had to pay for the evening supper, the room, and the breakfast, and pay we did through the nose. Six dollars! A general feeling of having been robbed spread through the little crowd. Six dollars was considered much too much. But we knew that the government had us over the barrel. We were sitting ducks with no chance to escape. Remember that we were in the clutches of the Depression, when one silver dollar was a real treasure.[1]

The second bell rang and we all trooped to the train. In the afternoon we arrived in Fairbanks, the end of the tracks.

Fairbanks then was a little town. The day after I arrived, I crossed it and crisscrossed it in a matter of minutes. Gold had been discovered nearby at the turn of the century, and by 1904 there had been enough people there to justify the presence of a priest. This had been no other than Fr. Monroe, who had proceeded immediately to build a church and a hospital.

The present pastor was Fr. Eline, S.J., a native of Milwaukee who had come to Alaska in 1920 and had spent seven years in Fairbanks. He was a short chubby man with absolutely no neck or, if he had one, I never saw it. He lit one cigarette with the butt of the preceding one both to save matches and to save precious time looking for another cigarette. On his desk were always several packs of cigarettes already open and with several cigarettes sticking out so as to save time. It made me wonder whether that could be called "madness in his method" or "method in his madness." But method it was.

He was a shrewd little town politician and was loved by all, be they Catholics, Protestants, Jews, Masons, or Nothings. It seemed that he was the unofficial mayor of the town. His counsel was sought by all. He was also most compassionate. People in need knew that Fr. Eline would never fail them. We sat in his room after meals and I was amazed at his wisdom. He died in Fairbanks in 1943.

The hospital built by Fr. Monroe was suited for the needs of the time. But time was marching on and the town was growing and so were the needs. The Sisters of Providence who were in charge told me that they were planning to add a wing that would be like a new hospital altogether, with modern facilities. This they did rather soon. The new hospital was a godsend to the city and its scattered surroundings. Patients were flown there from faraway.[2]

I spent five days in Fairbanks so as to make connections with the river boat that was scheduled to leave Nenana on a certain date.

When I arrived in Nenana expecting to leave that very day, I was told that the sternwheeler had suffered some damage on a sandbar and would be five days late. That was that. Take it or leave it. Fr. Hubbard had told me that in Alaska nobody is in a hurry simply because he may not be able to go anywhere he may want to go. How true!

The town of Nenana had seen better days. While the railroad had been under construction and for some time afterward, Nenana had been a big town by Alaska standards. Fr. Monroe (who else?) had hurried and built there a church solid as the Rock of Gibraltar. But gradually Fairbanks had taken over and poor Nenana had sunk almost to a ghost town. Yet it still had a post office, a school, a restaurant, and two general stores.

I was now stuck in Nenana for at least five days. What to do? First was to find who had the key of the abandoned church. Entering it was like entering a crypt, a hidden burial chamber, a haunted or a spooky cavern. How long was it since a human being had been there? I had no idea.

As I opened the door I was greeted by that smell peculiar to closed and abandoned buildings. Everything was so stale. I went down to the basement. The walls had a moldy coating like an abandoned catacomb. On the floor was a pile of blocks and an axe. I split a couple of blocks and built a fire in the wood stove upstairs. The noise and smell of burning wood and the warmth made me feel a lot better. It began to look like a home. I took one look at the big church, but I closed the door and left it as it was: cold, damp, sad, and forbidding. I would say Mass in the living room.

This time I did not want to make the mistake I had made in Seward. I went out to meet the people. Since the streets were empty, I went to the restaurant. There I found some folks and we soon established a satisfactory rapport. Yes, I would be in town till the boat arrived. Yes, I would say Mass every day at eight in the morning. As a result of that I had four people for Mass. For Nenana it was a howling success—I felt.

One of them was the former postmaster who insisted on paying for my breakfast as long as I was there. He was a born Republican. When Roosevelt took over, he lost his job. Between cigarette puffs he remarked in an audible, barely audible, voice: "Roosevelt killed the Republican party."

I had no comments. I was not even a citizen yet. But, if only to break the silence that followed, I said to him that the political pendulum might switch soon and then he would be back in the saddle.

"No," he answered, " this man is going to be in the White House till he dies of old age. Mark my words." I can see now that postmasters can also be prophets.

Thus my stay in Nenana came to be a pleasant one. I visited some homes and chatted in as friendly a manner as I could. One person asked me about my nationality. My accent was hard to trace. As I made apologies for my accent, he said, "Oh, no, Father, your accent is rather cute." This built my ego that had begun to crumble when the matter of the accent was brought up. He said that he was an expert in foreign accents, but that mine had him stumped. I was the first Spaniard he had ever met.

It was now September the sixteenth. The ground was covered with frost that broke under our heavy shoes. The breeze was nippy. The days were short and the nights were long. Winter was around the corner. Suddenly the whistle of the river boat filled the town with noise and filled my heart with joy. My deliverance was at hand. I bought a ticket for Holy Cross and brought my luggage to the boat. So did the others. We were less than one dozen passengers. The boat was the *Alice.* As soon as the loading was finished, the boat started down river, pushing huge barges groaning with cargo to be delivered to the local stores of the many villages along the river.

We were in the Tanana River, not in the Yukon yet. It was hoped that in two days we would reach the Yukon. The going was tough. The river was much too shallow at this time of the year and there was no end of sandbars sticking out everywhere. In spite of much sounding, we could not avoid hitting some of those bars. The experience of the captain and his associates was being put to a severe test. With grunts, cursing, yelling, and careful maneuvering plus my silent prayers begging heaven to give us an almighty hand, we finally made the Yukon and tied up at the bank in front of Tanana village.

---

1. Years later the railroad acquired better locomotives and the distance was easily covered in one day, so the Curry Hotel was closed. One day the radio gave the sad news that the hotel had burned to the ground. As far as I recall, no investigation was made about the nature of that fire.

2. In 1967 Fairbanks sustained a dreadful flood from the swollen Chena River. The hospital had to be evacuated. It survived, yet the trauma for the few sisters on hand was not small. Whatever the reason might be, the hospital was soon abandoned by them and was sold.

The Yukon River 4

The Eskimos have a word for the Yukon: *Kwikpak,* that is, "The Real Big One." The Yukon is listed among the big rivers of the world— roughly two thousand miles in length. It is to Alaska what the Mississippi River is to the states along its banks. If you live in Canada, the word *Yukon* makes you think of Yukon Territory, which is part of the Dominion. In fact, the river has its origin in Canada not far from White Horse. It flows in a northern direction and then turns west to enter Alaska close to the town of Eagle. It receives water from mighty tributaries like the Porcupine, the Chandalar, the Tanana, and the Innoko, to mention only the big ones. About thirty Alaska towns drink its water. Small towns, yes, very small towns some of them, but towns they are.

The Yukon supplies salmon and other varieties of fish in quantities that seem unbelievable. Salmon has become a big industry. In the winter the natives get other fish from under the ice, thus being assured of fresh fish all year around.

When the ice breaks in the spring, the river swells and carries in its current logs that come from the trees that have fallen as the banks have caved in; the natives get from the river the lumber they need to build cabins and boats and the wood they need to keep warm all winter.

Senator Gruening of Alaska died without seeing fulfilled his great dream: He wanted a dam built at Rampart to harness the might and riches of the big river. That dam would have made an artificial lake of some eighteen thousand square miles. Such a body of water exposed to the midnight sun would have raised the temperature, since water lets out cold more slowly than land does. The dam would have created electricity—so many watts in fact that we would hardly have known what to do with so much of it. To save the salmon runs, so-called ladders would have been built for the fish to swim with little effort. Other benefits would have accrued to the building of such a dam. But environmentalists sounded the alarm and the plan was scuttled. It was believed that atomic power would soon take over and fill the earth with all the electricity it wanted. Then, they said, eighteen thousand square miles was too much land taken away from the moose, the reindeer, the caribou, and all the fowl thriving in that area. So Ernest Gruening lost. He had traveled to Siberia in an official capacity to study the harnessing of the water coming out of Lake Baykal at Irkutsk and Angarsk, where the Russians have gone all out for electricity.

I had heard of the river and had read about it often enough. Now I was navigating its waters. A unique thrill went all over me when I saw it.

The week ahead of us was going to be this: We were going to travel day and night, stopping only at the towns to unload the cargo marked for each place.

If the boat arrived at 2:00 A.M., it was just too bad. The boat stopped; the gangplanks were properly secured; the wheelbarrows in interminable succession started rolling back and forth; you would hear the customary yellings of the foreman peppered with curses of all denominations; rattling, noises, etc., till, as if by magic, calm was restored. Then the whistles blew, followed by the rhythmic coughing of the engines. We were off again.

The captain was an elderly man, well built and with deep, penetrating blue eyes. He would invite me to the pilot house now and then just to chat. The first question he put to me left me in a quandary. He wanted to know what I thought of Roosevelt. Instinctively I put myself on neutral ground and answered that the president certainly knew how to get the votes. There was a moment of silence.

The captain broke it by saying, "He is a communist." Then he went on to explain that Roosevelt was not just an ordinary communist but a very dangerous one. The captain loved America and American institutions; America was a good country with a wonderful heritage. Now the president was going to destroy it all, and on top of that he was going to put us in the worst war the country had ever seen.

When I objected that the president needed the consent of Congress to do that, the captain said that Congress was soft putty in the clever hands of this master politician. And so on and on.

The captain had brought his wife along just for the trip. Sometimes the three of us would get together. She was extremely interested in knowing what makes a Catholic priest tick. That was the first time she had spoken to a priest. I think I waxed eloquent in defense of celibacy, total dedication to God, falling in love with Christ, and all that. This falling in love business made her turn to me and remark, "Oh, Father, I am sure you would make a wonderful husband."

"Oh, I guess I would," I blushed, "but, you see, I am already taken."

The captain gave his wife a dirty look.

We were navigating between the towns of Tanana and Nulato. These had been the stamping grounds of that giant of the intellect, the Canadian Jesuit priest Julius Jette, born in Montreal of aristocratic parents. He got what he had wanted; and what he had wanted was to come to Alaska to live and die in the midst of the Indians.

He had come here in 1898 and had died among the Eskimos of Akulurak in 1927. It was decades after his death before people began to stop talking about this priest. He was ever so gentle and refined. As for scholarship, suffice it to say that he wrote a monumental encyclopedia of the Indian language of the Yukon in several volumes. Nothing escaped his penetrating eye. Every modism of the language was traced to its roots. And he did all this in his own handwriting: limpid, clear, perfect.

Jette identified himself with the Indians. He would go ninety miles, pushing a tiny sled, to see a sick man. He claimed that a dog team was a hindrance inasmuch as it took too much time caring for them. By walking himself, once he reached the place, he did not have to bother with seven barking and voracious dogs. The biography of this man is waiting for the historian with time and talent to do it, though several articles have been published proclaiming the virtues of this Canadian hero.

Because of his talent and his close association with the founders of the Jesuit Alaska missions, he had been asked often to sit down and write a thorough history of these missions. He had chuckled pensively and shaken his head. He would not do it. "I could not do it." Why not? "Well, you see, the really interesting things would not be published, and what would be published would not be interesting." And then he would add,chuckling again: "Alaska is a madhouse without a keeper." This profound sentence made the rounds and made everyone chuckle.

It was daylight when we arrived in Nulato, so I had a good chance to sit with the two priests stationed there: Frs. Joseph McElmeel and John Baud. Fr. McElmeel, a native of Iowa, was then in his prime: a stocky, solidly built man with a broad chest and a heavy, square jaw. As a young man he had been an amateur boxer. He took me to the sacristy and served my Mass. Then we sat to chat.

Between 1935 and 1961, which was the year he died of a heart attack in Ketchikan, we were to meet many times. He served six years as general superior of the missions. In 1939 he flew to Kotzebue to receive my last vows in the Society of Jesus. When he was in a good mood, which was often the case, he would tell the funniest stories. Having associated with old-timers on the Yukon, he had heard enough stories to entertain you forever.

He was very exact and had a penchant for perfection in the discharge of priestly duties. He loved to quote the worthies: Saint Augustine, Shakespeare, Horace, and Fr. Jette, who was his model in everything. A rock-ribbed Catholic, he loved the church with real intensity. He was a penny-pincher and wanted every missionary to be likewise. Smoking to him was an abomination and drink was ten abominations. Women had to be kept farther than an arm's length, much farther, and he admired the wisdom of the man who coined the sentence: "Beware of wine, women, and song."

Unfortunately, he suffered from a rare affliction. He simply had to put his nose and his eyes into others' business and belongings. This caused head-on collisions which he actually enjoyed, or so it seemed to me at the time. But human nature is so complex.

Once, in a quiet peaceful mood, he told me that he had come from a very poor family. As a boy he had heard his mother tell him that she hoped that Dad would bring home something for supper; if he didn't, she did not know what to put on the table. The humility he showed while he uttered those words was most edifying. Perhaps his penny-pinching came from what he had experienced at home as a boy. Perhaps booze and cigarettes had jarred his sense of poverty. Perhaps a woman had tried to divert him from his religious vocation and he had reacted fiercely in his determination to remain loyal to the Lord and he never told me. With the strong faith he had, I always felt that he would have a high place in heaven.

As we sat together then in Nulato, he was very glad that I neither drank nor smoked.

Fr. Baud had arrived in Alaska two months ahead of me. We had never met. He was a Frenchman. He had the distinction of having gone through the First World War in the trenches on the firing line without being hit in the least. It had become so evident and so amazing to the rest of the soldiers that, when they were in actual combat, all wanted to be behind him. He had stood the whole bombardment of Verdun by the Germans. But he had become a bit shell shocked. A sudden noise, a bang of a door, would make him jump. He did not like to fly. All this caused superiors to let him stay in Nulato for many years, to save him the traumas of trips, changes, and new adaptations.

He had two excellent qualities: He was an artist—a painter above the ordinary—and also a saint. At the altar, while saying Mass, he underwent a manner of transfiguration that was evident to the people in the pews.

He died of cancer in Seattle in 1968 at the age of seventy-one. Other people, no doubt, die of cancer in Seattle, but no one has left the impression that he left at his deathbed. Doctors and nurses who treated him were awe-struck listening to him and seeing in his face the joy he showed at the thought of his imminent meeting with the Lord. His whole life had been a preparation for this last moment.

My visit with these two Jesuit priests gave me a big boost, and from Nulato the boat continued down river. We were getting close to Holy Cross, which was my final destination. When I saw the place from a long distance, I put all my belongings together to have them ready. So this was the place. I wondered how many years I would have to be in these surroundings. From the boat I could see many native children running around. Obviously they were having recess. There were many buildings and big ones. I could see some sisters in their holy habits mixing with the children. There was also farm equipment here and there. I was sure that the building over there was a barn. It all looked great.

Finally the boat tied at the bank and we began the process of unloading. I walked out packing two suitcases. Standing on the bank was Fr. Tomkin, the local superior. He showed signs of surprise when he saw me coming in as if I knew what I was doing.

After greeting him, I showed him the letter from the bishop. He read it twice and began to shake his head. It was all a mistake, he said, adding that it was obvious that the bishop was unaware of conditions on the lower Yukon. "You see," he continued, "we are three priests here whereas Akulurak has only two and one is dying. The bishop must have meant Akulurak." He read the short letter for the third time, turned it back to me, and told me to return to the boat with the suitcases and go to Akulurak.

Unmoved, I asked him how he dared to disobey the orders of the bishop.

"Young man," he said, "Alaska is different, entirely different from the rest of the country. Here we play it by ear. Only those on the spot are fully aware of all the circumstances. I am sure you are needed in Akulurak."

Totally defeated, I asked him if he knew where Akulurak was. He did not know exactly, but he knew that it was down river, and if I would ask in Marshall, people there would tell me. I took the suitcases and returned to the boat where I bought a ticket for Fortuna Ledge, also called Marshall, which was the end of the line for this boat. I reoccupied my little room in a state of great confusion. I was getting contradictory signals and it was hard for me to figure it out till the good Spirit made me feel that He had prepared me for things like this through Fr. Hubbard who had said that I would find myself often in distress, but to cheer up, because many others before me had made it.

I lay in my bunk hoping to doze off the whole affair, but the affair would not go away. So I left the boat and decided to explore the mission grounds.

Holy Cross had been known as the Pride of the Yukon. It was started in 1888 as an orphanage and developed into a first-class school. Both the Jesuits and the Sisters of St. Ann, who ran the place jointly, could be proud of the work. Holy Cross became the mother of the Jesuit missions in interior Alaska. It had a farm, cattle, a saw mill, just about all that could be expected in a well-organized mission.[1]

I asked to see Fr. Post, one of the three priests. I was led to the infirmary where he was in bed paralyzed. Bro. Horan was his nurse and was seated by the bed. When I explained my situation to Fr. Post, he quickly answered that Fr. Tomkin had made the right decision, because in Akulurak Fr. Lucchesi was a sick old man who was of no help for the trail.

Let me state here that both Fr. Tomkin and Fr. Post left Holy Cross the very next year. The former died in Fairbanks of a heart condition on October 4, 1936. The latter was taken to the States as an invalid and died in Spokane on December 18, 1940. Time proved that the bishop was very well aware of conditions at Holy Cross. In fact, the bishop had visited Holy Cross that very summer.

On my way back to the boat I met Fr. Prange somewhere between the buildings. He was the third priest. When I told him my predicament, he became indignant, not because Fr. Tomkin had made a right or a wrong decision but because he was a consultor and had not been consulted. I told him I was returning to the boat for good. He said that the boat would be there at least two more hours, so I had better go with him to his room and do a little chatting, which I did.

I had no idea whatever then of who Fr. Prange was. Once seated in his room, he took the floor, lit one cigarette after another and subjected me to an interminable litany of stories that had me spellbound. Now here was an orator, an articulate storyteller, a dramatic actor, a hypnotizer, all rolled into one and then some.

Later on, I was to meet him now and then. In 1937 we met in Marshall. He landed there before supper and went to the roadhouse. He had been appointed general superior. When he heard that I was in town, he sent for me. It was 10:00 P.M. We sat across the table by ourselves since everyone else had gone to bed.

What I am going to say is the truth, why should I lie? He began to talk and did not stop till 6:30 next morning. This is only part of it. I had been on the trail the day before and I was scheduled to leave for Pilot Station that morning. I had planned on a long sleep that would fit me for the ordeals of the hard trail in February. It was evident that a man, any man, met Fr. Prange at his own risk, because meeting him was hazardous to one's health. In the end his very name became a password. *Don't prange me* meant "leave me alone, please." I suppose the reason I was so upset was because I myself am prone to talk my head off, but there I had met my Waterloo. It was my inability to say anything that kept me boiling inside.

Fr. Prange left Alaska four years later and never returned to the Yukon. He became a chaplain in the McNeil Island penitentiary, where for many years he charmed the prisoners with his long stories about the Yukon. It was an ideal setting with the prisoners having nothing else to do and the chaplain entertaining them "world without end. Amen."

In his eighties he went blind. People would ask him what happened to his eyes. He had the answer ready: It had been his habit as a good Jesuit to see Christ in his superiors, he said. But of late he had to strain his eyes so hard to see Christ in them, that the poor eyes gave up in despair and went blind. He died peacefully in Tacoma, Washington, and this left me wondering. Would heaven be the same after he got there? I suppose it will depend on the system of communication among souls that is used there. Anyway, God is there in full command; all will be fine.

The *Alice* left for Marshall, a very long haul to go. When we arrived it was drizzling. Since that was the end of the line, I got my trunk and suitcases out. Anchored nearby was a smaller boat, but big enough to push two big barges. It was an N.C. boat, which stood for Northern Commercial (the company that supplied the Yukon Delta stores with cargo).

I spoke to the captain, who greeted me as if we were old friends. He told me to tell the crew to put my stuff on board. No, no charge at all. He knew all the priests and had the greatest admiration for them all. "Just come in, Father, and I'll take you to Hamilton. We'll be there in a couple of days." He added that Fr. John Sifton was in town. The boat would be there about a couple of hours. So I became installed in the boat and went ashore to meet the great Fr. Sifton.

Marshall had then a very small chapel with one room attached. This room was the living quarters and there I met him. I briefly told him my odyssey. He threw his head back in a hearty laughter that put me at ease instantly. He knew that Fr. Jette had been so right when he'd characterized Alaska as a madhouse without a keeper. He said that the same things happened to the government in Alaska; the Bureau of Indian Affairs pulled stunts that you wouldn't believe.

Fr. John B. Sifton, S.J., had been born in Alsace-Lorraine of German stock. After his ordination to the priesthood in America, he had spent nine years doing missionary work among the Indians in Wyoming, where he had learned two Indian languages. This facility for learning languages had prompted the superiors to send him to Alaska, where the missionaries complained that the Eskimo language was very difficult.

He had arrived in Alaska in 1912, and soon he had mastered the language but was reluctant to teach it. He had learned it by ear and felt that others could do the same. His common sense had become so apparent that he had been made general superior and had kept that job for thirteen years in a row. Now he was general superior again.[2]

While we were chatting now in his little room he asked me if I needed any money. No, I didn't need any. I told him I had one hundred dollars in currency and all bills paid. In the Depression that was a lot of money. His eyes beamed with joy and he asked to see that money. I passed the wallet to him. He took it, shuffled the greenbacks a couple of times, kept eighty dollars, and gave me back the wallet with a mere twenty dollars. He added with much relief: "My, Father, you sure came in handy. I was absolutely penniless."

My first reaction was that I had been robbed. It looked like highway robbery. But then upon reconsideration I saw that he was my legitimate superior and had a right to do just what he did. Also, this episode sobered me up. What was in store for me in Alaska if the general superior was penniless? What could I expect?

Finally, he outlined the trip for me. I had to wait in Hamilton for the arrival of Bro. Murphy, S.J., who would connect with the N.C. to take a load of cargo for Akulurak and would pick me up. There was a church and a room in Hamilton where I was to stay. The pastor, Fr. Martin Lonneux, S.J., just now was away visiting in Chaniliak and could be back in Hamilton anytime. I was to make myself at home there.

---

1. Like all institutions Holy Cross had its ups and downs and in the summer of 1956 it was closed. Holy Cross remained as a day school. Its buildings were dismantled. The boarders who had no place to go were flown to a newly built school in Copper Valley, halfway between Fairbanks and Anchorage. This school in turn was also abandoned in 1970 and later on it burned to the ground.

2. By 1938 Fr. Sifton lost his memory. He did not know the time, the month, the day of the week, whether or not he had had breakfast, and other such daily necessities. He died at Hooper Bay on October 20, 1940, at the age of sixty-nine. He died suddenly while he was making his customary examination of conscience before going to bed.

5

Traveling Down River

The N.C. left when it was already dark. Too bad, because I wanted to see what the country looked like. In the morning I found a stack of hot cakes in the little dining room. The Eskimo cook brought in bacon, toast, and all the coffee to be had. The weather was raw, chilly, miserable. But in that little dining room, life was a joy. The crew smoked and smoked but I did not mind. They eyed me with curiosity. I knew that all wanted to know who I was, so I chatted with them and told them many things.

We came to Mountain Village, where much unloading took place. While the crew worked, I went to the empty church, followed by a large crowd of children. They had been to school at Holy Cross and Akulurak and others were attending the local school, so they spoke English. I taught them catechism and told them Bible stories with other stories that made them attentive and happy. This I took as a good omen. But we had to part.

Back in the boat, we left Mountain Village and we headed for the flats. From now on we were not going to be near any hill, let alone any mountain. The river looked immense. As I stood alone on deck I saw the last flocks of geese flying south. The river was becoming wider. Here and there I could see sloughs leaving the main channel and disappearing in the willows. We were now on the delta of the Yukon. There were the northern, the middle, and the southern channels, all big rivers and all emptying a few miles away into the Bering Sea.

Our boat entered the northern channel that took us to Hamilton, a small Eskimo village which the natives called *Noonapilugak* or "Filthy Village," because in the summer it sits on mud. The sound of the engines brought all the people to the bank. This was a Catholic village. When they saw a priest on board, all got excited. No sooner had we tied to the bank than a dozen men came in to take my baggage ashore. They led me in triumph to the church, where we gathered to exchange greetings and impressions. A good many of those young men had been in our Akulurak school; they spoke English, but the older people spoke nothing but Eskimo. They showed me where the pastor kept things. Since there was a store nearby, I bought canned food with the twenty dollars I still had, so I was sitting pretty.

That very evening we rang the bell and everyone came to confession and to say the rosary. Now this was the heart of Eskimo country. My ears began to be hit by those impossible sounds. They said the rosary in Eskimo. In the Hail Mary they had the word *to-ko-ka-ta-thlim-ne* which meant "and at the hour of our death," seven of our words packed into one of theirs. In the Our Father it was much worse. We came to words like *a-shi-li-nil-res-tul-rest-kut*. The problem of even grasping those words appeared serious to me. As for the confessions, I told them to confess in their own language and I would tell the Lord to pay attention, which He would certainly do. I sat in a faraway corner and they were coming one by one, uttering those guttural sounds with great facility.

Since I was going to be there a few days, we set the order of the day as follows: Mass every morning at seven. Catechism for the children at 2:00 P.M. Rosary and sermon for all at 7:00 P.M. It worked like a charm.

During the day the children crowded my room. I filled many pages with Eskimo words, verbs, and sentences. It was a circus for them to teach me words. When I tried to pronounce them, they bent over with laughter. I remember having read from Chinese missionaries that children were better teachers than adults; an adult will let you get away with murder out of politeness. Though you mispronounce the word, the adult will tell you that it was good enough, whereas the child will make you repeat it all day till he is satisfied. He has no feelings.

I recall that after taking terrible beatings from those kids, my ego blew up and I challenged them to pronounce a few carefully chosen Spanish words that are real lulus like *torrejoncillo, ferrocarril,* and *cejijunto.* When they began to gag in their attempts, I mocked great surprise and laughed. Thus they learned that the whole world was not the town of Hamilton or Noonapilugak. From then on our academic occupation became less noisy and more profitable.

The evenings were wonderful. The church was full. First they had the rosary in Eskimo. Then I got up and began to explain different points of religion. The interpreter was a newly wed Eskimo who kept his eyes on the floor to concentrate better and then he would pass to the rest what I had just said. At the end I gave them my blessing and they trooped out in good order. I was impressed by their behavior, their devotion, their respect and love and admiration for the priest. It was clear that my predecessors had done a magnificent job in training them.

After all left, I was alone in the building. The blessed Sacrament was in the tabernacle. The Lord and I were left there to ourselves. That was my initiation to the many years ahead for the two of us living alone under the same roof, with only one wall separating us day and night.

For those who think that this was an ideal situation, let me inform them that living alone with the Lord, staying with the Lord, spending time in silence before the tabernacle, meditating or contemplating in silence without reading a book or saying the rosary, is the hardest occupation under the sun. Digging ditches under a hot sun is preferable to meditating in silence in an empty church. For one thing, the Lord does not talk back. If He does, it is to let the soul see herself as God sees her: ignorant, weak, blind, sinful. This view of self is anything but pleasing. The temptation is to look at the wrist watch, figure that one has been there long enough, stand up, and leave. There are few souls like St. John of the Cross who would go to the garden at 3:00 A.M. under a starry sky and sit on the grass till the sun got too hot for his bald head to bear.

Another important thing when one is living under the same roof with the Lord—not like in a great monastery or a convent but in a small, frame building with but one thin wall between the two—is this: Be careful how you deal with the Lord. There is a great danger of losing respect for Him and going about with a type of familiarity that breeds contempt, or at least disregard. If the soul allows herself to go down this far, she is running the serious risk of eventually losing her faith.

When the tabernacle means next to nothing, the state of the soul is alarmingly dangerous. One has to bear in mind at all times that the tabernacle contains the true God, and one has to act accordingly. It calls for slow and reverential genuflections, ejaculations that are like darts sent to the very heart of Christ, tender and affectionate looks that tell the Lord worlds in a flash, short prayers, and so on. One has to unite great reverence with great intimacy. I learned that early in my solitary life in the Alaskan wilderness.

My peaceful life in Hamilton was interrupted and brought to an abrupt end with the arrival of Fr. Martin Lonneux, S.J., the pastor of Hamilton. On his heels came Bro. Alfred Murphy, S.J., piloting the river boat *Treca* with two Eskimo boys in their late teens.

Fr. Lonneux was a Belgian, born on February 2, 1890. In 1924 he had come to Alaska to the Yukon Delta, which was not the same anymore after his arrival. A man of steel with a thunderous voice and a head full of plans, he made his presence felt at once. He was a carpenter, a painter, a cook, a mechanic, a builder, an electrician, and also a priest. With a clear French accent, he tackled the Eskimo language with all the might at his disposal. He soon knew that he could never preach in it, but he surrounded himself with the best interpreters in the land.

With their aid, he translated the catechism into Eskimo and then did the same thing with the Mass and Catholic hymnals and all manners of prayers. He had a typewriter made expressly to print those impossible Eskimo sounds that cannot be reproduced with our alphabets. The *Indian Sentinel,* printed in Washington, D.C., supplied the money he needed for this gargantuan plan. Mind you, he did all this without being able to preach in Eskimo.

Fr. Lonneux had a knack for putting people to good use. This virtue carried to extremes made of him a benevolent dictator, a benign czar, and a tolerable kaiser. He had four villages under his pastoral jurisdiction. He ruled over them completely. He was the mayor and the priest and the chief of police. He had very much to say about where they would fish and for how long. People went beaver hunting when he passed the word and not before. Also, not everyone could go beaver hunting. If the wife was pregnant, for instance, Lonneux decided whether the husband could go, depending on whether or not there was a fit place for her to stay in his absence. People could not leave to hunt seals before benediction or the rosary in the church. Masses and religious services were attended by all. He built in Chaniliak—his favorite station—a big, lovely hall where women could do their needlework around a hot wood stove, with good light and lots of floor space for the little children to romp. There was not the slightest doubt as to who was in command there. He was, and no one else.

But time is a silent file that abrades and wears things out. In time, as he grew old, he knew that he had lost his grip on the men. They began to drink and to miss Mass. He confided once to me that his people were getting out of hand. Actually, they were fine parishioners, very good people. But they were *doing their thing* without consulting him and they got away with it. No bishop or superior ever dared to interfere with his methods. They would visit him today and leave tomorrow. He was busy. He had no time to listen.[1]

As I said, he came home to Hamilton, where I was, and after a tasty supper that he cooked, followed by rosary in church for the people, we sat down by the stove to chat. He was a big smoker. It was before 8:00 P.M. when we began our conversation, I mean his monologue, and it was well after one in the morning when we went to bed. He got tired. I could see that he could not hold a candle to Fr. Prange.

He told me about his studies in the Society of Jesus, his early apostolate among the Indians in the States, his early years in Alaska, and finally, his present method. That was his favorite phrase: *my method*. He enlarged on how he overcame gigantic difficulties and how he managed to bring everything under control. He would repeat: "I am a man of experience, believe me." After having spent one whole night listening to Fr. Prange and half of one night listening to Fr. Lonneux, I began to wonder if Alaska grew those characters or if they came out that way from the wombs of their mothers. In the presence of Fr. Lonneux, I was a deaf mute.

With very little sleep that night, I got up early to say Mass, because Bro. Murphy told me that we had to start early, in the dark. After Mass I said good-bye to Fr. Lonneux and boarded the *Treca*, which was already roaring and ready to go. The boat was well loaded with cargo. It had a stove with an oven to do rudimentary cooking. Brother was at the steering wheel. Willy was the official deckhand, and Baltazar was the cook and deckhand. I was dressed like a clergyman, with Roman collar and all the trimmings.

The day was cold and cloudy. Chunks of ice were floating by. We were in the center of the Yukon Delta: a maze of rivers and sloughs crossing each other. Only an expert could pilot a boat there without getting hopelessly lost. Daylight came without a visible sun. Ours was the only boat in that immensity of rivers, willows, and sandbars. Where the banks were high, the noise of the engine echoed and reverberated all over. In time we came to the main channel, where the chunks of floating ice were bigger and more frequent. But our boat skillfully dodged and avoided every one of them. It was obvious that the steering wheel was in good hands. Thank God for that.

We were the only ones in that flat, vast solitude. It began to get dark. Baltazar, the cook, had on the stove cans of salmon caught in that very river, perhaps in the waters we were now plying. Salmon here is staple food. People can eat salmon three times a day every day. To break the monotony, they cook it or process it in different ways. The food of the dogs is also salmon. God, who is good and merciful, put the salmon here to give the people calories in abundance against the adverse weather they have to face. So we ate canned salmon mixed with canned pork and beans and washed down with coffee.

Finally, it got dark, really dark. We left the Yukon and entered the Akulurak slough at a place called Akorpak. What names! Will I remember them? Now we were going down a smaller river that bent like a snake moving on dust. It got pitch dark. Was there an end to the trip? Oh yes; we should be there in one more hour. But where were we?

I will tell you where we were. We were nowhere. During the war the army put four soldiers in Akulurak to monitor the weather and report to army headquarters every hour on the hour. The soldiers were getting supplies by air. The army planes had such a hard time finding the place that the soldiers had to be moved to Mountain Village, on top of the last little hill sticking out in that vast solitude of nothingness.

Finally, the lights of Akulurak became visible and eventually we hit the banks where the mission sits. There was a group of schoolboys who boarded the boat before the engine stopped. No one knew that a priest was on board. Within minutes the local superior, Fr. Paul O'Connor, S.J., appeared and we looked at each other like two bobcats. He had heard that a new priest was coming to the missions, but not for Akulurak.

He was extremely happy and showed it in a thousand ways. Now at long last he was liberated. You see, Fr. John Lucchesi, S.J., was seventy-seven years old and unable to do much work other than saying Mass. Fr. O'Connor had a good dog team to visit the vast district committed to us, and he loved dogs and loved the trail. Now, with me on hand, he could take off by sled and stay away as long as he cared to. It was too good to be true. He told me that he was very grateful to Fr. Tomkin for having sent me down river. Tomkin's loss was O'Connor's gain. I began to understand a little better the saying that God writes straight with crooked lines.

The father of the Prodigal Son did not show more joy than O'Connor did when he saw me under his roof. Surrounded by the boys, we marched into the living quarters. There were two stalwarts of the missions seated quietly at a table and eyeing me with much curiosity. They were Fr. Lucchesi and Bro. Keogh, whose real name was Chiaudano, both from Italy. We were to become very close friends as time went by.

I was given the last room available in the house. It was big enough for a cot, a table, and a chair, which was good enough. The bed cover was the skin of a brown bear. I loved that. It made me feel like an Arctic explorer. We talked for a while and went to bed. Fr. O'Connor was a slave to the doctrine that if you go to bed early and get up early, you will become a howling success. Who does not want to be successful in life?

Next morning he showed me around the place. First he took me to see the Ursuline Sisters, who were there as teachers and in charge of the girl boarders. It was great! Yes, yes, of course I would soon visit them and tell them everything I knew, whatever it was. Then we visited the classrooms. There were eight grades with the three Rs and a little more. Father cheered them up, telling them that I was a storyteller, especially scary stories. Great!

Then we went to the adjacent village, with some twelve Eskimo families, all Catholic, naturally. No, nobody knew where Spain was, but they were sure that she was somewhere, and they were quite right.

And so I took possession of my new assignment. I went to the chapel to thank the Lord for having brought me to such a lovely, beautiful place. It had taken me thirty-nine days from Seattle. In those days I had aged considerably and garnered precious experiences that were to help me a great deal in days and years to come.

---

1. Fr. Lonneux became sick in the winter of 1952 and had to be taken out of active duty. In the summer he was taken to Seattle to mend. By Christmas he could not stand being out of Alaska any longer. He prevailed with Bishop Gleeson, who took him to Fairbanks. In Fairbanks he began to talk about returning to Chaniliak to finish his writings in Eskimo, but he never made it. The Lord took him on January 21, 1953.

6

Welcome to the Akulurak Mission

The mission, started on Nelson Island in the village of Tununak in 1889, did not prosper and was soon abandoned, though Tununak was visited once a year by a priest. The missionaries found a better location on the Yukon Delta that was heavily populated. Being close to the Yukon River was a great asset for getting supplies.

They settled on the banks of the Kanelik River and built a house with a chapel. This was in 1891. Next year when the river ice broke, they were flooded. Bro. Cunningham looked for a higher bank and found it one mile away on the Akulurak River, and there they built. In 1894 they built a little convent and school.

The natives were astonished to see those white men and were very sorry for them. Then the Sisters of Saint Ann came in to start the school. When the natives saw the sisters, they breathed a sigh of relief. At long last the white men had brought in their wives. To them the truest part of the Bible is the passage from Genesis where God said that it is not good for man to be alone. Soon children were brought in as boarders and the work of the school began in earnest.

That whole area was then thickly populated with Eskimos, who were practically untouched by white presence. The land was ruled by medicine men who ruled with an iron hand. They were the custodians of the unwritten law. The presence of the Catholic school in their very midst posed a real threat to the preservation of said unwritten law. So they passed the word that the school had to go. Anyone allowing his children to go to that school would get sick and die. People believed then that a medicine man could kill by thought by sending invisible arrows that were deadly.

By 1898 the school had to close. No children were available. With the closing of the school, the missionaries also left because they were sure that the only way to penetrate those mentalities would be through the children. Get them before they are taught by the medicine men.

It seemed that God came to the rescue. In 1900 an epidemic decimated the land, and it was harder on medicine men. Few of them survived. In 1902 Akulurak was revived. In 1904 the school was refurbished and now the Ursuline nuns from Montana came to run it.

In 1905 Mother Laurentia came on the scene. That Irish nun was going to be the pillar of the school for some thirty-three years. She trained scores of girls who in turn became Catholic mothers.

In an effort to educate the natives to the fact that the priests and nuns were not husbands and wives, the quarters of the priests and boys were at the other end of the property. Out of curiosity I counted six hundred long steps between the two buildings. The nuns lived with the girls and the priests lived with the boys, and that was that. In the early thirties Fr. John Fox, S.J., started a community of Eskimo sisters in neighboring Hooper Bay. I say this to show how quickly the natives understood the doctrine of chastity, though they did not feel themselves called to practice it.

In 1919 another epidemic just about killed the few medicine men who were left. Also the numbers of Eskimo orphans increased considerably. Thus the school got filled to capacity. Soon, newlyweds raised in Akulurak began to fill those flatlands with at least a veneer of Christianity, which made it a lot easier for the missionary on his periodic trips by dog team.

There were no real villages then. People lived in small settlements, usually a few families closely related. They were living off the land and the water, so they chose their own little territory. After all, there are only so many rabbits and foxes and minks and fish to a square mile. The priest had to visit those little settlements by dog team to say Mass, preach, and give the Sacraments.

If he found children old enough to start school, he would plead with the parents or uncles and hope the child could be had. Then the child was taken to Akulurak to engross the numbers. Often those children had lice and were in a pitiful condition. Once I brought in a boy with long hair. I cut his hair and threw it into the fire. Then I told him to bend over so I could comb his short hair. I had two small boys flanking him with instructions to count the lice that would fall on the floor, and step on them and kill them. They counted and killed seventy-seven lice. How many lice went into the fire with the long hair, God alone knew for sure.

With the years, conditions improved. There were fewer lice. People were learning to take better care of themselves. Today's young people do not have the foggiest idea of how their grandparents lived. People have banded together in villages with a day school, a church, a store, and a movie hall. The girls wear lipstick and the boys sport neckties. If their grandparents came back from the grave, they would think that they were in another country with a different civilization. I am depicting what I experienced upon my arrival in Eskimoland.

When I arrived, I was impressed by the work done by my predecessors, who had started from scratch in a forbidding land of unbelievable poverty. Now we had the convent—an imposing building with a dormitory for the girls upstairs, a large hall with a huge wood stove in the middle, a big chapel, a big dining room, and a kitchen with a range that was a honey. Next to it was a warehouse for the immediate needs of the sisters. Then there was the beautiful building with the classrooms. Next came the big church that was used only in the summer and for Christmas and Easter. Next came the general warehouse with three hundred gunny sacks of flour and twenty sacks each of rice, beans, sugar, and farina, plus other sacks of diverse cereals. Next came the igloo-like underground to keep the one hundred sacks of potatoes supplied by Holy Cross in exchange for the seal oil and deer skins we sent them. Next came the carpenter shop.

Finally came the house for the fathers, brothers, and the boys, with its chapel, kitchen, dormitory, and large hall for the boys to play. Connecting the string of buildings there was a wooden walk. At some distance were the houses for the dogs. Near the back, all by itself, was the huge smokehouse to smoke the thousands of salmon caught every summer. At a short distance was the village. We were all one unit. If a villager misbehaved, he could be told to move away. The village was sitting on our property.

Fr. O'Connor was the local superior. Fr. Lucchesi was there in residence, practically retired. Bro. Keogh was then sixty-four. Brother was so stout that he could not tie his shoes, so he wore short skin boots that did not need strings. As a cook he had no equal. According to Fr. Sifton, who knew what he was talking about, Brother was the dandiest and dirtiest cook. Both the kitchen and the dining room were anything but clean.

He shaved every week whether he needed it or not—usually on Saturday. His room was so messy that one needed a guide to go from the door to the window. I asked him once if he had ever made his bed. He thought for a while and said that he did not remember. His bed was something else. He had several blankets—never sheets—and when he went to sleep he would lift more or fewer blankets, depending on the weather at the moment, and would crawl in over the rest. He could do anything and everything. He was a mechanic, a boatman, a painter, a violinist, a cabinet maker, and a top cook.

At one time there had been other Italian missionaries on the Yukon. Now Fr. Lucchesi was the only one left. When Fr. Lucchesi died, the good brother felt in his heart that life now was not worth much, so at sixty-nine he went to bed and told the Lord to please take him to heaven. The Lord obliged and took him on May 27, 1940. He had come to Alaska in 1900.

The other brother in our little community was Alfred Murphy, S.J., who had happened to be born in Calgary, Canada. His parents had lived in Everett, Washington, and had heard that there were good jobs in Calgary. They had gone to find out, but they discovered that Everett was better, so they had returned. In the meantime little Alfred, conceived in Everett, had been born a Canadian.

He had forgotten all about it, because he had returned to America in his mother's arms. But when the Second World War came upon us and he was the postmaster of Akulurak, he had to prove that he was an American citizen. Lo and behold, the record showed that he had been born in Calgary in 1886. Even so, the government was satisfied that he was American.

Brother Murphy was prefect of the boys. In addition, he was the head fisherman who supplied us with all the fish we needed, and he was also the provider of all the firewood we needed for the fourteen stoves that kept the mission warm all winter. He would go out in September about fifty miles up river with half a dozen men and in two weeks he would be back with several rafts of logs properly tied together. The logs were taken from the shores where they were waiting on a first come, first served basis. In the *Treca* first and then in the *Sifton,* this brother kept Akulurak supplied with wood and goods.

One of the first things I noticed when I settled there was the isolation from the rest of the world. There was no telephone, no newspaper, no streets, no cars. The mail arrived twice a month by dog team in the winter and by river boat in the summer. There was no mail at all in May because of the break-up, or between October 15 and November 15 because of the freeze-up.

A traveling doctor would show up about once in ten years and a dentist was an unknown entity. I asked what happened if we got sick. The answer was that we may just die. The nearest hospital run by the Bureau of Indian Affairs might or might not be reached. One had been built at Mountain Village, but it was soon condemned and moved to Bethel, a long distance away. There was hope that the little planes that had begun to fly between Fairbanks and Anchorage would eventually move westward. It was then a fervent hope.

As a result of this isolation, one soon began to unwind and relax. No hurry to go anywhere. Also I found soon enough that the weather was a sort of commander-in-chief in all operations. Boats had to sit it out on the opposite shore till the waves abated and the Yukon could be crossed. A snowstorm that lasted three days would keep everyone at home playing cards or chess or mending nets or building a sled. And rain in the winter was far worse than snow; it could be tragic if a warm wind would break the sea ice and the frozen land were covered with sea water and ice floes. People caught hunting seals were then in a real predicament. Even later on, when the planes carried the mail, the message was invariably this: "I'll be there first thing in the morning, WP," which stood for weather permitting. If the weather did not permit it, there was no mail.

One week after I arrived, we had the first snowfall of the season. Immediately, dog teams began to make trails in all directions. The men went out to set traps to catch black fish in small creeks. I was curious to see what those fish looked like, for I had no idea that there could be black fish. Sure enough, a man took me along and we came to a very narrow creek connecting two lakes. He broke the ice and lifted a trap that was two-thirds filled with wiggling fish about four or five inches in length and quite black. Those fish would be alive for several days out of water, and they were constantly wiggling like restless frogs.

The third trap had a dead mink. The man grinned at me and said, "This is what I was looking for." Minks go after those fish through holes they make in the ice. A mink can stay inside the water for quite a while in hot pursuit of fish. When he grabs one or more, he returns to the hole and comes out to enjoy his meal. Naturally, he has his own territory and digs several holes to be sure that he is always close to one of them, following the instinct that divine Providence gave him for survival. But then man comes along with his ingenuity and reasoning power to defeat that instinct. The hapless mink sees under the ice a trap full of fish and goes right in, hoping to get rich with so much loot. What happens is that the entrance becomes so narrow at its end that neither fish nor mink can figure out how to retrace their steps and get out. The fish wiggle there forever while the mink soon drowns.

We returned with two sacks of fish and one mink. The trap was made of long strips of wood that the Eskimo made out of ordinary sticks found by the river banks. The strips were held together with the sinew of seals. In other words, an Eskimo did not have to buy anything to set the trap. And here we were, with two gunny sacks of fish and one mink. Talk about living off the land—a frozen land covered with wind-swept snow the very sight of which would put panic in the hearts of civilized brave men. That was my first encounter with what could be termed Eskimo culture.

I had on ordinary shoes, and my feet got cold. My friend was wearing skin boots made of the skin of seals. Inside these he wore two pairs of socks. The socks went inside of a sort of moccasin made of rabbit skin lined on the outside with calico. Inside each boot there was a generous amount of dry grass. His feet, then, were resting on dry grass that kept them away from the ice or snow. He told me that he could be out all day walking on snow or ice without getting cold feet. This added another item to Eskimo culture.

If they wanted to wade in water or if they wanted to take precautions against getting their feet wet, then the skin boot was depilated and smeared with seal oil. That made the boot absolutely waterproof. Or the boots could have been made out of the skin of big fish. Those boots could be made long enough to cover the hips and they were practically weightless. This natural ingenuity meant simply that they did not have to buy costly rubber boots.

But there was a catch here. Not every woman has the natural talent to make stitches that are waterproof. Hence a girl who could make waterproof stitches was a sought treasure. Bear in mind that the man was always outdoors hunting, trapping, and fishing. He could do that if he could keep his feet dry under any conditions. On the other hand, it was only women who could make boots and repair them. It was an unbearable humiliation for a man to have to sew boots. He would rather be found dead than mending his own boots. So, when a man looked for a wife, one of the first qualifications of the girl was her ability to make boots that would not leak.

Women developed certain talents for making special types of stitches that were near perfect if not altogether perfect. They kept that secret to themselves and only taught it to their own daughters. Let's suppose that Mother feels that the son of Mary Jones would make an excellent husband for her daughter Ann. She would go quietly to Mary Jones and give her a pair of boots made by Ann for her son. Mary Jones would pass the tips of her fingers very slowly and knowingly over the seams. If her clinical eye told her that they were the real McCoy, she would keep them. When her son came home, she would present the boots to him, saying that those were the best boots she had ever seen, and they were made by Ann for him, yes, son, for you alone; what a joy to have a wife who can make boots like that. Right then and there the deal would be made and an affirmative message sent to Mary Jones. The next step was to see the priest and arrange the wedding. The girl's looks did not enter into the picture.

The last day of October the river was frozen hard enough to allow people to travel over it. I wanted to feel the thrill of crossing a river over the ice. When I went down the bank and saw the river like a well-paved road, I instinctively looked at both sides for oncoming cars. Right then and there I experienced an immense relief at the thought that I would never again have to be bothered with traffic. This was Alaska, the real Alaska; the land of freedom from a thousand cares that make life miserable for most of mankind. No traffic, no red lights, no left turns, no air pollution, no noise, no policemen, no currency, no rush, and no hurry.

We were near the shores of the Bering Sea. Our parish—district— had four thousand square miles with some seven hundred people. This gave us almost six square miles per person to breathe and swing our arms. Wasn't that terrific?

The snow kept falling. Now that the whole land was frozen solid and people could cross it in any direction by dog team, it was my turn to learn the mechanics of handling a dog team. Baltazar, who was the cook in the boat, was the man in charge of the dogs. He never learned to speak English, but he could understand it. He was then twenty, tough as nails, very knowledgeable on matters of survival on the trail, born and raised in the neighborhood and with an excellent sense of direction when the snow was falling and visibility was zero.

We hitched nine dogs, which itself was a work of art because they were big malamute dogs that had been chained for a long time and now they were desperate to hit the trail. I was told to hold the loose dog and lift his front so he could walk only on his hind legs. This was because if he put his four legs on the ground, I could not hold him; he would either drag me or run away.

The sled was tied to a post with a thick rope. The leader was the first to be hitched. He would hold the line straight and keep the other dogs from turning around in circles. When the nine dogs were hitched, they made an infernal noise with their furious barking. As soon as the sled was untied, they felt it and started on a mad gallop as if they were pursuing a rabbit. To hold the sled on an even keel, so to say, took a lot of expertise and muscle.

There was a comic side to it. Invariably, their bowels would move somewhere between the first and second mile. Usually, it was one dog at a time. Sometimes it would be two at a time. The poor dog or dogs wanted to squat and be relieved, but the others would have none of that and kept galloping at full speed. The result was that the hapless dog was carried away in that squatting position as though he were skiing on his hind legs. And so it was with all the dogs except with the leader. This little prince would slow down, turn aside, relieve himself, and then renew the running. All understood that it was the leader's right and privilege, and they respected that privilege. If there is honor among thieves, what do the thieves have that the dogs have not?

When Baltazar yelled, "Gee, gee, gee," the leader turned right immediately. When he yelled, "Haw, haw, haw," the leader turned left mechanically, as in a push-button operation.

If we met another dog team coming in our direction, we had to avoid a head-on collision that could have catastrophic consequences—like a maimed dog or dogs. A good leader led his dogs away from the fight. If both teams had a good leader, there was no problem. If one leader was not trained, he himself made for the team in front and the collision was unavoidable. The operation started a long way before the teams came close. If both leaders were seen maneuvering to avoid the fight, then all was well. If not, then it was a good thing if there were two men in one sled, because this extra man would hold the leader of his team and scare away the opposite leader. If there was no extra man, then the men held chains and waded right into the fray, hitting on the head those dogs already locked into a mortal fight. The chains did the work. After much cursing (if the men were white) or much yelling (if the men were Eskimo), the fighting dogs got untangled and the run continued. Some dogs may have limped a little or bled through their ears.

Eskimos did not curse. There is no cursing in the Eskimo language. The worst that an Eskimo would say was : "Oh, mena hona," which means something like "Oh, you despicable thing." Of course, later on when the natives fraternized with their white brethren and learned English, they soon learned how to swear like the best, I mean the worst, sailor. Baltazar stuck to his "Oh, mena hona" as long as I knew him. Myself, I constructed a grandiloquent sentence in Spanish and used it every time I thought it opportune. Often the Eskimos would ask what did I say, and I always gave the same answer: "It means, gee whiz." But they were not satisfied with my answer. There were too many words for just *gee whiz*.

After some time the dogs could not hold that galloping speed and gradually they settled to their natural dog pace. But if they would sight a fox or a rabbit or even a flying crow, or if they would smell those animals without seeing them, they would let out a few grunts and start galloping again.

In April, when the snow would be well packed and they would not sink, they could gallop for a long time, covering enormous distances in a short time. When the trail was soft and the snow was very deep and the load of the sled was heavy, the poor dogs just crawled and would look back at the driver in protest. Then the driver became the best dog and pushed the sled with all his might if he had any left himself.

It is very important that the dogs know and love the driver. I made it a point to feed them myself often, scratch their ears, pat them, caress them, bring them water to drink, fill their boxes with fresh dry grass so they would have a warm bed in freezing weather. They appreciated it visibly.

The first week of November brought low temperatures. The trail now was safe. Fr. O'Connor and Baltazar began to make preparations for long trips. The harness was in order; the sled was tops; dog feed was packed; the sled cover was in good repair; skin boots for a change were together in a sack, and the box with canned food was carefully tucked between the sleeping bags. The Mass-kit had been carefully examined to be sure that nothing was missing. In one of my trips I forgot to pack the small missal. Wine and hosts were a must. After a trip the Mass-kit was cleaned and the linens washed. It was easy to forget to replace every item.

One morning they took off and I was instructed to keep the mission functioning.

Fr. Llorente with Eskimo parishoners

John L. Lucchesi, S.J., born in Genoa, Italy in 1858, was seventy-seven and still saying Mass when Llorente arrived in Akulurak in 1935. He served as general superior 1909–1913 and again 1930–1931. After 38 years in the Yukon, he died in 1937 at Holy Cross.

The "big church" at Akulurak, used only in the summers and at Christmas and Easter

Paul O'Connor, S.J., the local superior when Fr. Llorente first arrived in Akulurak. He spent forty-five years in Alaska, died in 1979 at the age of 81 in Spokane, where he had grown up.

John Fox, S.J., founded a congregation of Eskimo sisters to help evangelize five villages in the Hooper Bay area, where Fr. Llorente conducted a seven-day retreat.

An Eskimo and her baby, with salmon hanging to dry. At Akulurak, thousands of salmon were caught every summer and smoked in a huge smokehouse near the banks of the Yukon River.

This fine dog team with sled was used by Fr. O'Connor and Fr. Llorente to visit their vast district in Akulurak.

7

Akulurak Stories

Actually, I had very little to do with the mission's functioning. It was already like a well-oiled train chugging on its tracks. Mass in Latin every morning, with the prayers in Eskimo. Catechism five days a week in the classrooms. The three meals at their proper times. The chores.

These included for the boys to saw logs and chop wood in the afternoons, to carry water in sleds from a hole cut in the ice, to cook smoked salmon for the dogs when they were not away, to sweep the hall and dormitory, and to replenish the wood boxes near every stove.

For the girls it meant for the oldest ones to make and repair skin boots, to do the laundry once a week, and to teach other girls how to do this; to help in the bakery and in the kitchen. For the small girls it meant sweeping and dusting so everything would be clean and to help with the dishes, to prepare the dining room, and so forth. Everyone had a task to do and every task had a supervisor.

As new children were brought in, they learned automatically to join the rest and do things properly. Everything ran so very smoothly! Mother Laurentia ran the girls' side with a firm hand and Bro. Murphy was a master prefect on the boys' side. Those children were taught the three Rs plus religion plus cleanliness plus work plus regimentation.

Once every four or five years one boy would be missing. It meant that he was not taking kindly to regimentation and was ready to risk his life to avoid it. The runaway was soon found and taken back and told to behave and be nice. But on one occasion it was not so. Two boys took off and were never seen again. There were no roads there. It was all tundra, a vast flat country crisscrossed by sloughs and dotted with lakes and ponds and swamps. When searching parties called off the search, it was unanimously believed that the boys had stepped on thin ice and never surfaced. Then came the guilt feelings and the weeping and gnashing of teeth.

Sundays were very special days. Both boys and girls put on their glad rags and were not allowed to do any work whatever. Of course, the word *allowed* is ironic, because if there was anything they really loved and relished, it was to be allowed not to do anything.

On Sundays there was the customary low Mass before breakfast. Then at 10:00 A.M. there was a solemn high Mass sung in perfect Latin, plus the sermon and all the trimmings. Before supper there was rosary with benediction. The rest of the day it was absolute freedom of movement—within reason!

As local superiors came and went, more prayers were added or were dropped. When Fr. Francis Menager, S.J., ran the place, devotions proliferated. Fr. Edmund Anable, S.J., and I were present once at a First Friday performance by Fr. Menager in the general chapel. It was a long affair with many incensations, songs, fervorinos, vocal prayers, more incensations, and more hymns. When it was all over, I whispered to Fr. Anable and asked him if our students of theology in the seminary would put up with all that. His quick, terse answer was, "They would mutiny to a man."

As I look back on it, I think that the subtle reason for so many devotions was that there was nothing else to do. Outdoors it was too cold for baseball or football. There was no TV. Movies had not arrived yet. Hiking was out of the question since going over the snow was painful. There was no library and no one would have used it if there had been one. So the founding fathers started entertaining the children in a religious manner that persisted for quite some time.

I used to entertain them with fantastic stories that I concocted as I was telling them. The boys did not need me so much for entertainment because their hall was visited by the villagers and other visiting Eskimos who brought them chewing tobacco and told them what was going on in the region.

But the girls were more isolated, so I would go Sunday evenings to have a circus in their big hall. As soon as I entered, they made a big circle with their chairs and benches, and the fun began. Did they

prefer laughing stories, educational stories, serious stories, interesting stories, or scary stories? The answer was thunderous: *scary, scary!*

They would lock arms for self-protection and self-preservation.
The small girls were firmly held by older ones. I would have only one
light. Then all purgatory broke loose. There were ghosts and
apparitions. There were wolves and bears going after little children
who were picking blueberries with their mothers because they had
nothing else to eat. There were exceptionally pretty princesses stolen
by ugly good-for-nothing, one-eyed men who insisted on marrying
them or they would cut their heads off, though the pretty girls wept
and wept and wept. And naturally the girls in my audience began to
bring their handkerchiefs to their eyes.

There were voices heard at night in a graveyard, and I imitated
those voices and repeated what those voices said. There were
medicine men who felt that they were losing their power, so they
would go to a graveyard on moon-lit nights to dig up some bones,
crush them with a hammer, and eat them; whereupon they regained
their power to make incantations.

There was the empty gray house that appeared suddenly in the
wilderness. Nobody was inside, yet the chimney was smoking day
and night—though there was no fire in the stove. When someone
walked in, an invisible foot would give him a terrible kick in the
pants, or a black hand coming from the ceiling would give him a slap
that left him only half conscious. Or maybe two black hands would
come and grab him by the neck and try to choke him. Of course, my
two hands would swing wildly all over the circle as if seeking whom
to choke; hence the locking of arms for self-preservation. Their
screams had to be heard to be believed.

After much fear of ghosts, finally I put them all at ease with the
latest discovery: It had happened in a town far away from Akulurak.
An Eskimo went hunting with snowshoes and got lost. He stumbled
into a graveyard with dozens of coffins lined up. (Eskimos in those
days never buried the coffins.) There was moonlight. The howls of
wolves were heard in the distance, but they were gradually coming
closer and closer. The poor Eskimo got caught between the coffins
and the howling nocturnal wolves. He said to himself, "What if a
ghost comes after me now?" And sure enough, a lanky ghost dressed
in white with terrifying eyes and very long fingers came out from
between the coffins and took after the Eskimo.

The poor man threw away the rifle and the snowshoes and ran

desperately to save himself. But the ghost was catching up and was getting closer, closer, closer till the man could feel the ghostly breath on his neck. But every time the ghost tried to grab him, the man managed to break loose till he ran completely out of breath and was forced to sit down on the snow.

The ghost then approached, patted him gently on the head, and said, "Why, friend, you and I ran some, didn't we?" The man answered between breaths, "Yes, we did, and when I get my breath back we will run some more."

But the ghost kept patting and caressing him and told him not to be afraid, adding: "We Alaskan ghosts are the friendly type. In other countries there are bad ghosts. But we Alaskan ghosts love people very much. Get up, friend, go home, and tell everybody what I have just said." And, saying this, he returned to the graveyard and was seen no more.

After this story, at least in theory, those children were not afraid of ghosts. Usually, they wanted to know more about the gray house in the wilderness. The goings on in that house took care of many a Sunday. Voices were heard saying this or that. Steps were heard usually in pursuit of the guy who got inside. Doors disappeared and left the guy in the dark and without exit; there were knocks, cries, pleadings, whispers—all by invisible people.

The girls kept asking why did people go inside. Well, those poor people were travelers who were starving and half frozen and when they saw such a beautiful house with smoke rising from the chimney, they knew that they could go in and have dry fish and tea and warm up. That's why. And they would answer, "Oh, I see."

But one day a guy came to town saying that he had a gray house that he wanted to sell for seventy-nine dollars and thirty-five cents. One widow with five little children bought it and moved in. The minute I said this, pandemonium broke out in the circle. They wanted me to keep the widow from moving in. And from all directions they were asking what happened to her and to the children.

Well, next Sunday we would know. "Oh, no, Father, you can't do this to us. We want to know what happened to them. Tell us, tell us, tell us." So I had to tell them: Just at midnight when they were sound asleep, someone was pulling the blankets from their beds, and whispers were heard, saying, "You get this one; I'll get that one." The poor woman got up and lit a candle, but an invisible mouth blew off the flame. Then things really began to happen . . .

But the girls were not the only ones. The good sisters had to have their fare, too. Only their fare was of an entirely different nature. While they were holding recreation in their living room after supper, I would show up with the writings of Saint Teresa under my arm. They were in their original Spanish and thus I was sure that we had the real meaning of the future doctor of the church.

The sisters were Ursulines, women of great faith, hope, and charity—a very selected group totally dedicated to their own salvation and the salvation of the girls entrusted to their motherly care, and all this for the greater glory of God.

Nuns those days had not heard the word *emancipation* and were the happiest group filled with the Holy Spirit—I mean, this particular group. Seated around the table by a warm stove, we would make comments on what Saint Teresa had written. Other times it would be Saint John of the Cross, also in the original. Other times I would take a theological treatise on sanctifying grace. Or a bulky manual on moral theology. It was obvious that the Lord was in our midst.

There we covered spiritual matters of great concern to us. There was nothing academic about it. No notes were taken. It was not a study class. It was just a relaxing, friendly conversation over what the saint said in this or that chapter. Thus we covered a lot of matter, like living in the presence of God while doing our daily chores by supernaturalizing everything we did or said; the evils of not living in the presence of God. Since we were created for the beatific vision, whatever helped us to achieve that supernatural end should be fostered, whereas whatever impeded us from reaching it should be avoided.

Then everyone would have her say about what helped and what would impede. A lively discussion could and would follow, and it was very interesting to hear what the Holy Spirit would inspire in some.

Saint John of the Cross, another doctor of the church, would come with a strong pitch for long visits to the blessed Sacrament. The question was how much time we religious in our active life could afford to spend kneeling or sitting in the chapel.

In the first place, unless a person is almost burning with love for Christ, there will always be one thousand and one excuses to stay away. It is almost certain that when confronted with an alternative, the Lord will lose out. There are always so very many things that can be done. We may not actually do them. But if an inspiration comes to go to the chapel to stay with the Lord, then those things pop out and scream and we cave in and leave the chapel to do them.

The question also was what to do in the chapel once alone, if the imagination was taking us millions of miles away. Saint Teresa complained that the imagination was the *loca de la casa,* that is, the crazy one inside our being.

How about saying rosaries? Or how about reading a spiritual book? But that was not the point. The point was to sit in the pew, rest our hands comfortably on or near our knees, put ourselves at ease, take full possession of ourselves, close the eyes, or look at the floor or at the altar, and be immersed in the presence of God. Should the imagination do too much mischief, then just tell yourself that you are there on guard duty; you are standing at the door of the palace of the King in the tabernacle as a sentinel guarding the entrance.

But again, no one can expect to walk into the church with a worldly mentality, almost a stranger to God, and kneel down and hope that God will pour over him Niagaras of graces and heavenly delights. It is against nature to go from ice boxes to hot ovens, back and forth between the two. To relish the presence of God before the tabernacle, the soul has to live that presence normally throughout the day.

The whole purpose of our comments on this was to avoid like venom the idea that one can hear Mass, say the rosary, receive holy Communion, say some vocal prayers, and that is all. A priest could be saying Mass without any personal contact with Christ. A nun could go through the spiritual exercises of the day without once meeting the eye of Christ. But lengthy visits before the blessed Sacrament could heal wounds and restore the soul to a healthy spiritual life, a life of intimacy with Christ. Then Christ will act through that person in a marvelous way. That person would thus become an apt instrument in God's hands to do wonders.

Those good sisters would wade into this wholeheartedly and come out with very appropriate comments. We all regretted that there seemed to be so much superficiality in our relations with the Lord. Of course, God knows that we come from clay, that we are dust and that to dust we must return. He cannot expect much from dust, true enough. But we are not only dust. We are temples of the Holy Spirit. Christ took our flesh in His incarnation and sanctified it and raised it to a higher level. We have in us the potential of being transformed into Christ. But, to do this, we need a lot of intimacy with Him, and this intimacy comes from close and frequent contact. How frequent can this contact be? Here again, the sisters would take over and all had their say.

One of them remarked how divine Providence worked. She had felt that coming to Alaska would deprive her of good sermons and talks by learned priests. And here we were, with such an opportunity to soar as high as we could into the very heavens. I told them that I was learning from them as much as they were learning from my comments. The credit in a remote way went to Saints Teresa and John of the Cross, but in a closer way, of course, it went to the Holy Spirit, without whom we can't even pronounce with devotion the word *Jesus.*

During the daytime I had long talks with Fr. Lucchesi, born on October 19, 1858, in Genoa, Italy, where he had become a diocesan priest. I learned from other sources that there had been a question of making him bishop and I am not surprised because Italy has more bishops than you can throw sticks at. But still, a bishop should have certain qualifications, and Fr. Lucchesi was talented enough to become a cardinal and be an ornament to the church.

At thirty-three he had become a Jesuit. Jesuits have to do all in their power to avoid becoming monsignors, bishops, archbishops, and cardinals. They join the Jesuit ranks to work, to do all the dirty work, to beat trails, to take assignments that no one else wants—and that was what John Lucchesi had wanted to do.

In case there was still a lingering possibility that he could be called by the Holy Father to be a bishop, Lucchesi had come to Alaska, that is, as far from the Vatican as he could go, in 1899.

From 1909 to 1913, he had been general superior and again in 1930 to 1931. With the exception of the year he had spent in Pilgrim Springs, near Nome, in 1925, he was always on the Yukon. Those were his stamping grounds for thirty-eight years.

He never managed to learn the language. The Eskimo constructions were too much for him, and when he tried to pronounce names of towns or say some commonly used expressions, his pronunciation was absolutely horrible. At forty-one a person is much too old to sink his teeth into a language like Eskimo.

Wherever Fr. Lucchesi was, he was always the local superior. There was much compassion in him, and a fatherliness and friendliness that endeared him to everyone he met. Yet he had a firmness of steel when it came to principles. Once at Holy Cross during supper the members of the community became less than charitable in their remarks. He called for silence and had one of them read from the *Imitation of Christ* till supper ended. That was the signal for future conversations during meals.

In his early years he had been lithe like a leopard. It had been impossible for him to sit in the sled on the trail. He would either run ahead of the dogs or push to help the dogs carry the sled. I asked him if he ever had met dangers on the trail. He said he had not met with dangers, but he had felt very miserable at times.

He recalled a particular time, how after a heavy snowfall the dogs had been so tired that they could not even crawl. So he had pushed and pushed till suddenly he had gone through some sort of nervous attack. He had sat on the deep snow and shouted in Italian with clenched fists that he was through—that he would go no farther, that he had had it, that he did not care what would happen, but that he was through right then and there. The attack mercifully passed. The Indian boy with him must have been scared to death, for Fr. Lucchesi was a saint and had never been seen complaining at anything. After a while he regained his composure and was himself again. It was part of that "distress" Fr. Hubbard had spoken to me about in Juneau.

Just as Christ had fallen with the cross on His way to Calvary but had gotten up and reached the top of the hill, so Fr. Lucchesi had renewed the pushing together with the big boy and in time they reached their destination. Well, was not that his own fault? He could have been bishop and sitting in a fine chair reading Dante's *Inferno* or some other great Italian book. He had chosen northern Alaska instead; what did he expect?

Also in those years the outboard motor had not been invented, so, as superior general, he had visited the Yukon stations in a rowboat and he alone had done the rowing. I gasped for breath when he told me in a matter-of-fact fashion that he had rowed from Nulato to Akulurak. The distance is six hundred miles as the river meanders. He said that it was easy: Just plant the boat in the middle of the channel and the water does the work. The worst had been the mosquitoes when he had stopped by the riverbanks. To save time, he had said by heart the psalms of the breviary in Latin. It was only to read the lessons that he had had to stop. This again made me gasp for more breath.

In his last years he suffered much from asthma and on top of that he got a nasty hernia that was constantly getting worse. At times his asthma became so acute that he went through the common signs of death. I anointed him several times. He suffered one of those attacks when Bishop Crimont was visiting us. There was no one else in the house, just the three of us. The bishop was sure that Father would die after the anointing, so he told me to help Father die a holy death by talking to him loud so he could hear. That meant that I had to improvise holy sentences and pious ejaculations so Father would die with those holy words in his mind.

I revolted inwardly but acquiesced and did the best I could. The bishop had known him for exactly thirty-six years and both were born the same year—why didn't he do it? Isn't a bishop better qualified than a priest just ordained? But it was not to be so, and I went through quite an ordeal. If Father and I had been alone, I would have preached to him for an hour if need there be, but doing it in front of the bishop did embarrass me more than a little.

Anyway, Father got better, slept well that night, and next morning he got up and had five hot cakes for breakfast. He never used syrup or anything sweet on his cakes, but only salt. For years he had trained himself to do penance and to deny his appetites of anything that would be appetizing. He slept on a bed with just a bearskin for a mattress.

My room was across from his. Many a night when his pain grew more than usual, he would address the Lord and our blessed Mother in Latin with words that were most touching. I had a personal conviction that he would be way up in the upper echelons of heaven. Akulurak had no medical facilities, while Holy Cross did have an infirmary, so he was taken to Holy Cross, where he died on November 30, 1937, at the age of eighty.

Every morning after breakfast a boy by the name of Clement Joseph, sixteen, would come to my room to teach me the Eskimo language. Some days I would have two boys, just to see if the two would agree. In time I had a little dictionary of words, verbs, and sentences. It was a slow-going affair. What I needed was a teacher who would give me general rules, like rules to make the subjunctive or the preterit or the gerund. But these words were Greek to them, so I had to go step by step, trying to figure it out myself.

When you ask an Eskimo in the negative, his answer is contrary to ours. If I asked, "You are not married yet?" and he said yes, it meant that he was not married yet. If I asked, "The mail plane has not come yet?" and he said no, the plane had already come.

Soon after my arrival in Akulurak I went a few miles with a big schoolboy to baptize a baby. I told the boy to ask the mother if the baby was boy or girl. After they exchanged some words he turned to me with a smile and said, "She says yes."

I asked again for clarification and was given the same answer. The trouble was with me, not with them. In those alternatives and in their mentality, the answer refers solely to the latter, never to the former. If I ask if a child is a boy or a girl and they say yes, it means that the child is a girl. If the child is a boy and I ask if it is a boy or a girl, the answer is no. So simple! Yet here I was a fully grown man and did not know a simple thing like that.

No wonder the old-timers among the Eskimos referred to the whites as stupid. They were stupid for many reasons: They did not speak Eskimo. They did not relish seal oil. They did not ride kayaks. They did not know how to make skin boots. They did not know how to take sweat baths in the *kazim*. Poor whites!

And I was a white. Or rather, I, being a priest, was not considered a white man. A white man to those early Eskimos was a tall man with a long nose who spoke a phony language, carried booze with him, owned stores, took their money, swore, went after their women, etc. Then the priest showed up. He had no women, had no booze, did not swear, did not care for money, said Mass and prayed a lot, spoke about heaven and hell; obviously, the priest was something else. Whatever he was, he was not a white man.

Once I had a group of Eskimos in my house practicing hymns for Easter. Someone from Mexico had sent me a little jar of the finest perfume so I would sprinkle the altar for Easter. I took off the cork and passed the jar by their noses. They were amazed at such a marvelous fragrance. One young lady remarked in a loud voice: "But Father, why do they send things like this to you when they know that you are not a regular man?" So there I was, totally emasculated.

Those early natives believed that the priest was a member of a different species. He was not Eskimo; that was certain. He was not white; that was obvious. Well, then, what was he? That was the question.

Fr. Treca was one of the first to settle among them. While he was eating, people gathered around him to watch how he ate. After he was through, he took out his false teeth to clean them. The people panicked and ran. To take out his teeth was something like taking his head off and putting it back. They feared him. Was he a regular man? Certainly not.

Fr. Menager started the mission in the village of Kashunak on the coast. The custom there was for the men every morning to walk about one hundred feet from the village and empty their bowels all at the same time in a long line, with loose dogs cleaning up behind them. But the priest never joined them. It meant to them that the priest was not a regular man and did not need any emptying of any bowels. Maybe he was a different type of human.

While I was holding the fort at Akulurak, Fr. O'Connor and Baltazar were making the rounds throughout the district which extended down to Scammon Bay on the south, to Mountain Village on the east, and to Hamilton on the north. The west was taken over by the Bering Sea. In that vast area were thirty-five villages, so called, because some of them were small settlements to accommodate a clan. Fr. O'Connor would return with a boy or a girl for the school.

Fr. Paul C. O'Connor, S.J., had been born in 1897 in Kansas. But his family had moved west and settled in Spokane, Washington, when he'd been a boy. He had come to Alaska in 1930. When I met him five years later, I was convinced that when God had made him, God had decided to do a good job, and God had succeeded. O'Connor stood about six feet, straight as a pine tree. There wasn't a flaw from head to toe. He was so handsome that when people met him, they stood still in wonderment. But God again, being perfect, did a perfect job with Paul this way: While Paul drew people to him with his irresistible smile, he kept them at an arm's distance and even farther with his quick anger. He simply loved to argue and in the course of the argument he would do everything in his power to crush the opponent.

It took me just one week to size him up. I decided never, but never, to contradict him. At times he would tell me something that normally would bring about a disagreement. With some other person I would beg to disagree and become quite vocal; but not with Fr. O'Connor. When his eyes narrowed and his lips quivered and his voice was raised, that was the storm signal. Knowing full well that I was no match for him, if the storm broke anyway, I simply put an umbrella over my head and let it pass. It takes two to make a fight. As a result of this, we went happily along together for the next forty years, meeting quite often.

Yet he was a very pious man. He prayed a lot. He was a priest's priest—always the priest. He wore his priestly clothes with pride and dignity. To the question of how he could be so pious and yet so opinionated, I always had the same answer: If he were not pious and if he did not pray so much, his quick anger might have pushed him to do some horrible deed. But his piety and prayer kept him under control. Women who would go for his looks would retreat in haste from his stern look. Thus the plates of the scale would not lose their poise.

In later years he mellowed considerably. Before the end, Fr. O'Connor was thoroughly supernaturalized. He was eighty-one and still looked quite presentable. His defiance was gone; his anger had lost its edge; his spirituality had grown; he prayed a lot. He went to his Maker on March 8, 1979, in Spokane, where he had grown up. After his burial I felt a bit like an orphan. He left an imprint in Alaska that will last for a long time.

8

Crossing the Line: Kotzebue

In the summer of 1938 I was sent north to another parish, Kotzebue. When you live in Kotzebue, you are above the Arctic Circle. It is a new world.

The late Senator Ernest Gruening loved to say that Alaska was much more than just a state. Alaska is an empire. He had in mind the vastness of the country with such variety of climate, peoples, fauna, flora, and geological formations. It looked as though God had begun to make the earth beginning with the South Pole. When he got to Alaska He was already tired and just threw everything around helter skelter. Between Juneau and the last island of the Aleutian chain there is the distance separating Atlanta from San Francisco. The ice-free ports of the south have little in common with the shores of the Arctic Ocean, where navigation is possible only a few weeks a year. There are primeval forests near the Panhandle and there are those vast regions permanently frozen—the permafrost so called. There are vast flat areas and there is Mount McKinley with its surrounding high peaks. Alaska has everything that a tourist craves to see.

Until 1929 the Catholic Church did not have a parish north of the Arctic circle in Alaska. In that year Fr. Philip Delon, S.J., with the help of Fr. William Walsh (a diocesan priest from Oakland, California) brought the material for a church with living quarters for the pastor. Fr. Delon was then general superior of the missions, a man of much zeal, like a good Frenchman full of energy, a bit of an idealist with the effervescence of a boiling pot, always planning, the type of man hard to control. He and his countryman Bishop Crimont saw eye to eye, so he was given the green light to go ahead as he saw fit.

Fr. Walsh, scarcely thirty and a six-footer, worked harder than the crew putting up the building. He was so tired that some mornings he could not wake up, though he put a noisy alarm clock by his pillow on top of an upside-down aluminum plate to increase the sound. When the building was up, he installed a telephone line connecting the houses of those who paid for it. The telephone rang in all the houses at once and there was no possibility of privacy, but it helped a lot to pass information and talk about things that needed no privacy.

One storekeeper did not approve of the Catholics moving in. When the workers were paid and went to his store to buy merchandise, he looked at them suspiciously and asked if that was Catholic money. When told that it was Catholic money, he would tell them to go somewhere else with it. He did not want to have his hands contaminated with Catholic money. The man who told me this was a Catholic. I asked him to pray tell me what was wrong with Catholic money. "Plenty," he said, "there ain't enough of it." I agreed.

Fr. Walsh was the soul of kindness and generosity. Everyone loved him. He went around with his stunning good looks and smiling eyes and, before he knew it, he had a congregation. Fr. Delon correctly guessed that there would be quite a few baptized Catholics who would surface the minute a priest showed up. One of his first converts was Louis Reich, Sr., a naturalized German married to Mamie, born on Herschel Island in the Arctic Ocean off the Canadian coast. You see, Louis had been a whaler and had spent much time in those waters dodging ice floes. Louis and I spent many hours together in his house. It was a sad day for me when I conducted the funeral services for the eternal rest of his beautiful soul.

On Columbus Day of 1930, Fr. Delon landed in Kotzebue in a plane piloted by Bro. George Feltes, S.J. Fr. Delon wanted to give young Walsh the thrill of his life by giving him a short ride over the clouds. The weather was not too good, so Bro. Feltes said that he would not fly. But there was a pilot, Ralph Wien, who would oblige. The three took off and in a few minutes they crashed to their deaths in full view of the curious onlookers.

The body of Fr. Walsh was taken to Oakland, where he was buried on a slope with the head facing the far north he had loved. So young and so promising! The Lord gave. The Lord took away. The name of the Lord be praised.

Fr. O'Connor cleaning fish with sisters of the Akulurak convent

Say, "Polar bear."

Fr. Llorente, left, with his brother Amando, also
a Jesuit priest.

John Hess, S.J., "the oldtimer's favorite brother," spent forty-eight continuous years in Alaska, surpassing any other Jesuit. A German, noted for his kindness and hard work, Brother Hess died in Sheridan, Oregon, in 1963.

Brother Alfred Murphy, S.J., left, boys' prefect at the Akulurak school, taught "the 3 R's, religion, cleanliness, work, and regimentation." Here, he is holding captured bird with Fr. Francis Menager, who was born in Normandy, France, and served Alaska missions for twenty-six years.

Fr. Delon was born in France in 1876, came to Alaska in 1915, started the first parish north of the Arctic Circle in 1929 with the help of Fr. William Walsh, a diocesan priest from Oakland, California.

On Columbus Day, 1930, Fr. Philip Delon and Fr. William Walsh crashed to their deaths while flying over Kotzebue in the *Marquette*, above.

Fr. Delon, born in France in 1876, had come to Alaska in 1915 and had been in Akulurak and Holy Cross. The sudden death of these two great priests caused no small consternation in the whole territory of Alaska.

To fill the gap in Kotzebue, several priests were sent in quick succession: Frs. Lafortune, Post, Baltussen, and Concannon; it was all patchwork until Fr. Francis Menager came and stayed five years. Then I succeeded him. Kotzebue was then a town of roughly six hundred people. There were thirty-nine white adults and forty factions, or so I was told.

After I became acquainted with the people, I went to the roadhouse and asked the owner, Paul Davidovich, how much would he charge for a first-class dinner with roast beef, mashed potatoes with gravy, peas or carrots, olives, bread and butter, chocolate cake, sugar, cream and coffee. Paul puffed at his cigarette and finally said that, if I brought in twelve people, it would be two dollars apiece. I visited the thirty-nine white folks and told them what a great thing it would be if all the whites got together properly dressed to chat and eat and be merry in the roadhouse for two measly dollars; we would be happy together, bury all hatchets, etc., etc.

Twenty-seven of us gathered at Paul's place and we hardly recognized each other. Such natty suits of clothes; such fancy dresses! Some averred that it took them a long time to find them in their closets after so many years. But they found them and they were wearing them. We sat in little groups chatting, and when the table was ready we trooped in to a most delicious banquet. It was so good that we repeated it shortly afterward. But twice was enough. Tongues wagged. We went back to forty factions.

In a way, Paul himself was to blame at least in part. He sat at the head of the table and proceeded to regale us with an account of the many things that had happened to him many years back when he was carrying mail by dog team from Kotzebue to Barrow, the northernmost town under the American flag. He had the finest team of dogs, of course, and they had to be the best to carry mail so far and under such weather conditions. One day a polar bear came out of nowhere and made straight for the team. Paul carried a loaded rifle. He took the rifle and, you won't believe this but it is a fact, the rifle went off by itself and the polar bear fell flat, deader than the proverbial doornail.

On another occasion he got lost in a storm in which you could not see your own fingers, it was so dark. But the leader smelled something and took him to an abandoned shack. That saved his life. He fed his dogs and broke into the shack to spread his sleeping bag on dry ground, that was what the shack had, just the bare ground with no flooring. He did not bother with the flashlight. He felt around with his feet and noticed that there was a log on the ground. He spread the sleeping bag using the log as a pillow. When he woke up in the morning the storm was gone, daylight filtered through. He got up in a fine mood and, lo and behold, the log was not a log at all; it was a frozen, dead man. Was he scared? Not one bit. He just prayed for the eternal rest of the soul of the poor guy. And he knew the proper terminology, too, because Paul was a Catholic born in Yugoslavia when that country (Slovenia) had been under Austria.

Paul was the son of a high official of the Austrian navy. His dad had taken him along on a visit that the Austrian navy had made to San Francisco. Paul, a teenager big enough to take care of himself, had gone ashore with other sailors and then never returned to the ship. Through hard work and good luck he had ended up in Kotzebue.

The world does not have paper enough to copy all the stories that Paul told his guests and friends around the wood stove of his roadhouse. The whites of Kotzebue had heard them, or many of them, and did not relish more of the same. Perhaps it was their fault, too. I personally never tired of listening to Paul.

The Catholic congregation in Kotzebue was rather small, but there were enough people to keep the pastor busy. There was a core of very loyal faithful. And there were enough children to make a lot of noise in the living room where I taught catechism. They were mostly half-breed children, sharp as razors. It was a joy to teach them. The Eskimos, too, because of their long association with white people, were sophisticated enough to march abreast with them in any field. The Eskimo spoken there had the same roots as the Eskimo spoken on the lower Yukon, but it was different enough to make it impossible to understand. Where one said *sa-bak-tun-ga* for "I work," the other said *cha-lle-un-ga*. *Unoako* (tomorrow) was *uvulakun*. English was already the prevailing and common language in the town because of the schools run by the Bureau of Indian Affairs.

I made it a point to visit every Catholic home at least twice a week. It was a good way for me to kill boredom and at the same time we became very well acquainted. On Sundays we had a Mass with organ and music. Every Wednesday people came for instructions. Children came to catechism after school every single school day, but catechism was only part of it. There were games and stories. The idea was to familiarize them with both the priest and the church proceedings so they would consider both the church and the rectory as their own home.

One family that gave me much joy came from Point Hope. Rachel, the wife and mother of four children aged four to sixteen, joined the church and took to it like a fish to water. Every afternoon she would go to church to talk to the Lord all by herself. I was convinced that she was favored with mystical graces.

Her husband was less pious and one day he told her that he had been told that no man could forgive sins; only God could, so the priest was a fraud. She told him to go to the sanctuary of the church and ask the big statue of the Sacred Heart, which was there with open arms as if to invite all to come to Him. He did. He went home and told his wife what had happened. The man had asked the Lord if the priest could forgive sins. The Lord had answered loud and clear: "Yes, my dear, he can." So he went back and told his wife. As simple as that. Next Sunday while I was preaching she saw the Lord behind and above me who told her: "What the priest preached is true. Listen to him as you would to Me." That was that. She came to my kitchen to tell me about it. I became a bit curious and asked for more details. She said that it had happened while I was preaching and that there had been a radiant halo around the head and face of the Lord. After that I felt that I had better prepare my sermons more carefully so as not to disappoint our Lord.

Every morning she came to Mass and holy Communion. Others did also. But there was a difference. The others received holy Communion with dry eyes. Rachel was a sea of placid tears that flowed silently. No handkerchief alone could handle that. I gave her small thick towels that passed for hankies.

There was also Effie Johnson, a widow, a full-blood Eskimo with a little boy. She had absorbed so much of the faith in so short a time that I was amazed at her progress. Effie died and we buried her with much sorrow. Next day Rachel came to my kitchen while I was making hot cakes to tell me that she had just seen Effie going up to heaven surrounded by angels. You can imagine my eyes of surprise. Here I was engaged in cooking breakfast—a rather animalistic occupation—and in comes Rachel with such a heavenly message.

I asked her to tell me more about it. She said that Effie had had the most heavenly look, with a smile impossible to describe, and that she had waved to Rachel, inviting her to follow. Rachel asked if that meant that she was going to die very soon. When I answered that God might keep her here for some time yet, her face lost a great deal of the gleam and looked disappointed. Rachel wanted to die that very day to see God.

There were Catholics among the thirty-nine white folks. There were also members of different religious denominations. There were nonchurch-going folks who kept to themselves their personal relations with almighty God. But the town had George Wagner, the amiable, well-read, generous to a fault, pipe-smoking official atheist. Every week on his way to the post office he came to my kitchen to chat. We had quite a game going on. He would start on a monologue which I interrupted intermittently with sentences like: "Not true"; "Entirely false"; "Figments of imagination"; "Tell it to the marines." Then I would take the floor and he reciprocated in kind. And so it went, week after week, in an atmosphere of mutual feelings of friendship.

He was running a mink farm on the outskirts of town. His clothes carried the smell of the mink wherever he went. When he took me by the arm to press his point, the smell became quite strong until in time I became used to it. The power of adaptation of our bodies is unbelievable. He has been dead now for many years. Nothing is impossible to God. Among the committee sent to the Pearly Gates to meet me, George Wagner could be one of them—if only his heavenly clothes will smell better than roses.

One summer the Ferguson brothers who ran a good store brought to Kotzebue a young bull with cute horns that caused a sensation in town. No Eskimo had ever seen a bull in the flesh. When the bull walked off the barge, all the dogs in town howled with fury. The natives stood at a long distance, ready to run at the slightest suspicious movement of the bull with such menacing horns. There was an enclosed piece of ground with high grass where the bull was placed, much to his delight, as he ate grass with real gusto.

Soon it was suggested that I, a Spaniard, should treat the town to a bull fight. The day and the hour were set and everyone came to the show. All stood outside the fence, naturally. I put on knee boots, a well-buttoned jacket, a leather cap, and took a cane that seemed strong enough to do the work. When the Eskimos saw me enter the enclosure and walk straight to the browsing bull, a general scream of fear emanated from the throng. Would some old ladies faint? But why should I be concerned with that?

I stood in front of the bull and hit him gently on the head with my cane. He raised his head in surprise and, still chewing the grass hanging from his mouth, he gave me a furious look. I became real angry then and insulted him to his face. I called him names and challenged him. When he wanted to renew his browsing, I became indignant and grabbed him by the horns. Here the howls of the people tore the sky. I proved to be much weaker than the bull; while I held tenaciously to his horns, he retreated backward and was dragging me in all directions. How humiliated I felt! But then I let go (I was out of breath) and stood firm in front of him. He did likewise. Then I let him have it with a couple of blows in the horns with my cane. He did not like it and ran in total defeat with his tail up in the air, while I stood there with my cane raised to the sky—a symbol of victory.

As I walked out and mixed with the astonished people, I heard myself mumbling that it was in the blood, etc. etc.

By the time the snow began to fall, the bull had grown a great deal and was really fat. One day he was butchered to serve as a source of proteins for the coming long winter.

My first winter in Kotzebue was a lesson in survival. The church was poorly insulated. The length and darkness and coldness of those Arctic winters have to be seen to be believed. It was obvious that the trouble was with me and not with the weather. Kotzebue was growing. The weather did not stop the growth. People born and raised there just loved it. Also people who had lived there a few years did not want to leave. So the weather was fine with them and so was the darkness.

The coldest day while I lived there was the day my thermometer marked sixty-three below zero for several hours. I took a basin half filled with water and placed it outside on the snow. In seconds the surface of the water was alive with motion till a sheet of ice formed before my astonished eyes. Two minutes later I broke the ice with the tips of my cold fingers. I simply had to experiment with it.

When the temperature is that low, there is no breeze, thank God. Then the smoke coming off the chimneys piles up on top of the chimney like a black thick cloud and there it stays, getting thicker and thicker. If there is a breeze then, it would be the acme of imprudence to venture outdoors. If the wind blows in those temperatures, anyone caught outside faces death by exposure.

From early December to the second week of January the sun does not come out. Around noon there is a crepuscular glow that allows you to see for a little while only. At 2:30 P.M. if the sky is clear it is covered with stars. Then the aurora borealis—northern lights—is frequently seen. One night it became an awesome thing to behold. The whole sky was lit. Then it began to revolve and rotate and change colors. The snow was taking on each color, making the whole thing eerie and ghostly. The natives whistled in the superstitious belief that whistling will drive the aurora away.

March is the month of the winter storms. I witnessed one that left me shaky. It lasted three full days, day and night, with howling winds and blinding snow. When I opened the door to see how it was outdoors, I faced a wall of snow blocking the exit. Thank God the door opened to the inside. To leave I would have to dig a tunnel, but I waited till the storm abated. The spire of the church had a good-sized bronze bell. The wind was so strong that it kept the bell tolling intermittently. It was impossible to sleep with the bell tolling as if to announce the recent death of someone in town . . . The noise of the chimney in the kitchen was nerve wracking. The whole building would shake in moments of increased wind velocity.

As far as I knew, nobody was outdoors. I felt like a prisoner in my own house. What is going on in the world? I had no radio. I was afraid to build a fire in the stove for fear that the building would catch fire. I put on my fur parka and knelt before the altar or walked back and forth between the door of the church and the altar to keep warm in the presence of God. I kept asking myself what kept people in Kotzebue. But it was a purely rhetorical question; I knew that those people just loved their home town or they would have moved away one thousand years ago. The problem was with me, a newcomer, not with them, who were inured to all this.

When at long last the wind died, I dug myself out and could hardly believe what I saw. Kotzebue looked entirely different. There were mountains of snow piled up everywhere between the buildings. To climb them, the people made steps of snow and continued their daily life as usual. I felt like I was living on another planet. That was Alaska, all right, the real Alaska; the Alaska people have in mind when they hear its name. No wonder Americans felt that Secretary of

State Seward was insane when he bought Alaska from the Russians. Seward should have been in Kotzebue one whole winter with his wife and half a dozen children to see what people on the Arctic have to endure. But now it was too late. We were stuck with Kotzebue, Seward or no Seward.

After the winter comes the summer, which in Kotzebue becomes another source of wonderment. From the first week of June to the first week of July the sun does not set. This means thirty days with the sun over your head or, if you prefer it, thirty days in a row without darkness. Then the problem is when to sleep. Children are in the streets with no concept of time. I used to see them looking for a place to lie down at any odd hour. The first time I saw it, I experienced a feeling of distress; it was so spooky.

The night is God's blessing upon mankind. It is the time to rest and to repair the losses of a long day's work. I know it is also the time for burglars and criminals to do their stuff. There are defenses against that. But against thirty continuous days of sunlight with no darkness there is no defense. Yes, you can put curtains on your windows. But when you are full of sleep, a knock or knocks at the door wake you up because the caller figures that you should be out enjoying the sunshine. And here is another anomaly: While you watch the sun in the sky at what should be midnight, you had better have a heavy coat on, because it is cold, very cold—cold enough to make you shiver.

On the fourth of July, the sun hides for a few minutes behind the Igichuk Hills on the Noatak River. Every day afterwards it hides for a few more minutes behind those blessed hills. Then the Kobuk River dumps all his ice in front of Kotzebue. This helps to smash the ice of the bay till winds and ocean currents leave it wide open for navigation.

In those days we were getting only first-class mail during the winter. It was flown to us from Nome once or twice a week. Now after the fourth of July the first boat showed up with mountains of boxes, mostly from Sears, Roebuck and Montgomery Ward. Women had spent much time all winter writing mail orders. Here they were now. A good many of those boxes were returned to Seattle. They were C.O.D. orders. People did not have the cash. When they ordered, they had a gut feeling that they might have ready cash to pay for them; alas, the cash was not there. That was the time to borrow money, but often enough there were no money lenders, so the boxes were returned. Back to Seattle went the dresses and underwear and shoes and kitchen utensils.

I saw that as a human tragedy. The Sears, Roebuck fat catalog came to be known as the bible of the Eskimos. The good catalog also served other purposes. In the outhouses there was always a generous supply of catalogs in lieu of toilet paper. We did not have running water in Kotzebue.

How was the problem of drinking water solved? In the summer there was no problem at all because it rained forever and we had fifty-two-gallon tanks to catch the rain water under our roofs. In the winter the problem was solved by sawing ice blocks from a lake nearby. Husky men with a good saw would pile up great quantities of such clean blocks, which were sold for so much a block—either come-and-get-it or delivered. I had them delivered and piled against the wall of the church near the door. That was my water supply. I had by the stove a fifty-two-gallon galvanized tank filled with water. When there was room in it for another block, I would carry it from outside and listen with a smile to the thunderous noise made by the ice as it cracked upon contact with warmer water. It was mind over matter, man against the Arctic.

In the summer Kotzebue became a trading center. People from the north came with their *umiaks*—skin boats— and built a city of tents along the beaches. They brought *moktok,* that part of the whale that to the Eskimo is the supreme delicacy. *Moktok* in the north can be compared to *akootak* on the Yukon. The fishermen of Kotzebue get a good supply of belugas or white whales, about ten to sixteen feet long. But in Point Hope and Barrow they get the sperm whale, which may weigh forty tons. Those people fill their *umiaks* with whale meat and come and trade. The people of Point Hope were all Episcopalians. Their archdeacon used to tell them that when they were in Kotzebue, they should attend the Catholic church, which was so much closer to theirs than other Protestant churches were. Our church was open to them in the short time they spent in our midst.

By the end of August we would hear that the big ice was already closing at Point Barrow. From then on, navigation was at your own risk. Such a short summer! At Kotzebue the water was open a little longer, so we could get more boats.

Kotzebue had no barber shop. I had learned to cut hair after a fashion. You have heard that in the land where all people are blind, a one-eyed man is king, so I became the unofficial barber. I never charged for my services, but I let it be known that if the man was married, one loaf of bread would be more than welcomed. And so it was; it came to me in bread often enough. If the man had no wife, it was all on the house, and I even swept the floor and disposed of the debris I collected.

Sometimes a man unknown to me would knock timidly at the door, asking if he had been misled. He had asked for the barber shop and had been told that this was it, but this looked to him more like a church. I invited him in with the good news that this was both: the place to clean the head and to clean the soul. This put him at ease.

When government boats came to town, some men would show up for a haircut. Some of them would not hear of a free haircut and would leave fifty cents, which in those days was considered a good fee. A white woman came once, but she was disappointed to hear that the pope would excommunicate me if he heard that a priest had anything whatsoever to do with women. She said she would not tell anybody. I told her that if she knew of a woman on earth who did not talk, to please give me her name and address and I would send her a letter of congratulations. So she did not part with her hair, but we parted friends.

9

Kotzebue and Beyond

In theory, my parish was Kotzebue. But that was the town. The real parish extended to all the land north of the sixty-sixth parallel, roughly the size of France. The population of that area would be, roughly again, some five thousand people. Outside of the towns of Barrow and Kotzebue, all other villages were relatively small in those days.

My friend John Cross used to take me along on some of his flights to Candle and Deering. There were some Catholics in those villages and they welcomed me with open arms. I said Mass in their homes. This afforded an opportunity to talk to the priest and settle many things pertaining to the salvation of their souls. Or they would fly to Kotzebue for a wedding.

Likewise, some miners from the region were brought to the local hospital. Those who were Catholic were delighted to find a Catholic priest. One of them died and we gave him a proper church burial, much to the consolation of his folks back in the States when they heard about it. Any Catholics brought to the Kotzebue hospital from anywhere received the ministrations of the priest. If they died, I would bury them after Mass. I do not recall a single case when the body was requested by the faraway family. Transportation then was a major problem. That meant that I had to dig the grave and make the coffin—things that were no problem to me.

Dr. Smith was in charge of the local hospital, run by the Bureau of Indian Affairs. We became friends the moment we met. He was the checkers champion. I told him that to an amateur chess player like me, checkers were peanuts. He despised chess. Before I knew it, he had me across the table playing checkers. He won most of the games, but not all, and it was agonizing to see him suffer when he saw himself in a losing position. He would shake his face in disbelief and start the long litany: "You got me beat . . . You got me beat . . . You got me beat." Once it was too much for his wife, who got tired of that wailing and snapped loud and clear: "I am glad you lost. It will do you good to take second place." The doctor pretended that he did not hear.

He told me that his name was not, or should not be, Smith. He said his father had been a fugitive from justice from Canada. When he had crossed the border into the U.S., he had picked the name Smith from the air and that was to be his name.

One day he asked me casually where did I have my tonsils removed. When he heard that I still had them, he wanted to see them. I had had no time yet to hear that he went about removing tonsils from any human being unlucky enough to fall into his medical hands. When he saw mine, he almost fainted and ordered me to show up next morning at nine sharp. Next morning I found him with his sleeves rolled up and ready to butcher me. I was then thirty-two. I can say in all truth that the night after the operation was the worst night in my whole life. When I went through the motions of paying for the operation, he was almost insulted. He would not charge me, a Catholic priest and a personal friend.

He got to the point where the very smell of the hospital got on his nerves and he wanted in the worst way to leave the building.

I have never been a cook, but my cooking was good enough for him. He loved to come to my kitchen at least one hour before dinnertime to talk and eat.

He was an agnostic. Maybe there was a God and he hoped there was one. But in his medical practice and medical studies he had come to the conclusion that the so-called God of the Christians had many flaws. For instance, by walking on two legs instead of four, we humans have many a disease that dogs have not.

Ideologically, he preferred a Russian political order to Western democracy. I once had to referee a battle royal fought between him and Governor Gruening in my living room. The governor was a Roosevelt man and a fighting Democrat. The doctor owed allegiance to no one and was free to state his beliefs. Gruening was a giant of the intellect. The doctor was a strong believer in certain causes. There they were locked in mortal combat.

Governor Gruening visited Kotzebue three times while I was there. He always made it a point to see me and to be seen with me. I inquired from certain sources why he acted that way since he was not a member of the church. I was informed that when Gruening had been about to be appointed governor of Alaska, the Alaska delegate, Tony Dimond, had objected to Gruening's anti-Catholic sentiments, which Tony went on to prove. Gruening had made a good defense of himself by saying that he, too, as a Jew, was a member of a persecuted minority, and that he was opposed to any form of discrimination, etc. He was appointed governor. When he landed in Kotzebue, he asked to see the Catholic priest and ever afterward we considered ourselves friends.

He also made a visit to our Akulurak school. Furthermore, he appointed Fr. O'Connor to the board of the Alaska Housing Authority, and when the U.S. Senate was holding hearings on admitting Alaska as a state of the Union, Gruening saw to it that Fr. O'Connor and Fr. Gallant had their trip to Washington paid so they could testify as two substantial Alaskans who knew what they were talking about.

Now in my living room he and Dr. Smith were battling over the merits and demerits of democracy. I sided with the Governor, but the doctor had known that I would, so our friendship continued in a "business as usual" fashion. He was glad to see me visit the patients. I felt in my bones that he wanted to believe. When I heard that he had died, I offered a prayer for the eternal rest of his soul.

There were other breaks in the monotony of Kotzebue. Hugo Echard, a German, was a married to Gretchen, an Austrian. Both were devout Catholics and lived on the banks of the Noatak River north of Kotzebue, where they had a mink ranch.

In one of his visits to town Hugo came to my kitchen to beg me to accompany him to the ranch to break the news to Gretchen that her mother had died in Austria. Hugo had just been to the post office, where he had gotten the news in a letter. He just could not go back alone with this news. And what are priests for, if not to help in such cases? So I went along. He had a very good dog team. I was glad also to see that country.

When we were close to the ranch, the dogs began to bark. Gretchen came out and stood there like an empress, tall, erect, beautiful. When she saw me, she suspected something and turned a bit pale. Hugo broke down and wept. Gretchen wanted to know what had happened. I walked up to her and told her that God had taken her mother to heaven. It was a painful half-hour. But she came out of it in grand style.

As she wiped her tears, she kept thanking God. Mother had had too many illnesses. She was much better off in heaven. When she had regained full possession of herself, Gretchen told us how good her mother had been. I was thinking of my own mother back in Spain. Mothers are good. Motherhood is a divine institution. Saint Paul wrote that women will save their souls by having children. He meant that since women were made by God principally to have children, motherhood is a good thing by itself; He gives women the grace they need to raise their families, if only women cooperate with God by doing it the way God wanted it to be done. It would be interesting to read a well-documented and well-reasoned doctoral thesis discussing whether man does his paternal job as well as woman does her maternal one. Something inside of me tells me that woman might come out the winner.

I spent a couple of days with Hugo and Gretchen in that Alaskan Eden in the woods with so much natural beauty, such primeval silence, such fresh air and crystal-clear water, so much elbow room. And then the mink ranch, with the animals increasing and multiplying in their own environment under man's care. I dreamed of building myself a log cabin there and living with nature under God's heaven, as Adam did before he messed it up through his own fault. It was comforting and reassuring to go to bed knowing beforehand that no noise would disturb one's sleep. No engines, no planes, no cars, no door banging, no steps, no coughs, no unwanted music, nothing caused by man.

On the other hand, one's sleep can be helped by the wind on the surrounding tall trees, the rain on the roof, the murmur of the water in the nearby brook, the twittering of the birds, and the distant howl of the forest wolf. To those who ask me how could those early biblical patriarchs have lived so many years, I answer that if I could sleep the way they did, I might yet surpass them. The length of our lives depends a great deal on the peace of our nightly sleep.

In my sermons I assure the people that if they are in bed by ten every night, they can count on succeeding in life; if they are in bed by 9:30, their success in life will be a tremendous one. Because so few people follow this advice, there is so much unrest and so many failures.

There were times when there was no lack of excitement in Kotzebue. One day in October the town was agog with the news that Warren Ferguson and Logan Varnell had disappeared under the ice of the nearby lagoon. In Kotzebue, that was something like telling America that the president and the speaker of the House had gone swimming and that skin divers were looking for their bodies. In a matter of minutes we were all running to the lagoon.

The ice of the lagoon was considered safe. You have heard how many people have been killed by supposedly empty guns. I myself once considered the ice thick enough and almost paid for it with my life.

Warren Ferguson was the owner of a prosperous store, of a commercial aviation company, and of a lighterage system to unload the boats anchored in the bay. He was a young married man who was revolutionizing the area with his never-ending enterprises. Logan was a married man, a prospector, a good seasonal worker, and the father of three children.

Warren had invited Logan to come along in his light truck to inspect something across the lagoon. Logan had been sitting by Warren. In the open truck there had been natives, going along to do the elbow-grease work. Before they had gotten to the middle of the lagoon, the ice had cracked wide open. The natives had jumped off on the ice and were safe. But Warren and Logan had sunk out of sight.

I went to Logan's house, where he was getting over the shock. Well, he did not get over that shock for months, but he told me time and again, and yet again, how it happened.

When the truck had sunk, Warren had told Logan to open the door. Those were his last words. Logan had opened the door and found himself under fifteen feet of water. He had had enough sense to fill his lungs with air just in time. Swimming carefully toward the open hole, he had seen that the tide was carrying him away. He had hit the ice with his hands. The natives had followed his motions under the ice and with two-by-four pieces that were floating off the truck, they had quickly cut a hole in the ice in front of him. One of his hands had come out of that hole. While one native had held that hand, the rest of them had made the hole big enough for Logan's head to emerge. Logan had taken a deep breath. The natives had dragged him out with great effort because his clothes were filled with water and weighed like lead. When he was out, Logan lay on the ice for some time in a state of total prostration. He was carried home, where he was put in a warm bed.

Warren never surfaced. Being the driver, he had been caught between the wheel and the seat and we all felt that he had drowned in a sitting position. After many hours of much work and ingenuity, the truck was lifted and recovered, but Warren was not found. He had managed to get out of the truck, but he had been carried away by the tide.

Sitting by Logan's bed, I heard him explain how he had felt in his bones that he was going to come out, not by his own efforts but with God's help. He was a nominal Catholic, that is, he had been baptized a Catholic as a child, and he had gone to church with his family, but as a teenager he had begun to take jobs everywhere and soon the church had become a thing of the past. Now when he saw himself in such mortal and imminent danger, he kept saying with closed lips: "God, help me." He had said that prayer with such faith and such intensity that he had felt inside of him strength to continue swimming and searching for the open hole.

Actually, everyone considered it a miracle that he could hold his breath for such a long time. Now Logan was determined to show God that he was grateful. "You can bet your last dollar, Father, that from now on I am going to be your best parishioner, so help me God." And God did help him.

First, he turned to his wonderful wife, Clara, a remarkable woman loved by all, who had never been baptized. Clara asked me to give her instructions so she could join Logan in the faith. Twice a week after supper I went to their house and we covered the whole catechism. Before Easter I baptized her. I also baptized little Helen and then little Bert. Their son Ingram had been baptized already. He was much older. Poor Ingram died in World War II in the Pacific.

In time, Logan moved to Seward, where he had a good fishing job; there he died, commending himself to God's mercy. Clara kept writing to me every year for Christmas till she died in California, her native state.

Remember that the truck sank at the end of October. At the middle of next May someone saw a floating, bulky thing moving to and fro between ice floes. The lagoon was connected with the bay through a narrow entrance, so we had believed that Warren's body had been carried to the bay by the receding tides. It was not so. That floating bulky thing was Warren's inflated body, which had been preserved that long under the ice.

The town now went through a second commotion. Warren's family contacted me to ask if I would consider conducting a formal religious funeral, though he was not a Catholic. I said I would, indeed, and next day the large hall of the church was filled with people. Hymns were sung. I delivered what I considered an appropriate eulogy. We offered prayers for the eternal rest of his soul, and moved in an orderly funeral procession to the nearby cemetery, where a final prayer was said. Thus we put an end to that terrible accident in the lagoon.

Warren had a brother, Archie, who took over the business. Though he was in his forties, he was taking flying lessons. It took him a long time to get a flying license, but finally he got it. Archie loved to act the clown. The whole Arctic was filled with the latest stories about Archie. I am going to tell one only.

During the war he was flying to Nome and as he was approaching the town he asked the tower or the station or whatever how was the weather. Now, during the war it was forbidden to give any weather except in an emergency. When Archie was reminded of this by the operator, he snapped: "Listen, buddy, when I am flying it is always an emergency."

One day in the summer I was visited by a sturdy character with a pipe and a weather-beaten face. He introduced himself as Jimmy Cross, a Scotsman by birth, now a gold digger in the Ambler Creek, a tributary of the Kobuk—way up in the hills. He was in the habit of coming to town every other year to buy many necessities and to mail his gold to the Bank of Nome. He himself had only a little boat, which he tied now to a bigger boat he hired to carry the big load he had bought. I hope I have made it all clear.

While we had a bite to eat, he told me the sort of life he was living. He had built a log cabin as far as possible from the next human being. He did not want to see anybody or talk to anybody. He had sought solitude and he had found it. His cabin had all he wanted: a stove, a bunk, a table, a seat made of a block, a gas lamp, and shelves enough to put all the grub he needed for two years. He was well provided with dry prunes, raisins, beans, pancake flour, pilot bread, canned milk and powdered milk, tea and coffee, sugar, and all the pipe tobacco he needed. He had a pair of good axes, picks and shovels, hunting knives, a rifle and ammunition, and a good supply of matches. Especially matches. To get caught there without matches would have meant death or nearly so. Also flashlights. Add to this a good supply of clothing and footgear, and you can envy Jimmy Cross.

During the long winter months he cut logs. He dug a hole in the creek. He filled the hole with logs, sprinkled them with gasoline, and set fire to them. When the logs burned, he dug up the thawed bottom and piled the dirt nearby. By springtime he had piled a considerable amount of dirt. Now with the creek running beautifully he washed the dirt and collected the gold. His usual catch was six hundred dollars a year, which was a lot of money in those days.

He would stay there all alone for two years. Then he would float down to town, where he bought more supplies for the next two years. The hired man with a big boat would take him up river again and leave him there with the cargo and would return to town. Very cleverly conceived and executed.

Jimmy was seventy-one years old, but what was that? He was a picture of health. Wasn't he scared? No. There were no thieves. How about bears? He had killed only one. By the way, the pelt of that bear came in handy as a rug for his bare feet when he went to bed. No stomachache or anything? No. His stomach was used to the same fare and never complained. What if he cut himself with an axe? Oh, no. When a man is all by himself, he is extra careful and is apt to avoid fatal mistakes. Wasn't he tired of always eating alone? Not at all. Eating alone has many advantages like not needing napkins, not bothering about slurping or not slurping, or burping or spitting, or what have you. Civilization—so called—has put people in a strait-jacket. Jimmy felt free to wiggle and move with no straitjacket impeding his movements. It was lovely. Then that blessed freedom to do what he wanted, when he wanted, if he wanted, for as long as he wanted. Money can't buy such blessedness.

But what was he doing for mankind? Here Jimmy almost lost his temper. On the positive side, he was contributing with gold so the government could keep itself financially solvent and help its citizens. On the negative side, he was bothering nobody. What more could one expect? I see.

Did he read much? Yes, indeed, he read a lot. By the way, he had recently finished a Catholic book on purgatory which he liked a great deal. He was a Presbyterian of sorts, and he loved God in his own heart. He was a believer. He had never accepted the idea of eternal hell, but the Catholic idea of purgatory suited him beautifully. A bad guy should not get away with murder even in the next life. Give the bad guy a good purgatory that will leave him soft as putty and that's it. Here we discussed at length the case of a man or woman who refuses God's love till the last minute and dies with his or her back turned to God. He listened to all I had to say.

When I told a neighbor that I had had a long visit with one Jimmy Cross, he smiled and told me that Jimmy was starving for conversation. When he came to town every other summer, people dreaded to see him come in because he would talk all day. It was a not-too-subtle compensation for the length of time he spent all alone thinking that he did not need anybody. Man is a social animal. We need each other. But it was educational to see a man who was different. We know that we are not all alike—thank God we aren't—and we are amused at the way some men differ from others. When I am busy doing something I consider important and at the same time have to answer the doorbell and the telephone, I sigh and yearn for a log cabin on the Ambler Creek, alone with the snow and the trees and the books. But then we are all different, thanks be to God.

Twice during my stay in Kotzebue I was called to Pilgrim Springs to give retreats and to give Fr. Edward Cunningham, S.J., a chance to get away for a short rest. Pilgrim Springs is south of Kotzebue and about sixty miles north of Nome. There was a boarding school with Ursuline nuns as teachers and two lay brothers. The school had been started at the time of the Spanish flu in 1918–19, when many children in that area had been left orphans.

Fr. Lafortune had acquired the land. In its midst there was a hot spring with medicinal qualities. The water came out so hot that it was almost unbearable. It looked to me like an oasis. There were ranges of mountains around it. The flat land where the school was located was covered with willows. In the summer there were luscious gardens with a variety of vegetables. The negative side to it was that it was off the beaten trail. It was a joy for me to mix with those lovely children, so well trained, so well mannered, so lively. A bath in the hot pool left me exhausted. I had to lie down for a while to regain my strength.

Every week Sig Wien flew in from Nome and brought mail and merchandise. One of my first visits was to the grave of Fr. Frederick Ruppert, S.J. He had been born in Germany in 1879 and had come to Alaska in 1918. In December of 1923 he was going to Pilgrim Springs by dog team, but he did not make it. He was found frozen a short distance away. He himself had let the dogs loose, hoping to follow them by walking, because the snow was too deep and they were making no headway. When the dogs began to show up at the school one after another, panic hit the school and a search party took off in the right direction, fortunately, for his body was found lying flat and facing upward. Much has been written about this accident and many versions have been given. He lies in the graveyard of the mission and close to him is the grave of Bro. John F. Hansen, S.J., who died in the Nome hospital in 1938. The school children made it a point to keep those two graves neatly ornamented as a sign of respect and veneration. Bro. Hansen had been with them for a number of years.

To these two must be added now the grave of Fr. Cunningham himself, my host, who died there on January 23, 1941, of a heart attack while he was shaving. He was a native of Baltimore, where he had been born in 1881, the very year my father was born. By looking at him, I figured more or less how my dad in Spain would be looking. Cunningham had come to Alaska in 1923 and had been stationed mostly at Holy Cross on the Yukon. He was highly emotional, a barrel of fun, an outstanding conversationalist, worshiped by the children everywhere.

But the poor man snored so horribly that I woke up several times in near panic. You know how it is when you are sound asleep and some strident noise wakes you up and you know not where you are. That was much more than sound snoring. It was a combination of wailings and screams emanating from a deep cavern. And it did not wake him up! I asked Bro. Wilhalm and Bro. Wickart how could they stand it. They answered that, after a few months of it, they would go to bed expecting it; then when it came, it did not bother them. To those who asked why didn't we close the doors of our rooms, the answer is that there was a general stove in the center of the house that heated the whole floor; by keeping our doors open, we all benefited from the heat.

Pilgrim Springs functioned until the spring of 1941, when Fr. Anable closed it with the approval of Bishop Crimont. The reasons were many. The building had deteriorated considerably; there was a lack of fuel; freight expenses had become prohibitive; the number of children had dwindled to the point where it was felt that the expenses incurred were not justified.

That area had been evangelized first by Fr. Joseph Bernard, S.J., a Frenchman who had built Mary's Igloo on a spot bought by Fr.

Lafortune. Fr. Bernard had covered much ground by dog team every winter. In Deering and Candle I met people who knew him and had received him in their homes, where he had said Mass. He had been a vigorous man with much zeal and great power of attraction. He had made friends easily and endeared himself to all, regardless of their race, color, or religion. His dogs had been well trained. If they barked when they were tied and he was indoors, one knock at the window pane sufficed to stop them automatically. When he spoke French to them on the trail, people figured that he was swearing at them or something because the tone of voice was out of the ordinary.

This priest, loved by all, had been called by the French army during the First World War to come to France and fight for the homeland. To the amazement of the missionaries, he had answered the call and gone to France, joining the army as an interpreter with the British. After the war, he had assumed that all he had to do was to go back to Alaska. But he'd been told not to return. I could never find out who gave him the order not to return. I say this because once when Bishop Crimont—himself a Frenchman—and I were alone, I did a little fishing around with this purely rhetorical exclamation: "Wasn't it a pity that the great Fr. Bernard never returned to Alaska?"

The bishop said, "Yes. Some did not like his going to France. But his class had been called by the French government, so he went." That was that.

I inferred that the bishop had approved of Bernard's going to France. Who told Bernard to stay put in France? If my suggestion is worth anything, I'll say this: The general superior of the Alaska missions during World War I and up to 1923 was Fr. John Sifton, a German. If he and the bulk of the missionaries disapproved of Bernard's decision to leave Alaska to fight the Germans, we have here a force capable of resisting Crimont. Fr. Bernard died in France in his late eighties.

World politics seemed to influence the Alaska missions on another matter, also. In 1938 Bishop Crimont made every possible effort to have a French Jesuit appointed as coadjutor with the right of succession. He first tried Fr. Auguste Coudeyre, with no results. Then it was Fr. William Levasseur, but he got nowhere. The Americans in the field wanted "home rule," so to say, and there was an impasse.

As the months rolled by in a frustrating silence, it was "leaked" that if the Jesuits did not soon come to an agreement, Rome would appoint a non-Jesuit bishop over them. Suddenly, things happened. The provincial of the Oregon Province, Walter Fitzgerald, S.J., who happened to be in Rome, was called by the general superior, Fr. Wladimir Ledochowski, to his desk to be told that the Holy Father had chosen him as the coadjutor with right of succession to Bishop Crimont. After Bishop Fitzgerald's consecration, Crimont told him that he only had the authority that Crimont would give him, and that he was giving Fitzgerald no authority whatever. The next year, Coadjutor Fitzgerald was told to make a detailed visitation of all the northern mission stations and come back to Juneau with the report. Fitzgerald did exactly that. When he laid his report on Crimont's desk, Crimont held a consultation with the two other priests living in the house, but did not want Fitzgerald to take part in the consultation.

On the Feast of Pentecost of 1945, we heard that good Bishop Crimont had been called by God at the age of eighty-eight. Bishop Fitzgerald presided at the funeral and, acquiescing to the wishes of Crimont, had him buried in the chapel of the shrine of Saint Therese some miles north of Juneau.

Lunch followed the funeral. Bishop Fitzgerald told the two priests that he was now in charge and was calling his own helpers, so they were thanked for past services and advised to return to the States. And with that came the end of lunch.

10
Bury Me Next to Fr. Jette

In 1941, Fr. O'Connor was transferred to Kotzebue and I took his place back at Akulurak. The bishop sent Fr. Francis Menager, S.J., to help me. He would be mostly in the house while I did the traveling by dog team.

In October the usual training of the dogs began. Fr. O'Connor was heavier than I, so I'm sure the dogs appreciated the change. On October 30, I went out with several dogs and I took an eighteen-year-old boy by the name of Elias who was in our school. The purpose was to give those dogs a good run to keep them in good shape. Everything was going fine. We were crossing a big lake that was frozen solid, so the dogs were having a good time running and barking, when suddenly the ice under us broke and we all disappeared under the broken ice.

Things like this do happen and when they happen it usually means death unless the water is not deep. Our water was so deep that we could not touch bottom. Now many things happened. I was dressed with a thick jacket and had on knee boots. I had learned to swim in Hayden Lake, Idaho, and this was an asset. But to swim with knee boots that get filled with water plus a jacket that gets soaked, plus the fact that we had just eaten and were digesting our food, plus the sharp edges of broken ice cutting my hands and face, plus my worry for poor Elias, who could not swim . . . All this conspired to put me in that state of soul which is well nigh impossible to describe.

The sled disappeared under the ice. The first three dogs were walking and breaking ice, while the other four had only their noses above water because Elias was hanging on for sweet life atop them and grabbing the tow line. I would put my elbows above the ice, but when I tried to climb, the ice would crack and break apart. We had hit one of those spots that do not freeze with the rest for several reasons.

As we measured it later, we were ninety-seven feet from shore. I have no idea how long it took us to get out. I know that twice I gave up and was ready to sink, but twice I made an extra effort. While struggling to get out, I remember I told the Lord that it was a dirty shame to have a young priest like me drown like that since there was such a shortage of priests in the church, and it took many years to make a priest. When nothing happened, I told the Lord that I offered up to Him all the prayers that were being said for the missionaries. Just then my elbows hit solid ice that did not break. I struggled and climbed and stood and took a few steps and was safe. At that very moment the dogs followed me with Elias in tow.

The water trickling down from our clothes soon became icicles. The dogs shook themselves several times, became dry, and were ready to resume running. But they absolutely refused to turn around and return home. They had not been out long enough and they wanted more running. I had a feeling that if I had had a gun then, I might have shot them. With much urging and dragging, they finally took the hint and began to walk, and I mean walk, as if they were one hundred years old.

It took us quite some time to get home. When we arrived, I saw in the eyes of the people that they could not believe what they were seeing. Elias and I were more dead than alive. He went to his bed and I went to mine, but it took two people to undress me. I drank a glass of wine to warm the insides and wrapped myself with blankets to warm the trembling and shaking members of my poor body, which at that moment was not worth a nickel. My whole abdomen was frozen and insensitive. Touching it and touching the wall gave the same feeling. For five whole hours I was frozen.

My mind was not unlike the minds of those poor people who are tortured by putting them before a firing squad and then firing guns that have no bullets, and doing it time and again so as to keep them wondering if this time will be the real thing. I was drowning. For five hours I was floating with broken ice. My mind was in a dream, a scary dream. I kept asking about Elias. The answer was that he was doing fine, but I wondered if they were telling me that so I would not collapse altogether. After five horrible hours I began to perspire in earnest. Thank God. Next morning I got up to say Mass, but I could not keep my arms raised. My fingers were full of cuts.

This close call told me that God wanted me around for a while, since He had made such a miracle. We called it a miracle. When word spread around, the natives said that the priest had made medicine and had come out alive.

The thought that I could have drowned sobered me considerably. It would have meant that all my plans, ambitions, preoccupations, and cares would have come to a crashing end. From now on I would be more preoccupied with doing God's holy will at all times than with doing mine. Things that up to then meant very much to me suddenly lost their luster and value. The only thing that would accompany me on my journey to meet my Maker would be the manner of life I had lived. Everything else would be of no account. Unfortunately, all those good resolutions have a way of losing strength as time rolls on. Time can have a devastating effect on resolutions that are not renewed daily or nearly so.

Elias also came out of it miraculously. We did not have any bad results. No pneumonia, no arthritis, not even a cold or a cough. For many years afterward, every time we met, we smiled knowingly. I married him to Rita Stanislaus of Alakanuk. They raised a family. Rita survived him.

On December third of the same year, 1941, I received an S.O.S. from my neighbor Fr. John Fox, S.J., the pastor of Hooper Bay. He sent Jimmy Droane, one of his parishioners, with Father's dog team to take me to Hooper Bay because he was sick. Jimmy had eleven dogs, but they were so poorly fed that I did not expect much from them. It is better to have seven well fed and trained than eleven that show their ribs.

The first day we covered only fourteen miles to Pastolik, where we slept. The second day we reached Uksukalik. The third day we were fortunate to make Kapothlik. The fourth day we made it to Scammon Bay.

By now I was very well battered. The poor dogs were not pulling and the snow was fresh and deep. We had to walk alongside and give the dogs a hand. One of them lay down totally exhausted, so we let him loose and we never saw him again. I was walking mechanically, almost unconscious of what I was doing. I told the Lord that every step I took had to count for one sinner who needed conversion. When the step was not too deep, I figured that a light-weight sinner had been saved. When my foot sank to the knee, then I knew that some real heavy-weight criminal had been brought back to the fold. I was amazed at the large number of sinners walking this earth.

When we reached Kapothlik, I was dismayed at what I saw. There was only one cabin, with three families inside. There was no room for any of the things we had in the sled. I walked in with the Mass-kit to say Mass there in the morning. Was there room for the sleeping bag? They thought there might be, so I brought it in and so did Jimmy.

After warming up a big can of pork and beans, we called it supper and I proceeded to have a short instruction. Then everyone spread something on the floor and we made as though we were going to sleep. I could not stretch my legs without hitting somebody, so I had to bend them. When we were all asleep (or should be) an infernal noise of barking dogs kept us awake. It was the dog team of a friend of the family who was coming to sleep in the cabin. When he opened the door, knowing that there was not one square foot on the floor that was not occupied, I closed my eyes tight and steeled myself for the worst— like being trampled under foot because it was dark. Yet the man found some hole where he literally holed in and silence came again.

Next morning I said Mass on the only flat space there was, namely, a sewing machine. How in the world a sewing machine had landed there was a mystery to me, but it sure came in handy. I could not stand erect while saying Mass because, though I am only five-foot-eight, I would hit the ceiling. Bent as I was, my head was between the tails of the skins of mink, fox, land otter, and lynx. Those skins were the bank account of those people. They were precious.

The sanitary conditions of such a place I leave to your imagination. Being young does help in overcoming such apparently insurmountable hurdles. In our fifth day between Scammon Bay and Hooper Bay, I was not sure at all that I would make it. For one thing, I was half starved, yet I had to push the sled.

When night set in and we did not know exactly where we were, I offered myself to God and begged Him to take that trail as my purgatory and let me get into heaven instantly to share in His divine life in the company of the angels and saints. Suddenly, the dogs and sled disappeared. Jimmy threw himself behind and caught up with them. I stood behind like a statue, totally speechless. We had come unexpectedly to a sharp, high cliff. Jimmy yelled at me from down under, instructing me to let myself down carefully so I would not be hurt. I sat on the snow and moved to the edge till my feet were dangling. Looking up to a dark sky and commending myself to God, I let myself slide and I fell in a ball, rolling till I hit a flat space.

Following my ears, I came to where Jimmy was calling me in total darkness. We were pleased to ascertain that we both were unhurt and we renewed our march to Calvary. Knowing that God is the God of the broken-hearted and of those who come to the point of despair, I begged Him to lead us to Hooper Bay that very night, because if we had to spend the night where we were, I could not possibly make it.

Then it happened. To this day I have no reasonable explanation. A flash-like lightning shot from the ground ahead of us toward the left. The dogs saw it and made for it. And there was the trail. From then on it was smooth sailing to Hooper Bay. We had been saved.

Fr. John Fox, S.J., had his quarters in Hooper Bay, the center of a vast district with five fairly well populated villages, and all were quite Catholic. He conceived the bright idea of founding a congregation of Eskimo sisters to help him evangelize those villages. His plan was to train those sisters himself and then put them in twos in each village. The idea caught on. He gathered a group of Eskimo girls who had finished their education at Akulurak and Holy Cross. The cream of the crop, we might say. He had Annie Sipari as superior of the group. She was an exceptional woman by any standards. Besides being capable of leading the group, she could run a dog team or haul wood or fish and process the fish or set traps, you name it. Bishop Crimont approved the rules and gave his heartfelt blessing to the congregation, which was named the Sisters of the Snow—so it was all official.

Fr. Fox had called the scattered sisters to Hooper Bay so that I could give them a seven-day retreat in silence. When Jimmy and I arrived half-dead late in the night, Sister Annie Sipari opened the door. One look told her that I immediately needed a hot bowl of soup and a bed. How I thanked the Lord when I saw myself cozily wrapped in bed away from cliffs threatening to do me in.

How about Fr. Fox himself? I am sure he was under the weather, but the minute he saw me, he revived and told me that he was going away to spend a week in Chevak. Next day I found myself in charge of operations.

It was a great joy for me to give four meditations a day to those sisters. At the end of the week I had passed on to them just about all I knew about God, Christ, Mary, the holy Eucharist, together with the main points of the catechism they were supposed to teach in their villages.

Our retreat was not without some excitement for me. A man came to tell me that his wife was having a baby but the baby could not come out. He begged me to follow him and give a hand in the matter. After recovering from the initial shock, I went along meekly.

As I entered the poor cabin, I was saddened by the look of pain in the poor mother, who was in a bunk covered with a blanket. There were women around the bunk. All turned to me as the life saver. I closed my eyes, raised my arms to the ceiling, invoked the name of the Lord, and imparted my blessing. Before I was altogether through, there was a sudden excitement. A woman struggled somewhat and presently brought out a healthy baby boy screaming to high heaven. The father of the child turned to me and said, "I knew that the priest could do it," which to me meant that he knew more than I did.

After the baby was washed, I told them to put some clothes on the little thing. To my consternation, they did not have anything to put on him. With an air of unbelief I remonstrated that they had known that the baby was due. Hadn't they anticipated it? Didn't they have any baby clothes ready?

A woman more articulate than the rest put me at ease by telling me in a quiet monotone: "You see, Father, some babies are born dead and we wait until the baby is born. If he comes out dead, those baby clothes would be useless. If he comes out alive, then we scrounge around the neighborhood and we always find something."

A couple of days later, they brought the baby for baptism. I called him Louis like my father. Years later I was in the habit of asking Fr. Fox how was Louis doing. When he told me that Louis had developed into a husky hunter, I quit asking.

The last day of our retreat, the Japanese attacked Pearl Harbor. We had begun the retreat in peace and we ended it in war. Fr. Fox returned next day quite excited and ordered the people to put blankets around their windows at night in case the Japanese war planes would come. I nearly died laughing. I asked Father if he thought we were worth one single bomb. And how could the Japanese know that we existed? He said that they had spies everywhere and, you see, with our lights we could lead those planes on their flight to wipe out Fairbanks. So that was that: Every window was covered at night. I renewed my objections by saying that those lights could save the lives of dog mushes lost in the tundra in a dark night. He retorted that the Eskimos know the country like the palm of their hands and do not need to see the lights of the faraway village. I caved in.

Those Sisters of the Snow were fine specimens, but the experiment lasted only fourteen years. Some of those sisters contracted tuberculosis, a very common disease among the Eskimos—so common, in fact, that it became a threat to their very survival. After World War II the U.S. government embarked on an ambitious plan to stamp out the disease altogether. As many as four thousand natives were at one time in sanatoriums. Most were taken to Washington State until the native hospital was built in Anchorage. The result was that the community of the Sisters of the Snow was crippled as some had to be taken to sanatoriums.

Other sisters figured that they could still teach catechism and at the same time be married. Bear in mind that the average Eskimo woman is at a loss if she is not carrying a baby in her arms. When her children start growing, she looks around for some baby to hug. Those good sisters saw their women friends carrying beautiful babies. The temptation was too much for some of them. They would send a note to Father telling him: "One man here distracts me." When decoded, that message said that the man had a crush on her and she had one on him and that life was miserable because those crushes were fast becoming unbearable crosses. The next thing was the wedding.

Good Fr. Fox had his crosses, but he carried them valiantly. One girl from Holy Cross joined the community and eventually took the habit as a novice. In due time it became obvious that she had no real vocation. Fr. Fox explained it to her and told her that, since she had no vocation, she had better take off the habit, put on her civilian clothes, and return to her family. When she arrived in Holy Cross, people asked her why had she come back. In her simplicity and faulty English she answered that she could stay no longer because Fr. Fox had told her to take off her clothes. It took some time to clear up the ensuing embarrassment.

In time there were only four sisters left, and two of them were in the hospital. Some missionaries wondered aloud if the experiment was worthwhile. Unfortunately, they were speaking from hearsay. Then Bishop Fitzgerald came along and, after some soul searching and much questioning, decided that the best thing was to disband them.

I always felt that the attempt was a beautiful one. For one thing, those sisters did much good in those villages. Then it showed that the natives were becoming of age spiritually. Such Christian terms as chastity and consecrated virginity were also for them and they accepted them. It had not been so long since the first missionaries who had come to Akulurak had been pitied by the people because they had not brought their wives along. Now the grandchildren of those natives were themselves abstaining from husbands for the glory of God. A long step had been taken in a rather short time.

The mere presence of an Eskimo sister spoke of the supernatural. It showed that there is a hereafter where people are neither married nor given into marriage because our lives there will resemble the lives of the angels. It isn't all eating and drinking and working and getting married and raising children. All these things are restricted to this valley of tears. There is a heaven. The holy habit of a nun speaks of it without words. It is a symbol, a sign, a reminder, and also a warning. This spiritual message alone was worth the time and money Fr. Fox spent building the convent. He built it with the money he received from friends in the States without ever asking the bishop for one cent.

When the order to disband the sisters came, Father obeyed at once. But it was a big blow to him. For years the mere mention of it brought heated discussions, but he obeyed and continued working with the same zeal and determination that characterized him. To this day Fr. Fox has the distinction of having lived in Alaska longer than any other Jesuit priest.

When I finished the retreat, I returned to Akulurak with Evan, who had come with my own dogs to get me. The trip to Scammon Bay made me thirsty. The village has a crystal-clear creek where I drank water to excess. As a result I did not sleep. Next day the weather turned bad and we were fortunate to make Kaveagameut, a former village which had dwindled to just one cabin with one family living in it. I entered the cabin very sick. There was no fuel. The walls were coated with frost. Our breath was like a chimney. Outdoors the night had closed in and the storm was howling. Soon my pain became unbearable. It was pleurisy, as I was told later.

I crawled inside my sleeping bag and called Evan to tell him that I was dying but that he should not be scared. All he had to do was to put my body in the sled inside of the sleeping bag and take me to Akulurak to be buried between Fr. Jette and Bro. Keogh. He answered that he would do it. But in the morning I felt better. We took off and the more bumps the sled was getting, the better I was feeling. So we arrived in Akulurak in the pink of health.

11

The Winter Trail

At Akulurak I was told that I was losing Fr. Menager, who was to go to Hooper Bay to replace Fr. Fox, while the latter would go to the States for a few months to rest.

Fr. Francis Menager, S.J., had been born in Normandy, France, twenty years ahead of me. He had become a priest in this country, taught philosophy, and in 1927 he had gone to Alaska. In our brotherly chats he told me that he had been assured that he would replace Crimont as bishop of Alaska. With all humility he had begun to prepare himself inwardly for the coming episcopal task. In the intervening time, Fr. Philip Delon, S.J., then general superior of the missions, had been killed in the October 1930 plane crash at Kotzebue.

Fr. Menager at that time had been between Kashunak and Hooper Bay and could not be reached. So Fr. Lucchesi had been appointed superior general *pro tem* until Fr. Menager could make it to Holy Cross which was the next year. The plane that crashed in Kotzebue, the *Marquette,* had been replaced by another, and Bro. George Feltes, S.J., a trained pilot, had been commissioned by the bishop to fly it. Fr. Menager had felt that as superior general he should have the say about the disposition of this second plane. For one thing, he had begun to take flying lessons in Fairbanks. When the bishop had heard this, he had sent word to Menager to keep off that plane completely. Only Bro. Feltes was to fly it. In the Kotzebue crash two priests had got killed; there was no need to tempt God and have more priests killed needlessly.

Fr. Menager had his own version about the whole affair, but the bishop did not take his side. Fr. Menager—for reasons he kept to himself—had gone ahead and had the plane sold. Here the good old bishop had hit the ceiling and demoted Menager from his high office and further sent him to be pastor of Kotzebue, which then was the remotest Catholic post in Alaska.

Fr. Menager knew that his episcopacy had gone sour, but he was genuinely spiritual and priestly to accept it. Not only that, he went ahead doing great work as a missionary, because not only was he spiritual, he was also a very talented man. He had an acute philosophical mind, was a voracious reader of big books, had a fine tenor voice, played musical instruments, and learned the Eskimo language quite proficiently—so he was a man for all seasons. As a Frenchman at heart, he was effervescent almost to extremes; a great entertainer, though like all extroverts he had his ups and downs.[1]

When Fr. Menager left Akulurak to go to Hooper Bay, his place was taken by Fr.Norman Donohue, S.J., one year younger than I. He was to stay at the mission quarters to study the language, while I would take the trail and visit the villages and settlements with a big boy named Ralph and nine dogs. Ralph was not as good as Baltazar for the trail, but Baltazar had just died of consumption.

It was my turn now to fill the shoes of Fr. O'Connor. While I was not a novice on the trail by any means, I made preparations to save myself from as many traps and pitfalls as possible. The trail is always dangerous. In 1911 Brother Paquin, S.J., had been driving his dog team between Saint Michael and Stebbins when a sudden snowstorm had fallen upon him. He had been found later frozen, half covered with snow. In 1923 shortly before Christmas, Fr. Ruppert, S.J., had been found frozen to death. He had tried to reach Pilgrim Springs but failed.

Fr. Joseph Treca, S.J., had covered as much territory by dog team probably as any other missionary. At age 72 he had gone by dog team from Akulurak to Nelson Island and back, a trip that had taken the whole month of April. A few days after his return from that awesome trip, he had gone to baptize a baby a mere twelve miles away. On his return the dogs had got lost in a sudden ground fog that had blinded them and prevented them from seeing or even smelling the narrow trail between thickets of willows. As night came, he had been forced to spend the night in the open. He caught a severe case of rheumatism in a hip. The leg eventually became gangrenous. In Seattle he had the leg amputated, but the operation proved to be too much for him. He died there on September 16, 1926.

In time, snowmobiles were not much better. Fr. William McIntyre, S.J., was on his way to Sheldon Point when he ran into what the pilots call a "white out," that is, a white fog so thick that it is absolutely impossible to know north from south, sky from ground, right from left. Father stopped the machine simply because he feared that he might be going over sea ice. When he was found two or three days later, his feet had to be treated in the hospital for a long time, and he was fortunate to save them from amputation. And the very same thing happened to Fr. William Dibb, S.J., when his machine broke through thin ice and he got his feet wet. He was also fortunate that he did not have his toes amputated after a long hospitalization. The trail shows no mercy.

I was officially appointed welfare agent for the wide area I was to travel. I had to report cases of people sixty-five or over who were in need. Since everyone was in need, my problem was to prove that they were sixty-five years old. Likewise I had to report cases of orphans, of widows with small children, and of people blind to a certain degree. That degree became a thorny business, but I tackled it the best I knew, I suppose.

Fortunately for me, I had the early records of baptisms that went back to 1890 or thereabouts. But this brought another problem, because the name given by the priest in English meant absolutely nothing those days and the child grew up with more than one Eskimo name. It was customary then, when someone in the family died, to change their names so the dead person could not come back to harm any of them. The dead person knew people by their names. But if he or she came back to get even, the dead person was stuck: There were not any such people around. They were different people with different names. Very simple and very complicated.

I had to disentangle the mess. I had to prove that Pasgatak, who was also called Jimmie, in reality was that boy who in the baptismal book appeared as Joseph Kaurtutailinok. I did this by finding out how many Eskimo names his parents used. If his parents had at least one name that had been well known, then this was the guy for sure. Once I established this, I had overcome the hardest hurdle. But the baptizing priest had put down the age of the boy, say, as ten. Was he eight or was he perhaps twelve? Against this obstacle I had a ready solution.

A very well-known man going by Francis Lee (who in reality was

Joseph Ekoyungilinok) had been born on a well-known date. I would ask the old man who was older, he or Francis. If the man said that he had already married when Francis was a boy, my problem was solved right there.

Now came the problem of when he was born. He remembered that his mother told him that he was born when the geese wanted to come. This meant the month of May. Or when they were picking berries. This meant the month of August. Or when they were catching mink. This meant between November first and Christmas. Or when they were catching fish to smoke. This covered June and July. If one was born during the big moon, that was January. So I was sitting pretty.

You see, when I sent my first records to Juneau, they were all sent back. They were faulty. They were too vague. To make it worse, the name of the recipient was not the same as the name of the father. It all looked like a fraud. Bear in mind that the agents in Juneau were from Iowa or Kansas and did not have the slightest idea of how the Eskimos handled their family affairs. Since the intent of the law was that any American citizen who qualified for old-age assistance should receive it, I saw to it that they would receive it. After some trials and errors I developed a system that always worked. I would walk into an extremely poor log house with an old man sitting on the floor in a corner. This was the dialog that took place between us.

"What is your name?"

"Akomogagolok."

"You have an English name?"

"Yes."

"What is it?"

"Philip."

"That's great. You are Philip Akomogagolok. Where were you born?"

"I don't know."

"When you were a child were you very far away from here?"

"No."

"That's fine. You were born at Akulurak, Alaska. How old are you?"

"I don't know."

"Are you as old as Ekoyungilinok?"

"I am much older."

"Very well. What was your father's name?"

"Kuskanayak."

"And your mother's name?"

"Attulak."

"Are you married?"

"Yes."

"What's the name of your wife?"

"Which one?"

"Oh, you have more than one wife?"

"Yes."

"How many do you have?"

"Three."

"Where are they? I don't see any around here."

"They died."

"Do you have a living wife now?"

"No."

"Do you have children?"

"No."

"Who feeds you?"

"My son."

"But you just told me that you have no children."

"This son is not my son."

"Oh, I see; you are raising him, are you?"

"Yes."

"Is he related to you?"

"Yes."

"How is your health?"

"Bad."

"Is it very bad?"

"When I want to chop wood, I cannot. When I want to walk, I tire right away."

"Oh, I see. Do you also spit blood?"

"Sometimes."

"Very well. With this information I am going to see that you get food and some blankets. Is there anything else that you want?"

"Yes."

"What is it?"

"Chewing tobacco."

"Oh, yes, by all means you will get chewing tobacco; leave that to me."

Back in my room at Akulurak I would sit at the typewriter and fill the official forms, answering every single question and giving chapter and verse in every case. I had all the details. This last one was: Philip Akomogagolok; son of Anthony Akomogagolok and Anna Attulak; born on May 14, 1869, at Akulurak, Alaska; a widower; consumptive, is taken care of by a nephew.

The clerks in Juneau would process the case in a hurry and one day there would appear in our post office a check for twenty-five dollars in favor of Philip Akomogagolok with instructions that if the recipient did not know how to write, he should write a cross in the presence of two witnesses who had to write their own names and addresses.

When the first checks began to arrive and food and blankets and chewing tobacco could be had in exchange for that piece of paper, the recipients wanted to know who sent that. The answer was: the government. But they did not have any idea what *government* meant. They were born and raised on those infinite flats, making a living the hard way. They did not know if they were Americans or Germans or Chinese. They were they and that was their land. There was no need to go any further. Those were the beginnings. It did not take them long to learn. Within a few years they knew that the mail plane brought checks which meant food, which meant life.

I was also marriage commissioner. This entitled me to perform marriages not only as an ordained Catholic priest, but as an official of the government. I have to admit now that in those days I was inclined to be legalistic. A man was living with a woman. They were young. He had lost his wife and she had lost her husband. Now suddenly they were cohabiting. I had in my suitcase all the proper forms to perform a marriage. I would walk into their little cabin and sure enough she was cooking and he was making a net in a peaceful and harmonious environment.

"How long have you been living together?"

"Two months."

"Don't you think that it is time to get married properly?"

"I don't know."

"Well, my goodness, are you thinking of living together like this?"

"Maybe."

"Well, gentleman, you had better make up your mind. There is a law . . . You are baptized Catholic and you have been around the mission long enough to know that men and women get married properly."

Here the poor man began to look very much concerned. He looked at the floor in deep reflection. Then he looked through the window. Then he turned his pleading eyes on me and asked: "Father, won't you let me try her one more month?"

This question tells worlds. To us, white men, stupid men that is, and to me in particular, a priest, not even a man that is, this question sounds unchristian, pagan. But put yourself in his shoes. There were many things he wanted to know before he married her properly. Was she a good cook? Did she know how to sew boots that did not leak? Did she get angry at the drop of a hat? Did she know how to skin a fox or a mink or a seal without making a mess of it? Would her relatives become intolerable in-laws? Was she lazy? Things like these were much more important to that man than sex was. Sex had nothing to do with it, or at least it would take the last place on the list.

The missionary has to know these things to appreciate the actions of his scattered parishioners. How did I solve this case? I, in turn, looked at the man with pleading eyes and told him that I had known that girl since she was small and that she was average: neither the best nor the worst. And if he did not marry her properly, her uncle Nuyarpak would come and take her away from him.

He reflected again and decided to marry her then and there before me and two witnesses. He came to realize that he knew her well enough to take the plunge. So they got married and lived happily ever after, as the saying goes.

The time to start visiting the district by dog team was about the middle of November. After Baltazar was gone, I took Ralph Jones, a tough, nineteen-year-old Eskimo, short, wide, ambitious, and with a pride taller than a mountain, who would not take second place in anything. He had been in our school and was bilingual.

With nine dogs we would start on a week trip. In the first village there were three cabins. I would stay in the biggest of the three and Ralph was free to choose. We would arrive late in the afternoon.

When supper was ready I never tired of watching the same ritual. A cloth or canvas was spread on the floor. A huge deep platter was placed on it. An enormous pot of boiled black fish filled the platter to overflowing. The family sat on the floor around the platter and each one began to pick one black fish. They took that little fish with their fingers and ate it till there was nothing left but the tiny bones. In due time not one fish was left and all the bones were piled up in a big dish. A rag was passed around for each one to clean fingers. Then came hot tea, pilot bread, and a can of lard. Each one helped himself. They spread lard on the pilot bread, ate it, and washed it down with tea. That was supper.

After everything was removed, I would give a lengthy instruction on God, Christ, the sacraments, or whatever. If some of them had been in Akulurak, they had heard all those things already. If they had not gone to our school, then most of what I said was quite new. The old folks were all baptized, they said, and when asked who baptized them, the answer usually was Kutlik. That was Fr. Joseph Treca. With his French accent he had told the people that he was *Catolic*. The French find it hard to pronounce the *th* sound and they say *Catolic*, which the Eskimos corrupted into *Kootlik*, and that became his name. He had put in twenty-two years in those flats, crisscrossing them and speaking the language in a way that people understood him. He had been kindness and generosity personified and his memory was still very much alive.

By the time I would finish instructions, people were sleepy and so was I. But before going to bed, we had confessions. I would dress up with my fur parka and gloves and would go outdoors so nobody could hear. All the people would come out one after the other, beginning with those from the other cabins who had come for the instruction, so they could go home immediately after confession. If the night was dark, I would be staring into nothing. If there was a moon or if we had a starry sky, I would be staring into the heavens while hearing those confessions. Whatever we had, it was cold and I could be shivering. I never ceased being impressed by divine Providence, who used the priest as an instrument to bring Christ to those people under such strange circumstances.

In preparation for sleep we went through another ritual. Everyone left the cabin one after the other and soon all were back. I would spread my sleeping bag on the floor and soon the cabin became silent like a grave. How long did we sleep? There was never an appointed time to get up. The nights were extra long. Getting up was probably the worst time in the day, because of the problem of washing and other private matters. Sooner or later we all gathered around a little table where I said Mass after they finished their vocal prayers in Eskimo. All went to holy Communion.

For breakfast there was hot tea again with pilot bread and lard and a dish of cornmeal. Eventually, tea gave place to coffee. For some reason that I did not know, they bought only Hills coffee, and if this brand was not available, they reverted to tea.

After breakfast there could be a baby to be baptized or a youngster who could be taken to the Akulurak school or an old man or woman who was certainly sixty-five or over and therefore entitled to the twenty-five-dollar monthly pension. Those days twenty-five dollars was a lot of money. Little by little the checks were getting fatter and fatter.

I would visit the other cabins and settle some last-minute little family problems. The man was drinking too much. The woman was lazy and did not do her chores. The child was sick and needed hospitalization. Maybe we could contact the doctor by radio at Akulurak.

One couple wanted me to settle their constant misunderstandings and things went like this:

"My wife does not want to wash my clothes."

"Why don't you wash you husband's clothes?"

"Because he does not want to buy me soap."

"Why don't you buy her soap?"

"I give her money but she buys other things."

"Why don't you buy soap with the money he gives you?"

"Because he never gives me enough."

"Why don't you give her enough money so she can buy soap?"

"I give her as much as other men give to their wives, but she eats too much."

I did not have the heart to ask her if she ate too much, because she was so stout that she could hardly go through the door.

The problem was settled in this way: When he went to the store with his pelts, he would buy soap himself and give it to his wife to wash his clothes. They looked at each other with relief and we passed to other matters.

The man begged me to tell his brother who lived in the next cabin some twenty feet away not to come to his house while drunk.

Couldn't he tell him himself? His brother was younger. He should have some influence over his younger brother.

No, it did not work; he had told him often, but it did not work. But if the priest told him, then he would stop for sure, because he had been in the mission school one year and he would respect the priest.

The problem was settled this way: I called the younger brother and faced the two of them. Bill was the older, Jim was the younger.

"Say, Jim, when are you going to stop coming here when you are drunk? Bill says that you are always drunk and come here to bother his family."

"Is that what he said? Bill is the one who goes to my house to bother me."

Bill: "I never."

Jim: "You always."

Bill: "You call me to your house when you are drinking."

Jim: "You bring the pot of hooch to my house when you brew it."

Here I have to intervene and to tell them that I am sorry I am not Solomon. How about shaking hands and promise before me that you will not bother each other again? They shake hands. Then I turn moralistic and insist that drinking like they do is the worst imaginable thing they can do, etc., etc.

Once I took the bull by the horns and smashed a wooden container of home-made brew with an axe that was lying on the snow. But it was a chance that I took. I never did it again. I was out on those flats surrounded by people who considered drunkenness one of the necessities of life. Those people were convinced that God had made them for one purpose only, namely, to get drunk; when they were not drunk, they knew that they were not fulfilling the purpose for which they were created. Anyone who dared to tamper with their drinking habits was taking his life in his hands. The wife and the children would be peacefully sleeping at night when the husband would storm in totally drunk, screaming like a wild animal, kicking the wife and the children out of the cabin, and forcing them to go outdoors on the snow.

I made a survey about the Alaska jails and found that most inmates were there because of drinking. In my sermons I would tell them that if they would not drink, they would be saints, because when they were sober, they were the finest people on earth.

Learned studies have been made to try to explain why people living on the Arctic have such propensities to abuse liquor. I used to sit at my desk in a pensive mood trying to figure it out myself.

For one thing, they did not read and did not write, outdoors it was freezing, it was very hard to make a living, they were bored to death, and so on. What would I do if I did not know how to read and write? The winter months in Alaska are more tolerable if one has good books that take time to read and ennoble and enrich the soul. What would I do if I had to go through the ordeals those natives were undergoing?

I remember one night at Akulurak when Fr. O'Connor and I finished a game of chess around ten o'clock. He filled his pipe and took a look at the window. A snowstorm was raging and was blowing snow on the window panes. He turned to me and asked if I would blame a man for getting drunk on a night like that. I understood.

My life was in serious danger twice when two Eskimos took after me with loaded guns. What saved me on those two occasions was that they were quite drunk and their reflexes did not work as fast as mine did. Tampering with a drunk Eskimo is a very serious business.

When Ralph and I finished in this village, we hitched the dogs and left for another, by the name of Nunalrapak, which was considered a metropolis because there were seven cabins with as many families and it had a big *kazim*, that is, a community cabin half underground with a round roof over it that made it look like an igloo. It was a long trip with the wind on our faces. The dogs hated to face that wind and so did we, but life was like that.

We arrived just before dark and we settled in the *kazim* because the houses were too small, though we ate black fish with one of the families. After supper the *kazim* was filled with people. First we had the ritual instruction on religious matters. Then while they were saying the rosary in Eskimo, I was hearing confessions at the entrance of the *kazim*, a narrow tunnel so low that one had to crawl, and with a bearskin as a door. (In fact, the Eskimo word for *door* was the same as that for *skin*.)

Then they brought in the big drums and a native dance followed. I sat in their midst and beat a drum just as they did. That made them happy. It became hot inside; we were sweating. The people drank water like camels. In due time the women left with the children and we—men only—remained to have a well-deserved sleep. We spread our sleeping bags on the floor shoulder to shoulder—so to say—and an elderly man took upon himself the task of putting everyone to sleep by telling in a monotone a long story. Off and on he would break to ask, "Are you following me?" and when no one answered it meant that he had succeeded and then he stopped his monotone. Now it was his turn to fall asleep.

Those long stories more often than not were pure fantasies, but

they believed them. Not only did they believe them; they got angry
if you questioned them.

"Once upon a time a woman gave birth to a baby. She called a
medicine man to ask him how should she raise that child in
accordance with native traditions. The medicine man came and saw
the baby and became quite scared, because he saw in that baby
something that he had not seen in any other child. He told the woman
to be sure that at night—every night, yes every single night—she had
a light in the cabin, and that light had to be on at all times. If that light
would ever go off, then a most horrible thing would happen right
away.

"The woman was curious and asked what would happen, but the
medicine man told her not to ask him. But she asked if the child would
die if the light went off. He said no. Would the devil come? He said
no. Would her husband die? He said no. Would someone in the
family get sick? No again. Would she die? Yes. Would she die right
away or only after a long time? Right away. Would she die with much
pain or only with little pain? With much pain. If she died suddenly,
how could she have much pain? Because it would be both a quick and
slow death. But how can one thing be at the same time quick and
slow? Because the light had gone off. But if the light would go off and
she would get up to light it again, would she die? Yes.

"So that woman was so persistent that the medicine man lost his
patience and told her the whole thing, and the thing was this: If the
light went off, the very moment it went off, the baby would eat her
alive, and it would take some time for the baby to swallow her whole;
that was why it would be a quick but slow death, and this would
certainly happen if the light went off during the night.

"So the woman was very careful to keep that light on all night.
But, alas, alack, lo and behold, one night the light went off. Suddenly,
the mouth of that baby became wider than that of a shark and with
teeth every bit as sharp. His body grew suddenly. He took his mother
and slowly he ate her, because she grew careless and allowed the light
to go off. After he swallowed her, little by little his body began to get
smaller and smaller and smaller until it was again the little body it
had been before he had eaten her up. He had no more big teeth. Then
the medicine man told the father of the baby that there was no need
to keep the light on all night now, because the baby was fully satisfied
and did not need to be satisfied again. But the name of the baby had
to be changed. Now he had to be called Shark.

"The father asked the medicine man if the baby would be a good or a bad boy. The medicine man said that he would be little bit good and little bit bad. But he should never get married, because if he married, he could have only daughters—never a son—and that would make him mad, and once he got mad, he could very well do worse things yet."

When the story teller came to this point, he asked if they were listening. Two only answered and with grunts so subdued that he figured he had accomplished his task and stopped.

We were nine men in the *kazim,* which had no window. Darkness was absolute. Somehow my alarm clock did not go off. My bones began to complain so badly that I began to suspect what had really happened: We had lain on those uneven boards for twelve hours. A man broke suddenly into our dungeon and shouted, "Ka-war-pak-tu-chi," that is, "You are oversleeping." We were indeed. One hour later we had Mass in the *kazim,* with practically everyone there.

Then I spent the rest of the day going down from hut to hut to chat with every family. There were always little problems to settle. They all had great confidence in the priest to settle everything. While this was somewhat flattering to me, in reality it put a heavy burden on both my wisdom and my prudence. Some things have no human solution and in those cases I referred the matter to almighty God, to whom nothing is impossible.

There were children who should have been being prepared for first Communion by former Akulurak pupils. But they were not doing it. How about sending those children to Akulurak? The parents did not want to. They loved their children too much to see them go away. I understood.

There was the case of the big girl living with a married man.

"But, Teresa, why do you live with him?"

"Because he asked me to."

"Why don't you go back to your grandma?"

"I don't know."

"Do you want me to tell the man to take you back to Grandma?"

"If you want to."

"Where is the man now?"

"He went to catch seals."

"When will he be back?"

"He did not tell me."

"Is his wife glad that you are living with him as a second wife?"

"She is not glad."

"Then, why are you making her sad?"

"I don't try to make her sad. I only obey him."

"Why are you obeying him? He is not God."

"At first when he asked me, I said no. But when he asked me too many times, I said yes."

Here I was, a Spaniard trying to unravel an Eskimo triangle! Anyway, in time she went back to her grandma in another village. She was an orphan.

There were more instructions that night in the *kazim* and more prayers. Also more dancing to the rhythmic tom-tom of the drums. Eskimo dances have nothing in common with our dances. One man can dance alone and entertain the crowd. He sits on a bundle of clothes and in that squatting position he turns and wiggles and twists and the crowd loves it. I suppose the original purpose of such dancing was to get warm. When outdoors it is snowing and there is no heat in the cabin, any exercise will be welcomed. If you add a dash of folklore to that exercise, you have the roots of drama and entertainment. That night my alarm clock went off properly. The sounds and noises that one hears when nine people get up from a long sleep are better left to the imagination. Saint Paul said that he aimed at making himself all to all, that is, that he mixed with people in all walks of life to bring them closer to God. I recalled addressing myself to him with the question: "Paul, dear, did you also sleep in *kazims* like this one? Answer me. Or rather, please do not answer me, because I do not want to hear voices in a dungeon."

After Mass and breakfast, Ralph and I hitched the dogs and off we were. For a while the going was good and it was a joy to see the dogs so lively. Then the clouds were getting darker. Then snow began to fall. Ralph assured me that he was not afraid; he knew where he was; by going straight we would hit our village in three hours or maybe four. A good Eskimo will always leave a loophole, and in their language there are many ways to say *perhaps*.

Unfortunately for us, the snow kept coming thicker and thicker. The dogs began to slow down and to look to us, which is a manner of danger signal. There was brush that made it much worse. How about going back? No, our tracks were already covered and we now had the wind on our backs. We stopped to drink the hot cocoa we had in our thermos bottle, and it did revive us quite a bit. Ralph also gave the dogs some chunks of frozen fish, which made them shiver at first but gave them some pep afterward.

Now both Ralph and I became dogs and pulled the sled with all our might. After an eternity of that, my strength caved in. Then I put on all my clothes, I mean the over parka, the mittens over my gloves, and the fur cap over my knitted cap. I told Ralph that I had had it and I sat on the sled. He assured me that he had not begun to work and that he was going to start now, so he grabbed the back of the sled and began to push very hard. The dogs felt the push they were getting and walked a little faster—but it was still walking. I knew in my heart that Ralph was lost—totally lost.

My feet began to be so cold that hitting one foot against the other did not produce warmth but pain. I began to shiver all over. That could easily be my last night on earth because we were lost and it was already dark.

Knowing in a vague way that humanly speaking I had no escape, I turned as usual to heaven. The colder my body was getting, the warmer my soul was becoming. It had been my dream in Spain to be found dead in the wilderness half covered with snow while the pure snow from heaven was falling and covering my remains. Well, I did not know what would happen to Ralph, but I sensed that I was being done in and I offered myself to God. Then it happened.

God seems to delight in waiting till the last minute as if to prove that He is ever alert and watches over our needs. The dogs pricked their ears, let out a few nervous grunts all at the same time, and started on a mad rush onward so fast and so suddenly that Ralph lost the handles and was left behind. It became then my turn to take over. I stepped on the brake, which did not stop them altogether, though it slowed them enough for Ralph to catch up.

The dogs had smelled the reindeer herd that was but one hundred feet away but could not be seen because of darkness. Now the dogs barked madly and made for the herd. While Ralph held the sled, I held the leading dog to keep the team from jumping on the astonished deer. For a while all was excitement, but the deer turned one way and we forced the dogs to turn the other way and a collision was averted. By then my strength was sapped. Yet I saw light at the end of the tunnel and, like the dogs, I became very much alive again.

What made me ponder then, and still makes me ponder, was the suddenness of it all and how those dogs, which by all human standards were more dead than alive, showed that they were very much alive—that they were strong, powerful, capable of great things, but they themselves had not realized it. I myself became a new man. It reminded me of that middle-aged man so stout that he could hardly walk. Yet once while he was crossing a meadow where a bull took after him, he ran for the fence and jumped at a speed that beat all Olympic records. Which means that we go through life at half throttle and that we have within us talents and strength seldom tapped.

The dogs were frustrated with regard to the deer, but they smelled the smoke coming from the cabins of the reindeer herders a few miles away. The thought of a good night's sleep made them trot. They were headed for that oasis, which to us was still invisible, but to them was very close, as their noses were telling them. Soon we saw the lights and soon we reached our salvation.

Ralph's humiliation had to be very deep, but I never brought it up. The fact was that we were not headed at all for the reindeer camp and on the trip he had insisted that he knew where he was. A prudent silence fell over the whole affair.

When we reached the cabins, I jumped out of the sled and entered the main cabin where Emily Afcan was washing dishes after supper. She told me afterward that I looked like a dead man. Emily had grown up in our school and I baptized some of her children. Her husband was the main deer herder. Those days we had a four-thousand-deer herd that belonged to the people of the area, including our Akulurak mission. Off and on we would get some deer carcasses to have deer stew for the children, who considered it the finest delicacy. In time the deer disappeared due to mismanagement. The federal government took over, and since the federal government is an intangible, invisible entity, the deer, which were used to people, not to invisible entities, wandered away for good.

Anyway, the important thing for me now was that Emily was in the kitchen, where there was a generous supply of deer meat. Without saying a word she put the frying pan on the fire and soon there were deer steaks filling the air with the finest odors this side of heaven. She also had fresh bread and coffee. I stripped to my woolen shirt and began first to thaw and then to eat. I told Emily that if she ever needed my help in any way, not to hesitate but just come to me and ask. She said nothing. As I kept eating, I told her again that if she ever needed my help not to hesitate but to come and ask me point blank. For the third time I told her that if she ever . . . And then she cut in to say, "I heard."

That night the people said the rosary while they were coming to confession in another cabin. In the morning we had Mass with holy Communion. A good breakfast followed. For the fourth time I told Emily that she had saved my life and I was anxious to show my appreciation. The intelligent lady that she was, she smiled but said nothing.

Seven years later I was the pastor of Bethel, on the Kuskokwim River, where the Bureau of Indian Affairs had a hospital for the natives. One day I was called by the doctor to come and see if I recognized a woman who had been pronounced dead on arrival. The mail plane had brought her from the Akulurak territory. As I entered the morgue, one look told me that she was Emily. She had died of childbirth. When the family was contacted, it was decided that I go ahead and bury her in Bethel. There were no morticians. Each minister took care of the dead of his flock. First I bought lumber and made the coffin and with the help of a native I placed the body inside and nailed it. Then two boys helped me to dig the grave. The funeral followed and we took the coffin to the grave in a pick-up truck used by the airlines to load and unload the planes. When I returned to the church with the pick and shovel, I knelt in a pew and broke down.

---

1. In 1953 Fr. Menager's health deteriorated. He suffered from bronchitis and was told to go to Seattle for a checkup. The doctors told him never to return to Alaska. He died in Sheridan, Oregon, on June 29, 1965.

12
Quiet Nunakhock

It may be asked what purpose was served by this traveling all over the flat country where so few people lived. The answer is that gold is where you find it. If the people did not come to us, we had to go to the people. Actually, we did build some chapels in some strategic places, but they became useless in a short time, since those people were quite nomadic.

We had one chapel that promised a great deal, the one at Nunakhock built by Fr. Donohue. Next to the church we had a log cabin heated by a stove made out of a drum, a fifty-two-gallon oil drum, that is. The fuel was willows cut on the river bank quite a distance away. That cabin became a school for beginners taught by an Akulurak girl who had completed her eighth grade.

The houses in the village were made of lumber brought in from Seattle, through the instrumentality of Fr. O'Connor, who for fourteen consecutive years held the chairmanship of the Alaska Housing Authority which built countless houses all over Alaska. Those cabins were small, but adequate to the needs of an Eskimo family making a living in no man's land.

The village numbered 175 people, all Eskimos and all Catholic. I wanted to spend some time with them to give them a thorough instruction on the tenets of the faith. The best time to do it would be during the freeze-up, when they were very much forced to stay home but before the land froze solid and they would be on the go by dog team trapping and seal hunting.

I arrived in Nunakhock in the last days of September and was there exactly eighty-six days with their nights. The village had no store, but there was one quite a distance away where a village had been at one time. I was the only white man, assuming that I was white and a man. I had no radio, no phonograph, no electricity, and no running water. Naturally, there was neither telephone nor TV. All I had was myself and my health. Under my wooden bed I had some boxes filled with raisins, dry prunes, rice, canned milk, and similar items. Both to cook and to heat the room I had a coal oil stove. The only valuable item was the typewriter which was responsible in many ways for keeping me in my sanity, because out of that typewriter came many articles for a Spanish magazine. The whole building, made of logs, was about twenty by sixty feet with a thin partition and a door. Fifty feet were church and ten were the living room or living quarters for the priest.

As soon as I arrived, we set the order of the day. School in the morning and afternoon, five days a week. Mass every day at 7:30. Rosary and sermon every evening at 7:30. It worked beautifully. Bear in mind that those people had no entertainment whatsoever other than their native dances at night. Every afternoon I would go to the little school room and teach both English and catechism, with some music to break the monotony.

After supper people trooped into the church and filled it. They had eaten seal oil, so the smell of seal oil permeated the very walls, floor, and ceiling. That smell in the air could be cut with a knife. After the rosary in Eskimo, there would follow a rather long explanation of the Catholic faith. I was fortunate to have with me William Tyson, a former Akulurak pupil who without any doubt became the best interpreter in the land. He was so good that while he spoke the eyes of the people were fixed on him as though he were an apparition from heaven. Now and then we would add benediction with the blessed Sacrament. The burning incense helped dispel somewhat the odor of seal oil—for me, that is, because for them seal oil was a delicacy, almost a necessity.

Next morning at the sound of the church bell, most of them came in well wrapped in their fur parkas. There were prayers and songs in Eskimo.

After they left, I had my own breakfast and sat to read or type. People would come with their little problems. There were baptisms and even some weddings. When I felt like it, I would dress up and take a walk on that infinite vastness of nothing somewhere between a gray sky and the permafrost. That was the real Alaska, no doubt about it. We were always three—God, the guardian angel, and myself. What conversation there was had to be among us three, and I loved it. As usual I did all the talking. When I was some distance away, I would take a close look at the village. All I could see were cabins lined up alongside the bank of the river. There was a silence that always intrigued me. Total silence all around, one day after another, forever silence. Well, not quite. Whenever a dog team would come near the village, all the dogs took up the howl to let the people know that someone was coming. Then silence again.

Saint John of the Cross would have loved to be the pastor of that village. Perhaps that would have helped him to reach even higher in his reach for the Divinity. There I spent eighty-six days without mail, newspapers, or news of any sort.

Gradually, I began to take possession of myself and to find things within me that had escaped me up to that time. God and my guardian angel were telling me things that the soul alone heard. Every night, after the people left the church, I was left alone with the Lord. Not having anyone to talk to, and sensing the need to talk to someone, I decided to talk to the Lord in the church. To save fuel and light, I would dress up as though I were outdoors and walk into the church with a flashlight to guide my steps. The only light was that of the sanctuary. The world then became still and the Lord and I were all alone. First it would be the stations of the cross, with no time limit for any station. Then I would kneel till I was tired and walked back and forth or sat down.

The main question was what to do with all the time I had on my hands. Without a vocation to be a missionary, a priest in a situation like that would crack and run. But, with a clear vocation from God, everything fits into place. I simply loved that situation and began to feel sad at the thought that some day it would come to an end. When God calls, he gives whatever it takes to carry it through.

I was told of a priest in the Bavarian Alps who was sent by his bishop to a town lost in the woods, with people characterized by lack of polish and refinement. In time he became so depressed that he knelt before the tabernacle and said: "Lord, I can't take it any longer. This is not for me." But then the Lord wanted to be heard and said in an audible voice: "But, son, I love this place and this people. What is good for Me, shouldn't it be good for you also?"

During those eighty-six days I discovered another thing I had not realized. Seal meat had been more or less abhorrent to me because of its looks. It is so black and has such a fishy taste that I had put it out of my mind and mouth for a long time. Now these generous natives were bringing me chunks of freshly cut seal meat along with smaller chunks of fresh blubber as white as pure snow. Their intention was flawless; they simply wanted me to be well fed and nourished as long as I was in their midst.

The men would go out to sea, way out from the shore and over the ice till they reached broken ice floating indolently over undercurrents of water. There they settled with a rifle on the ready. A seal would pop up its head to breathe; instead of air it would get a bullet. When the man had a few seals, he would call it quits and come home with a sled load of them.

If someone asks how did he go to the water to fetch the seal, let him know that the Eskimo carries with him a small kayak and a hook at the end of a rope. He puts the kayak in the water and reaches the seal before it sinks; he hooks it by the nose and paddles the canoe to the edge of the ice where very carefully he lands safely on both feet.

I used to boil seal meat with rice and throw in an onion to take from it some of the fishy taste. With a little salt over it you have a delicious meal. At first it is a forced meal. Soon it is sort of indifferent. Finally, it becomes tasty. The meat has a lot of calories that keep you warm and peppy. Then it keeps the body perfectly lubricated, that is, you are not easily constipated and it does not physic you either; so it is ideal.

As to the blubber, it depends: When it is cut from the seal, it is the nearest thing to bacon out of the hog and it both tastes good and gives you more calories than you need if you lead a sedentary life. But after some time, it becomes rancid and it is not for me. The natives, though, loved it regardless of age. Boiled blubber turns into seal oil that is kept in containers and becomes staple food for them like chili sauce for the Mexicans. Whatever they eat will taste better for them if dunked in seal oil. Eating without seal oil, for them, is like eating without a piece of bread for us. Something is missing. So I told them that I would take blubber only if it were brought to me the same day it was cut off the seal. They understood.

There were days in Nunakhock when the weather was ideal: There was no wind; it wasn't snowing; the temperature was very tolerable. After several snowstorms there was near the church a high pile of snow which the children used for fun by climbing to the top and then sliding down on their pants.

While the children were at school, a lady who was supposed to be ninety years old, Mrs. Amokan, properly dressed in furs and skin boots with a calico dress over the parka, would come leaning on a cane and sit on top of that snow and remain so seated for a long time. I would watch her through my window panes. The more I watched her the more amazed I became. She was a statue of peace and serenity. She looked vaguely anywhere, but mostly she would have her eyes fixed in the horizon without making any move. There she sat as if Michelangelo had modeled her as he did with his famous Moses. She wore no glasses. She had no wrinkles. She was stout and her face was a picture of health. Everything in her exuded, as I said, peace and serenity.

She never went to any school nor did she ever learn to read and write at home. All the libraries of the world meant absolutely nothing to her. She did not know if she was an American citizen and she never heard the word *America*. Nobody ever told her that there were wars between nations, because the only nation she knew was the area comprehended between Hooper Bay, Mountain Village, and Saint Michael, that is, some twelve thousand square miles of land green in the summer and frozen in the winter, with some three thousand people. That was her world. She had great-grandchildren, not many, because mortality then was very great. She survived her peers and was now a relic of the past. Her face showed no tensions, fears, anxieties, or ambitions noble or otherwise. Neither did she give any indications that she had a care in the world. She sat there like an empress on her throne showing total self-dominion, as if she were expecting the tribute due her by her vassals or even by distant kings as an acknowledgment of submission. Would that I knew what she knew about Eskimo customs and practices and beliefs and the stories she heard from medicine men. Too bad all this would go with her to her grave.

Her native language was absolutely pure inasmuch as it had never been contaminated with any English words. While I could sustain questions and answers with Eskimos who knew English and spoke Eskimo with a Western construction, it was impossible for me to penetrate her mentality. Once I went to her and told her that she kept herself very well. She answered that I looked like a boy to her. That was all. She lived in her inner world—a world that was one million miles away from mine.

When Bishop Gleeson visited us on another occasion, I told him about her and asked him if he would confirm her. He said he would. In the line of people to be confirmed could be seen, the last, Mrs. Amokan advancing unperturbed. I was feeling in my bones that she did not have the foggiest idea of what it was all about, though she had been coming faithfully to my instructions, passed on to her beautifully by William Tyson. She had been baptized by *Kutlik* when she was a grandmother—I suppose—and the Sacraments do work in the soul in many marvelous ways. As I saw her approach the altar, I whispered to the Lord: "You do it, Lord. I am not equal to it." She also received her welfare monthly check without ever learning accurately from where it came or why it came.

There she was again, seated on top of that snow pile so serene and so well self-possessed.

I asked a mortician once why was it that so many corpses looked better than when those people were alive. He said that it was because a corpse was totally relaxed. Our faces show the undercurrents of tensions within us. These tensions cease with death and the face shows it. Well said, I told him. At least it satisfied me. All worries end with death.

All worries seemed to have ended inside of Mrs. Amokan and yet she was still alive. How to explain that? I don't know. All I wanted was to achieve through asceticism and the practice of virtue that peace and serenity and relaxation that Mrs. Amokan had achieved in a mysterious way in the midst of a non-Christian environment among ancient Eskimos who lived off their bows and arrows in one of the most hostile environments known to man.

I had to leave Nunakhock for Akulurak, a very long trip if the trail is not good and now the trail was only so-so. I hired Willie Augustine, who had the best team in town and was known to be a top driver. We took off early because the days were very short. No sooner had we started than it began to snow. He assured me that there was nothing to worry about because he had a compass in the back of the sled. I sat in the sled and he did the driving. The snow was falling gently but steadily, which made visibility nil. There were no tracks to follow. Everything was covered with snow.

In time we hit the village of Anarchik, where we stopped for dry fish and tea. We took off again into an invisible world with the snow getting thicker but no wind, thanks be to God. In the sled I began to let my imagination do as she pleased for a while. Then I put order in my thoughts and concentrated on carefully chosen subjects. The dogs kept their pace. Willie was silent. The snow was covering us, but we shook it off and kept going and being covered with more snow, which we continued shaking off rather monotonously.

What if we got lost? Getting lost is one of the worst sensations, because on the trail it can mean almost certain death. Fr. O'Connor had been lost once only a few miles from this very trail. It had been snowing. Then it got windy; then he and his guide had not agreed on which course to take. In the sled they'd had a nine-year-old boy for our boarding school and finally the leading dog had not known which way to turn—or rather had not wanted to, because the right direction had been facing the wind and he had not wanted to face it.

Night came and they stopped till they got numb and had to continue on, simply to get warm. All next day they wandered, blinded by the storm. Night followed. The cans of pork and beans, frozen solid as cement, were useless.

Next day the storm had continued as usual. Tempers became extremely short. Father wanted to turn one way and the guide suggested another one. Where were they? Father thought that he knew and so did the guide, till they became like zombies. The guide told me that Father had told him to stop by the sled till he went alone to look for a landmark that did not exist. The guide lost sight of Father and feared the worst, so he followed him and caught up with him. After a few more hours of meandering in the blinding snow, the dogs stopped by a building. They were safe. They could not have found a better place. It was the N.C. store run by Andrew Prince, one of our parishioners married to Olga, who was the best cook in the neighborhood.

Fr. O'Connor walked into a warm store and thawed out while Olga prepared a delicious hot meal. After they ate, they went to sleep for many, many hours. They got up and put on dry clothes.

There were other stories: Fr. Norman Donohue had been driving a lively team alone and—one of those things—he lost the sled. The dogs took off by themselves so fast that soon they were out of sight, not to be seen for two more days. It was thirty-six degrees below zero. But Father was young and he was a good hiker. He found an empty cabin with some wood and oatmeal. That took care of that night. Next day he walked to another faraway cabin with a smoking chimney. With help he was able to find the dogs, which had become caught with a tangled harness in the willows. They had decided to sleep instead of killing each other.

Fr. John Fox did it differently. He decided that he could not do his work in his vast district if he had to depend on the weather. Assuming that the weather would be bad every day of the year, he planned his trips according to what he considered the best for the people and never mind the weather. As a result of this, he was forced to sleep on the trail five times in his very first winter. But Fr. Fox did not mind that at all. With the constitution of an ox, he crawled in his sleeping bag under the stars. Next morning he continued on his trip none the worse for the ordeal. He told me that once he had become quite exasperated when he'd woken up from his snow grave to discover that he was only one mile away from the village.

I begged the Lord to spare me the anguish of having to spend a night in the open. I knew in theory the mechanics of how to spend the night on the snow. But I was apt to stop for the night when I was sweating. I couldn't see how I would avoid pneumonia. The Lord did not want me to see it; He providentially spared me the horrid experience.

I was going over thoughts of this sort while Willie kept the sled headed in the right direction in that blinding snow. In time we hit the village of Nunakak, where we stopped for dry fish and tea. Should we stop there for the night? Oh, no, Father, we will make it all right. So we were off again.

Now we came to the Kwimilik River, which at that spot was nothing but a frozen white expanse of infinity. With sunshine we could have seen the faraway low banks, but the persistent snow darkening the horizon made this impossible.

The question now was: Can we hit the mouth of the Kanelik slough? You see, the compass leads you in the right direction, take or leave two miles. If you can't even see a quarter of a mile, the compass is of small help; if we were to hit the willows instead of the slough, we could wander forever.

Willie would stop the dogs every one hundred yards and, standing on the loaded sled, he would turn his binoculars in all directions. Another one hundred yards and he would repeat the operation.

I felt that now it was my turn to save the situation. God is the God of the poor, of the needy, of the helpless, and of the desperate. After everything else fails, He steps in and tells Lazarus to get up and walk.

And Lazarus gets up and walks. So very simple! So I went to work with my guardian angel, who told the Lord one thing or two and, sure enough, Willie spotted a windmill. That was all I needed. I knew we were near Arovigchagak. From there I could reach Akulurak blindfolded.

Another hour and we were there in the dark with the snow still falling. I looked at Willie and told him: "Friend, with you and my guardian angel, I can go to the North Pole."

This reminded me of the farmer in Minnesota who had a garden that was the envy of the neighbors. A minister was going by and stopped to admire it. Being a minister, he felt he had to bring God into the conversation, so he said to the man: "Brother, you and the Lord are doing wonders with this garden," to which the man replied: "Reverend, you should have seen this garden when the Lord alone had it!"

13

Summer in Akulurak

To all appearances, nature in northern Alaska during the winter months is absolutely dead. All its rivers and its numberless lakes and ponds and marshes are buried under a thick coat of solid ice, so thick that planes use the ice to land. The whole land is covered with snow. Nothing is green. Nothing stirs except the ptarmigans, which could be called the doves of the Arctic. Even they turn pure white during winter and are hard to see. An occasional crow may be seen flying low. Its blackness is a striking contrast to the surrounding snow. As the months go by, one gets used to the silence of nature—a silence not unlike the silence of the grave.

Then summer comes. Everything is life and excitement. The rivers break loose from the grip of the ice that flows in heavy chunks toward the sea. Migrating birds fill the air. Green grass starts growing and the willows cover themselves again with green leaves. The Eskimos have their nets and their boats ready to catch the salmon that will come in the minute the last chunks of ice clear the waters.

At Akulurak the month of May was a feverish one. Bro. Murphy was getting the boats and the crews ready. The sisters were readying the knives and the tables to cut the fish. The boys were busy preparing the poles to dry the fish and the smokehouse with the stoves and the wood—green and dry—to cure the thousands of salmons anticipated. At the beginning of June Bro. Murphy would leave for the fishing grounds on the Yukon where he set several fishwheels at strategic places. Soon he would start the daily trips to Akulurak with loads of fish.

In that small world where everybody knows everybody, Bro. Alfred Murphy, S.J., became an institution. He was there for thirty-eight years. He provided the mission with salmon and firewood and did all the freighting, besides being postmaster. He was a genius for mathematics, but he could not spell. His English was not too grammatical. He spent a great deal of his free time saying rosaries.

As the years were going by, he developed the belief that he would work in the summer but would spend the winter reading magazines. For many years he was prefect of the boys. His reading became a form of drug, an addiction, an exaggeration. He could not recall anything he read. He had to read for the sake of reading. During the summer he gathered from his friends piles of pulp magazines to be read in the winter, like the ants gather for their winter months.

I saw in a national magazine that *Argosy* was in trouble with the Justice Department, which was debating whether *Argosy* should be permitted to use the U.S.A. mails because in their contents there was some objectionable material. *Argosy* was one of the magazines stacked by Bro. Murphy for winter reading.

I was in charge at the time and I felt that it was my responsibility to put an end to that. So in his last trip in early October 1943 I had his two sacks of pulp magazines burned. When he came and saw what had happened, he and I went through a very bad half an hour. For a week he was moving around in a trance. Slowly he came to his senses. Grace prevailed. Since he had to read, and since our house library had only spiritual books, he read them all or nearly all and the change in him soon became noticeable. His outlook was more supernatural.

I would say that he underwent a conversion for the better. He had been using eighteen pounds of pipe tobacco every year. Now of his own accord he quit smoking, although he told the Lord that if and when things in the boat became much too hard to handle, he would reserve the privilege of filling his pipe to cool off and get hold of himself; that was what he did.

Eventually, his eyes began to hurt when he read, so he quit reading but not praying. He was so absorbed in God that it was evident that he was living in His divine presence. He told me that he was saying an average of forty decades of the rosary every day. A short time before Bro. Murphy's death, Fr. O'Connor and I anointed him. When he died, he looked like a saint to me.

Until I meet the Lord face to face, I will not know whether I did the right thing when I burned Murphy's magazines, or whether I placed the brother in spiritual jeopardy. The Lord, and only the Lord, will have the last word on this.

We built a fishing camp on the banks of the Yukon where we spent seven weeks processing the salmon. The boat brought the fish in; the girls cut it; the boys hung it; the sisters supervised the girls and I supervised the boys; everything ran smoothly.

We had a chapel with the blessed Sacrament reserved. There we had daily Mass, daily rosary—visits by individuals and in groups. The presence of the Lord in our midst set the tone for our behavior. On Sundays we would fill the boat and go for a picnic to Alakanuk or Kwiguk or both, where the children met many of their relatives and friends.

By 1940 John T. Emel in Alakanuk and the N.C. Co. in Kwiguk had their own separate canneries operating quite well. The Eskimos were paid first by the fish and then by the pound. Likewise in Bristol Bay there were several canneries operating and some of our people went there. Soon the living standards of the natives began to rise. Other canneries followed suit. We ourselves came to build a regular cannery at nearby Saint Marys under the able direction of Fr. Edmund Anable, S.J.

Thus the natives found themselves living in a cash economy. Their cabins became respectable homes with linoleum on the floor, good stoves, beds from Sears, curtains on their windows, and outboard motors of their own. Then the sleds began to be replaced by snowmobiles. People left the flat lands and settled on the banks of the Yukon. Even my beloved town of Nunakhock came to the Yukon; the church was dismantled and the salvaged material was brought to the Yukon to help in the buildings going on there. Progress and Western civilization began to catch up with the Eskimos of the Yukon River.

In the last visit that Bishop Fitzgerald made to Akulurak in 1947, he saw the condition of our buildings and decided that we had to look for a more suitable location. In the winter the ground at Akulurak swelled with the frost; in the summer the ground thawed and sank. This made the buildings acquire lopsided positions that forced the doors to become inoperable. The floors likewise were uneven. It all became very messy.

We told the bishop that the banks of the Andreafski River had good gravel and trees that guaranteed good foundations, so he ordered that a suitable place be picked up on the Andreafksi River.

In the summer Bro. Murphy and I with three Eskimo boys went and took a look. We went up and down with our boat and we finally settled on the spot where Saint Marys is now. We sank the ritual four corners with what we considered proper nomenclature, a sort of "hands off, everybody." It was quite dramatic for us to navigate back and forth surveying the land as if it were all ours.

To whom did that land belong? Alaska was then *territory*. It all belonged to Uncle Sam. But we were Alaskans, natives in reality since the purpose of the buildings was for the betterment of the natives, so the land was also ours with squatting rights. The only provision on the part of the government was that while we could use the surface, the government reserved to itself the right of ownership of any minerals ever to be found in the ground.

Bishop Fitzgerald died and nothing was done for some time. In the meantime, I was moved south to Bethel, on the Kuskokwim River.

14

Bethel and Beyond

The Kuskokwim River, with its 680 miles as the crow flies, is the second largest river in Alaska, beating the Tanana River by sixty miles. It originates near Bearpaw Mountain, not too far from Fairbanks on the North Fork, and at Mount Gerdine, not far from Cook Inlet on the South Fork. It passes through McGrath, Sleetmute, Red Devil, Aniak, Kalskag, and Akiak, and practically ends at Bethel. From Bethel it widens and dies in the bay that bears its name.

Ocean ships of up to eight thousand tons come from Seattle to Bethel. The big ships could not navigate any farther, so they unloaded there. It is a flat, bleak land with the evils of the permafrost. Nothing grows there. During the Second World War the army built a city of Quonset huts and an airfield, thus adding to its importance. Stores went up, school buildings, a judge, a marshal and a jail house, and finally a fairly good-sized hospital owned by the Bureau of Indian Affairs. A white person would be admitted in an emergency. The airlines made Bethel the center of operations for a very wide area all around.

The spiritual care of Bethel and towns around had long fallen to the Moravians, who had arrived there as far back as 1885. Slowly, Catholics had begun to move into Bethel which was visited by passing missionaries. I myself spent three days there in the winter of 1937.

In 1942 Fr. Francis Menager, S.J., was given the job of organizing the Kuskokwim mission with headquarters in Bethel. He bought a twelve-by-fourteen-foot cabin that was dubbed the Black Hole because the walls were covered with tar paper and only had a tiny window. He added a room to store his belongings. Then he had a little chapel built which he called "a gem," but it was too small.

When I replaced him in 1948, the Black Hole was so depressing that I had to do something soon if I was to keep my sanity. I acquired two Quonset huts—one for living quarters and the other as storage. The town then did not have over six hundred people, but it was growing so the buildings were inadequate. Missionaries going to the coast had to pass through Bethel. There was need of a real building with two or three bedrooms for visitors and guests. This was done by my successor, Fr. Norman Donohue, S.J., who also built a bigger church.

In time Bethel grew out of all proportions for the location, that is, the ground is not suited for a good-sized town. The river swells at break-up time when the ice comes thundering and cutting at the silt banks. There are bad floes. But Bethel became the metropolis of the Kuskokwim.

I found Bethel quite agreeable. Once or twice a week I would go to the Bureau of Indian Affairs building, where a good gathering would form: the teachers, the hospital staff, and other disparate elements including me. Some would play pinochle or bridge and others would just chat. Politics was the main subject of conversation unless the title of heavy-weight champion would change hands or some local event was big enough to merit lively discussions.

Disputes were settled by a bet. New York City has less than nine million people, but according to others it had more. Bolivia is a landlocked republic, but according to some it was not. James Madison was the fourth president, though some were sure that James Monroe was. The *World Almanac* was admitted by all to be essentially correct and it settled all disputes and caused some silver dollars to change pockets. It all would end with coffee and cake so we would go home in good spirits.

I was the only one who went back to an empty home—first to the Black Hole and then to an empty Quonset hut. Some said that this was not fair; that the church should allow the priests to marry; that God Himself said that it was bad for man to be alone, etc. There I was sitting pretty listening to it all and thanking God from the bottom of my heart that I was single. But I could not bet them one dollar that I was happy the way things were with the church and priests. Only those with a vocation know it. The others beat the air in the dark, while thinking that they hit the bull's eye by quoting the Bible or repeating what someone said somewhere.

They went home, husband and wife with or without children, which is perfectly all right. I went back through the dark streets all alone and went into the little church with the sanctuary lamp glowing. Those were two worlds. God had chosen them for one thing and He gave them what it took to live happily; I did not question that, but God had also chosen me to be a priest and had given me what it took to live my priestly life with great joy. Their joy and my joy sprang from God Himself, I am ready to admit, but when I knelt at night before the sanctuary lamp, my joy was of an entirely different nature. What God tells a priest kneeling in front of the tabernacle cannot be explained well to those who are not initiated.

God is a mystery. The priest is a mystery. The greater a thing is, the more mysterious it is. Life is not just digging ditches, eating, drinking, and mating. There are other realities. Saint Paul lost his temper a bit when he said that the animal man does not understand the things of the spirit, just as darkness cannot understand light and vice versa. It is a form of tragedy that some people pity the priest and some priests pity those people. God wants us all. I am very grateful for my parents, but I am equally grateful for having been called to be a Father with a capital *F*.

At Bethel I used to visit the hospital regularly. There I found Eskimos from Catholic villages who were delighted to see me. If they died there, I would take care of the coffin and of the grave. I remember well the time when a man who had been several years in one of our Catholic schools came down with galloping consumption and had his days numbered. He had strayed from the church and said that now he was nothing. I visited him frequently.

Probably he expected me to bawl him out and to give him a bad time. Instead, I entertained him as well as I could with anecdotes calculated to bring a chuckle. Then I brought to his memory the happy times he spent in school and how hard life can be to people as we grow. Then I prayed for him a lot when I was alone in church. One day he sent for me to hurry and come. I did, and he was sinking but his mind was clear. He told me that he wanted to receive the last rites. We gave him a solemn funeral. Back from the grave I entered the church to thank God for having used me to bring that soul back to Him. These souls are the children a priest begets, and for this he is called Father.

In the summer months hundreds of Eskimos from the coast came to fish not far from Bethel. There were Catholic colonies that gathered together in long rows of tents. On Sundays they would fill the little church that was too small for so many.

One of those Eskimos came to see me one day and told me that he had by the river bank an outboard motor to take me to their camp to baptize one baby. When we arrived at the camp, a large group formed around the tent where the baby was ready for baptism. I performed the ceremony slowly so that all could follow it and I explained many things during the performance which I used also as a catechetical instruction on the sacrament of baptism. When it was all over, I packed everything in the little box and began to say good-bye one by one with a warm handshake.

While we were marching in procession back to the boat, a man approached me and begged me to please baptize his baby also. I showed surprise. Why didn't he tell me at the beginning that there were two babies to be baptized and I would have baptized both at the same time? Now it was his turn to show surprise. He faced me sternly and asked why hadn't I asked at the very beginning if there was more than one baby. The fault, then, was mine, of course. The man who had come to Bethel with the message spoke of one baby. In my Western mentality *one* meant the singular, not the plural. But in their mentality *one* meant that particular one without excluding others.

The white man had better learn and be sure that he left absolutely no loopholes, because the Eskimo just loves those loopholes and Bethel was in the heart of Eskimoland, so there!

It reminded me of the white man from Nome who was building the reindeer herds and had been away from Nome out in the fields for some time. He wanted his mail. He called the best educated Eskimo in the crew working for him and asked him how long would it take him to go by dog team to Nome and back. Well, it would be two days each way plus one day in town. Five days. The white man told the Eskimo to go to Nome and go to the post office to see if there was mail for him. After five days the Eskimo arrived with an empty sled.

"Did you go to Nome?"

"Yes, sir."

"Did you go to the post office?"

"Yes, sir."

"Did you see if I had any mail?"

"Yes, sir."

"Was there any mail for me?"

"Yes, sir. Lots of mail: letters, papers, boxes, everything."

"Why didn't you bring it?"

"Because you told me to go and see. I saw it. You have lots. Do you want me to go back and bring it?"

On another occasion at the Akulurak school, I was in my room reading when two teenage girls came with a verbal message from Mother Superior. When I saw the girls, I proceeded to ask them several questions about their families and other things. They answered them all, giggling and having a good time which encouraged me to keep them giggling by asking still more questions. Finally, I ran out of questions and asked them what they wanted. The older of the two giggled again and said verbatim: "Our reverend Mother told us to tell you that the bakery is on fire."

But why hadn't they told me that at the very beginning? It was all my fault. Instead of listening to them from the very beginning, I had asked them questions that had nothing to do with the bakery being or not being on fire; they had been waiting for an opening in the conversation to deliver the message. What I should have done the minute I saw them was to ask them if the bakery was all right. Then the fire would be put out in a hurry and no nonsense about the health of their families. Many times I vowed that I would never get caught again, but those vows proved to be useless.

My first Thanksgiving Day in Bethel had an emotional side to it. There was an elderly white couple who could not afford a turkey. There was also a half-breed couple who could not afford one either. There was a young bachelor taking flying lessons who could not either. There was a spinster who lacked the facilities for eating the turkey. And there was me. After a semiconfidential inquiry, I found them most receptive to the idea of our getting together. One would bring this and the other would bring that and I would bring the turkey.

I went to one of the local stores and asked about the turkey situation. The owner had all sizes. I asked for an eighteen-pounder. What was I going to do with that big bird?—he wanted to know. When I explained to him that the turkey was my share of the dinner, he stood thinking for two seconds and said, "Well, Father, I am not what you might call a religious man, I am sorry to say. But, so help me God, I am a believer, and I'll be blessed if I am going to show up at the Pearly Gates with empty hands. Here, take the bird; it is on me. But wait, I have a bigger one. Take it and tell those folks to enjoy it." It was a twenty-two-pounder.

When the great Thursday arrived, we all sat around a big table and enjoyed the evening enormously. And there was so much turkey left! We had agreed to come to the turkey dinner ravenously hungry, and possibly we were, but I have yet to see or hear of a turkey that is finished in one meal, no matter how many sit at the table.

About sixty miles southeast of Bethel there was the NYAC gold mine. Since there were a good many Catholics working there, I was flown now and then to say Mass for them and stay a few days to teach catechism to the children. They were getting good wages, so the last day they would pass the hat and give me easily one hundred dollars. The setting was beautiful. The Tuluksak River went by and filled the land with willows. They had their own school. When the school was over, all the children came and we would walk between the willows with our catechism lessons. I had my meals with the crews in the main dining room. The cook was a Yugoslavian. The last day he would come to shake hands and would leave in my hand a check for twenty-five dollars. He said he wanted to do something for God, but he left it to me to do it for him, which I hope I did.

One seventeenth of October I sat in the mail plane with the pilot and another passenger for NYAC. There were some three inches of snow on the ground. When the pilot came to land, he made the horrible error of stepping on the brake so that the landing wheels could not turn. Something had to give, so the plane took a complete somersault and came to rest on its back. This left us head down and feet up—a very inappropriate position, indeed. There were six cases of gasoline loose on board. One of them hit me in the head and scalped me somewhat.

To this day I have no recollection of how I came out, but I did, and, as I did, I stepped on the fabric of the wing, which tore with a tearing noise. There was blood all over the snow. Where did it come from? I was fine. I touched my bare head and was shocked to see my hand full of fresh red blood. The other two men were pinned down by the boxes under their seats. I worked frantically to get them out and I succeeded. The propeller was all twisted; from the engine gasoline was trickling down which could ignite and blow us to smithereens. When the pilot came out, he took a look at the wreck and let out a good solid American expletive which I choose to delete and which surprised me because I was full of gratitude to God for having kept us alive. I surmised that the pilot would be the same. My clothes were full of blood. People came and were aghast at the sight of me.

There was a young miner who had a flying crate built just for him; a plane so small that one healthy man could easily lift it. They bundled me in that crate. The pilot got in and sat between my wide apart legs. It was already dark. They wired Bethel that we were coming and would land by the hospital. To find out whether he was flying in the right direction, the pilot would light a match now and then to look at the compass. We were going in the wilderness in a dark cloudy night in the hope of eventually seeing the lights of Bethel.

I offered my life to God and united it to His on the cross. With this I relaxed a great deal. Finally, there was Bethel. As we came in, we saw a man swinging a lantern to indicate that that was where we were supposed to land. I asked the queen of angels to please send a few of them to land us safely. She did. Our crate surprisingly landed smoothly and came to a beautiful stop.

The doctor told me that head wounds look bad because they bleed so profusely, but if the skull is not touched, they do not amount to much. The skull was fine, so I had nothing to fear, just some stitches, and he put me to bed to calm myself. Next day still in bed, I noticed that I had small pieces of skin gone from here and there which had gone unnoticed. This made me think of the Mexican Indian dentist who advertised painless tooth pulling. He had built a special chair with a contraption calculated to divert the patient from the tooth being pulled. When he felt that the tooth was coming out, he stepped on a pedal and the patient would get a good pinch in his buttock. He would jump, scratching himself and wondering which was worse, the tooth or the other thing. It had to happen, so it did happen. One Indian had a lower tooth pulled. When he felt the pain in his seat, he yelled, "My goodness, I didn't know that teeth had roots that deep."

Above Bethel is the town of Kalskag. Actually there are two Kalskags: Lower and Upper. The lower one was all Russian Orthodox, served by a native priest from the Russian Mission on the Yukon, so I left it alone. The upper one was all Catholic, made up mostly of former Holy Cross students, well trained in the faith; good singers in church; a very fine congregation. It was a real joy to celebrate Mass in that church.

Next to the church there was a little cabin for the priest. I settled there like a king on his throne. There was a bed, a chair, a table, a stove, and a bench for visitors. Shortly after breakfast people began to come to chat. After school the children would come to catechism. All went very smoothly. No collections were taken yet in church, so I had to make a living off my typewriter, which I did, thanks be to God.

There were two old-timers who were my delight. They had grown up in Holy Cross and knew every priest, brother, and sister who had lived there from the beginning. Fr. Robaut was probably their favorite. They pointed to me the spot on the Kuskokwim where he had built a cabin shortly after the turn of the century.

Fr. Robaut and Fr. Tosi had been the first two Jesuits to come to Alaska back in 1887. The next year they had started the missions of Nulato and Holy Cross. Fr. Robaut had been a heavily built man who ate enormously. He had needed all that food to keep the great energy that he was consuming every minute of the day. When he would travel by dog team, he would start maybe a couple of hours ahead of the driver, who would catch up with him halfway to their destination. In his cabin on the Kuskokwim, Father would call the people in the evening and speak to them in Eskimo for three hours, explaining the Catholic doctrine and repeating and repeating until the people understood everything.

One can imagine how tired the poor man must have been when he went to bed. This explains why he did not wake up in time to put out the fire that started around his stove and burned the cabin to the ground. He lost practically all his belongings, including the pile of papers on which he had written his Eskimo dictionary. He escaped alive, but totally destitute. He broke down and wept, not so much for the cabin as for his Eskimo writings. If it had not been for that fire, maybe Father would have stayed on the Kuskokwim and there would now be more Catholics in the area.

The old timers' favorite brother was John Hess, S.J., who had come to Alaska in 1913. He was a German, the kindest man in the neighborhood. From sun up to sun down Bro. Hess could be seen doing maintenance work on the large piece of property owned by the mission. One superior had wanted cows, so Hess had built a barn. Another superior had decided against the cows, so Hess had torn down the barn. The next superior would say that it had been a mistake to get rid of the cows and he wanted the cows back, so Bro.

Hess would rebuild the barn in no time. Another superior had ruled against the animals, any animals, so down had come the barn. Good Bro. Hess did obediently what he was told and did not get angry at all. He just worked in silence.

When I heard this, I felt that he had been superhuman; it reminded me of the story I was told about a millionaire who was approached by two men looking for work. He had no work for them, really, but he wanted them to keep busy and earn an honest living, so he told one of the men to paint a room and keep putting on new coats of paint until told to stop. The other man was told to build with brick and mortar a wall that had to be six feet long, six feet high, and two feet wide. When he finished it, he had to demolish it and build another one on the same spot, but he had to try to improve on the previous one till he came out with a wall so perfect that it did not have to be destroyed. Both men were guaranteed a higher salary every week.

The painter gave about fifty coats of paint to the walls of the same room. He went to the boss and asked how many more coats of paint he wanted. The boss became angry for being interrupted in his thoughts and asked in turn why had he come without being called. The shaky and timid painter muttered that he would like to know how many more times he had to paint those walls. The angry boss went into a rage and said: "Keep painting until the four walls meet"; whereupon the erstwhile timid painter went into a rage himself and told his boss to go to hades and please do not return. He threw his brush on the shiny shoes of the boss and quit.

The builder of the wall had already demolished three walls and had had them rebuilt, so when he heard what had happened to his friend, he went to the boss and told him point blank that if he did not have a more humane work for him, he—the boss—could go plum to hades and stay there forever. He threw the trowel at the feet of the boss and quit. Which goes to show that Bro. Hess was a superhuman.[1]

In contrast to Hess, my two old friends told me about the antics of Bro. James Twohig, S.J., who had been born in Ireland and had come to Alaska way back in 1893. A master boat builder, he had built beautiful boats. But something about the brother had made him quite intractable. He had been five times at Akulurak, two at Holy Cross, two at Nulato, and one each at Pilot Station, Nome, and Tanana. Three times he had been sent back to the States with the request that he not return to Alaska, but three times he had cried himself back.

When he was sent back to the States for the fourth time, superiors took the hint and kept him in California, where he died at age seventy-nine in 1932. Today he would be called a workaholic. Sundays to him were dreaded days because there was no manual work permitted.

When he went around with an axe on his shoulder or a hammer in his hand, people gave him a wide berth. He told Fr. William Judge, S.J., when they were navigating on the Yukon that he—Twohig—would throw him—Judge—overboard if Judge were not a priest.

When the big sternwheeler pulling several huge barges loaded with freight tied by the bank in front of Holy Cross, the good captain overlooked the little rowboat of Bro. Twohig caught between the river bank and a barge. Brother took an axe and cut the ropes holding the whole complex. The sternwheeler with the barges began to float down river. It was a long time before everything was brought back to place at the unloading bank. The captain went livid and wanted to know who was the So-and-So who had cut the ropes. Axe in hand, Bro. Twohig stood before the captain and said that he had done it and what was he going to do about it. The captain saw something in Brother's eyes, for he caved in and left the scene in silence.

My two friends had very kind words for Bro. Edward Horwedel, S.J., who had come to Alaska at the turn of the century. He was prefect of the big boys at Holy Cross and was a first-class worker who could turn his hand to anything. He carried authority with him, though he was small in size. Perfect order was kept at Holy Cross all the years he was prefect. Many of those boys were taller than he was; but they stood in front of him as if they were little children. After he was replaced, the big boys would get out of hand now and then.

After spending a couple of weeks in Kalskag, I would fly to Aniak. This little town is located in an area covered with high timber, which means accessibility to firewood and plenty of it. Since the place is one of the coldest in the region, firewood is truly a godsend. The Catholics of Aniak were also originally from Holy Cross and nearby Pymeut. Aniak had a good chapel with a living room attached to it and the church property was surrounded by trees that made it look somewhat bucolic. It was the ideal spot to have a good night's sleep.

The town also had a store, two in fact, and a roadhouse. These two items were very important. I could buy groceries or I could have a good hot supper in the roadhouse or both. It also had a landing strip for big planes. There was a sawmill. There were trappers. There was a school and a weather station. All this brought a number of white folks into the town.

I said that Aniak is a very cold spot. Once the pilots of a big plane were detained three days in the roadhouse until the weather went up to forty-eight below zero. The regulations stipulated that no flying would take place if the weather were under forty-eight below.

I had to leave for Anchorage in that plane and I had no idea when the thermometer would go up, so I stayed very much around the roadhouse. The three pilots needed a fourth to play pinochle, but they assumed that a Catholic priest would not play cards, so they were sort of sad. I heard them whisper. When I told them that I was a shark at pinochle and I said it deadpan, they set a chair for me and the games began. It was twenty-five cents to a game, which took long to win, and ten cents if you got set. After three days, when the weather improved and the plane took off, my partner and I came off the winners with a grand total of one dollar and eighty cents to the good.

Lest someone think that all I did there was gamble, news came to me that a family of Eskimos living two miles away in the woods had a baby who was not baptized; they wanted him baptized right away. I could not go by dog team. At fifty below zero it is very dangerous to take the dogs out for fear that their tender underbelly parts may freeze. A dog takes very good care of himself when he is loose or if he can curl up and warm those delicate parts with his own breath by burying his long nose between his hind legs. But if he is prevented from doing this in those low temperatures, he may cripple himself and die. So I had to walk, not run, mind you, but walk because running causes perspiration which could cause pneumonia if other things concur.

I dressed myself in such a way that the only parts of my anatomy exposed to the weather were my eyes. As far as my experience goes and from all I have heard, the only part of the body that does not freeze is the eye. Its aqueous chamber stays liquid no matter what. I set myself a steady pace and arrived at the cabin, which was so hot that I undressed in a hurry clear to my shirt sleeves and even then I began to sweat. We baptized the baby and had a nice visit. To go back to town I dressed up in the porch of the cabin that had no heat to avoid again the sweating that goes with putting on those furry clothes.

Aniak evokes to my memory the quiet evenings all by myself near a warm stove facing the tabernacle. The colder it is outside, the warmer the feelings when there is a pile of wood by a stove that works properly. Nature is asleep in total silence. Nothing moves. The dogs are in their wooden boxes keeping warm. There is no wind. Planes are not flying. People are in bed. Nobody knocks at the door of the church. I had had a long sleep the night before, so I was not too sleepy. There was a bearskin near the altar that made the ideal cushion for me to sit on, while my back rested on the side of the altar itself. There we were: the Lord and I alone in the silence of the night with the stove sending waves of heat. Was there on earth a man (or woman for that matter) happier than I was? If there was, congratulations and more power to him.

Was there on earth a priest more pampered, more coddled, more spoiled than I was? I doubt it. You see, the cloistered monks and nuns have to follow a schedule with a time to retire and a time to rise. If they wanted to be alone with the Lord beyond those times, they needed special permission that might not be given. But I was placed under such favorable circumstances that it was up to my generosity with the Lord to be there five minutes or five hours. I had done my day's work (I gambled only three times in several years) and now at night I was in a position to do all the contemplating that my soul thirsted for in the favorable environment of silence and peace. If I got tired of sitting, I would walk slowly between the door and the altar. The noise of the steps on the bare floor helped in a way to give one the feeling of life. It was not a graveyard; there was life.

---

1. By the way, Bro. Hess spent forty-eight years in Alaska *continuously*, thus surpassing any other Jesuit. He died in Sheridan, Oregon, on March 19, 1963, on the feast of Saint Joseph, patron of hard workers.

15

Holy Cross and McGrath

Since Aniak was close to Holy Cross and small planes were flying every week between the two places, I availed myself of that opportunity to visit our big school. Twice I gave the sisters an eight-day retreat in silence. It was comforting to my soul to be able to rise above the everyday catechism classes to children or the Sunday sermons to adult Eskimos and soar a little in those conferences to the sisters who wanted to hear again what the saints had written about following the Lord closely.

Once I wanted to make my own retreat at Holy Cross, but I found the place too noisy. Wasn't there a remote cabin in the woods, an abandoned cabin where I could spend a whole week all by myself, possibly by a brook with clear water? Oh yes, there was and a dandy one. Across the Yukon and up the Innoko River there was a river island with tall trees. Joe Benedict, a neighbor, had built there a small log cabin that he used during the hunting season. But the cabin was probably in disrepair because he had not used it for some time. Joe was contacted and was glad to hear that somebody would use it.

But there was another problem. The island was infested with bears. Was I a good shot? Not really; rather, I did not know; maybe I was if I had to. This problem was solved easily. I was loaned a rifle—a Savage brand—and bullets and I went to the hill to try it. I hung a coffee can from the branch of a tree and I was delighted at the number of times I hit it from fifty feet. If I could hit a tiny can like that, I certainly could hit a bear. Of course, there was the difference that the tin can stood still, while the bear might move; plus the fact that the can did not mind me, but the bear might object vehemently to my presence in his territory. But did not bears avoid man, period? Some do, some do not, especially if they are angry or hungry.

But didn't I dread spending those long nights in the woods all alone? Maybe Satan objected to my asceticism and would send legions of demons to make horrible noises to chase me out of there; hadn't I thought of that? We had much fun bringing in all the dreadful possibilities. As for Satan, holy water would take care of him, and I could bless the river.

And how about cooking? Of course the cabin had a stove, but it might be rusty and full of holes. I answered to this one saying that I was not going to the island to feast, but to fast and do penance. In fact, I would take only bread and carrots. I said carrots because they had harvested a good crop of carrots. I had not eaten carrots for ages, and there they were so appetizing. Bread and carrots, period. So the island was named on the spot Carrot Island. Sister Mary Ida, the cook, could not believe it.

By the way, Sister Mary Ida made a name for herself as easily the best cook in Alaska. Her cooking was out of the ordinary. I happened to be there when I celebrated my silver jubilee as a Jesuit and she came out with such culinary productions that I was left speechless. When I told her that all I wanted were carrots and some bread, she acquiesced.

Bro. Aloysius Laird, S.J., a veteran of those waters and a close friend of mine, made it possible for me to make the trip. We towed a rowboat with a bigger outboard motor and up we went. He knew the place. First he fixed the stove and stove pipe for me. We gathered some wood and I had a sharp axe to keep myself busy. We spread the sleeping bag on the bunk. I had a coal oil lamp and matches. I had a Mass-kit with hosts and altar wine. I had absolutely everything I needed.

When I looked at the box with the carrots and the bread, I saw with astonishment (and with gratitude, the whole truth be told) that the good sister had included bacon and eggs and a small frying pan. That was the motherly instinct, I knew.

Bro. Laird shook hands with me and begged for prayers, many prayers, for him and for his intentions, which I gladly promised. He left me alone with the small rowboat tied by the bank in case I called it quits and decided to return to civilization in a hurry. He was supposed to return for me on a certain day at a certain hour after eight days. Instead he returned after three days just to check if all was well with me, which it was. So after promising him once more that I would pray for him, he left. He said that the folks at Holy Cross were worried and had sent him to check.

Life on Carrot Island got off to a flexible schedule. To bed when I was tired. Up when I had slept enough. A good fire. To the river to wash. Meditation till I felt that I had had enough. Mass with thanksgiving. Breakfast. The breviary. Wood chopping. Spiritual reading. Meditation again. A walk in the woods. A couple of carrots with bread and water from the river. A siesta. More breviary. The rosary. Spiritual reading. To the beach. This meant that I was to spend considerable time beating a path on the wet sand between the river and the bank. I marked a length of some one hundred feet and I paraded back and forth with no time limit.

It was chilly. We were in the middle of September. The yellow leaves were falling like snow. A cold breeze rippled the surface of the water. Flocks of geese were migrating south and leaving me all alone. I had warm clothing and dressed properly, so the breeze did not bother me. The only noises were those of nature: the breeze on the tree tops; the squirrels up and down the trees fighting for food and territory; the flying geese; occasional fish jumping off the water; little birds chirping here and there.

The long nights started early and they were a bit awesome. The silence then was total except for a faraway sound that I took to be that of an owl. Near the cabin there was a big denuded log lying there just to serve as a chair. I sat on it after dark till the night was really dark, then I went inside the cabin, built a fire, and sat by the coal oil lamp to finish the breviary and meditate.

My idea of going to Carrot Island was to tell the Lord that here was a whole week when I had absolutely nothing to do except listen to Him. In our daily lives we have time for everything except for prayer. The Lord is forever waiting till His turn comes, but it seldom comes because there is always something else for us to do. Here was a whole week. "Speak, Lord, for Your servant is listening." Usually, the Lord waited till He had me pacing the beaten trail on the beach. There it was where His divine inspirations were the loudest and the toughest. To be another Christ is to carry the cross.

All too often Christ is a stranger to us; we see the Lord as distant, like an abstract being lost somewhere in the clouds. This explains why some priests say Mass daily and end up leaving the priesthood and in some cases losing their faith. There is no knowledge of Christ, no attempt to study Him more closely, no effort to attain to a close intimacy with Him. In other words, Christ and the priest are not personal friends.

The fault naturally is with the priest who lives immersed in worldly matters from morning till night.

I invite every priest to spend one whole week in solitude with the Lord in a spirit of faith and humility. The Lord will fill him with divine light so he may see things the way God sees them. Perhaps one of the first changes the priest will see is the disorder that rules his life. He will see that he must detach himself from every manner of tyranny: tobacco, booze, TV programs, trashy reading, fancy food, and traveling. Give the Lord a chance. Keep silence. Meditate at the foot of the altar. God will do the rest.

In Carrot Island—if I may say it—I dared to put the Lord to the test. "Speak, Lord, for Your servant is listening," as the boy Samuel was instructed to answer when he heard the voice of God calling to him.

The power of God manifests itself in talking to the soul without words. God bathes the soul in light. The soul sees, comprehends, understands, and at the same time feels divine strength coming to her rescue. This is accompanied by deep interior peace. The soul realizes that this is good for her and becomes insatiable, wanting more and more of it. But she also notices that the Lord will not be manipulated in any way. He is the boss; He is in full charge and no nonsense. If the soul turns to her former, worldly pastimes, she finds herself again poor, ignorant, blind, weak, and she then realizes that the fault is all hers. She must go down on her knees again and beg like the Prodigal Son. This is the reason for yearly retreats where the soul assesses her losses and gains.

Christ will tell the priest that he—Christ—expects him to aspire to total transformation into Him. Only then will God the Father perform through the priest the works He performed through His divine Son. In God's plan there is but one Priest, the High Priest Jesus, and every other priest on earth must become one with Jesus. When God the Father looks at Jesus, he sees all other priests in Him; and when he looks at the priests, any priest, He sees Jesus in him. God said over the waters of the Jordan that He was well pleased with His Son, Jesus. He will be likewise pleased with each priest in proportion to the likeness of Jesus he bears within himself.

Those priests to whom Christ is a total stranger are a contra-diction in terms—something like a policeman who is in cahoots with the burglars. One thing we must bear in mind: Being another Christ means poverty, much suffering, being lonely, being misunderstood, being persecuted, bearing pain, and being disgraced. Souls are bought with suffering, and not with any suffering, but suffering supernaturally united to the sufferings of Christ. From this come redemption and salvation. Having a good time is hardly a Christian way of life. Priests must not be of this world while they cannot escape being in this world.

God understands that priests, being human, will throw a tantrum now and then; it is the nature and character of the tantrum, for there are tantrums and tantrums, just as there are passing tantrums and there is rancor, bitterness, protracted egotism, and finally open rebellion. Christ in Gethsemane screamed with bloody tears, begging the eternal Father to spare Him much of what was coming. But He squelched any semblance of rebellion by adding: "Not My will, but Yours be done." This is the program for every priest when the going is rough. This is the recipe for saving souls.

One evening I was pacing back and forth on my sandy path as usual. I was reflecting on the goodness of Christ and on my badness. The contrast began to build within me admiration, pain, and sorrow till I could hardly breathe.

It was more than I could take even physiologically. Just at that critical moment, my nose came to the rescue by starting a profuse bleeding. This made me take a few steps to the river, where I poured cold water all over the head and face and the bleeding stopped completely. In very short time I was back to normal, though I feared returning to my meditation for fear that it would start all over again. Such is the weakness of our mortal nature that it can't take as much as one would like.

Later I asked a doctor about it and he told me that God put within us many a valve of escape to help us live longer. There are capillary vessels strategically located between arteries and veins that break whenever the pressure becomes exceedingly great, thus preventing fatal strokes. I am just repeating what he said; being a doctor, he probably knew what he was saying. My pouring cold water over the head and face diverted my mind from what I was thinking and relieved the pressure.

Leaving the cabin for the first time in the morning, after the long night, was a moment of some concern. What if a couple of bears were marauding around the cabin looking for something to eat? The door itself was flimsy and the window was even with the floor, which disturbed me somewhat. A bear could demolish the whole thing with a blow of his mighty paw.

I wished I had there a friendly dog, friendly to me, that is, but a dog that would chase the bears away with his furious barking. Joe Benedict, the owner of the cabin, had his own dog team while he lived in the cabin; the bears had no way to make a stealthy approach. I had to depend, instead, on the good offices of my guardian angel.

After eight days and two hours in that solitude I heard the engine of a boat coming around the faraway river bend. I was sure that it was Bro. Laird, but often enough we are sure of things that just are not so. It was the very superior of the Holy Cross school, Fr. William McIntyre, S.J., with a couple of big boys. They had an empty sack on board. Why the sack? Well, you see, it could have happened that the bears ate me and that they would have left some of my bigger bones strewn all over the grass. The sack was to take those bones and bring them to the mission for Christian burial. The piety and depth of the thought touched the innermost parts of my being and I was very appreciative.

Was I glad to leave? Yes and no. Yes, because man is a social animal and can take only so much solitude. And I am so social that one of my faults is to monopolize the conversation wherever and whenever the opportunity presents itself. And no, because I dreaded to return to the nitty-gritty of daily life with all that it entails. I had not shaven during that week. I did it in a hurry when people at the mission told me that I simply had to.

Fr. McIntyre was a native of Alaska with blue eyes and rosy cheeks. He was born in Douglas and raised in Juneau, across the canal separating the two towns. He was as Irish as they come and his sense of humor was simply out of this world. Most of his priestly life was spent on the lower Yukon, where he endeared himself to all with great ease. He replaced me at Alakanuk in the sixties. I went to Alakanuk with three hundred dollars. When I turned the district over to him, I turned over to him five thousand dollars, which he accepted with some smart jokes that I already forgot.

From Holy Cross I flew to McGrath on the upper Kuskokwim, the western end of my district. Fr Menager had procured a Quonset hut as church and living quarters. There the natives are not Eskimo but Indians, two races quite different in build, traits, language, natural abilities, etc. Here there were quite a few Catholics among the white population. McGrath is one of the main trunks in the communication system both by air and by boat. It has an enviable central location that makes the town quite important.

It is surrounded by forests of small trees which make it the ideal habitat for the mighty moose. The river makes a horseshoe around the town and there is a very fine airport with all its facilities. The FAA has a regular little town with its rows of neat, cute, similar houses for the employees. There is good soil for anyone who cares to raise a garden.

The Quonset church served its purpose for a while, till Fr. John Wood, S.J., arrived on the scene after my time there. Fr. Wood built a regular church with all the trimmings plus proper living quarters for the missionary.[1]

I had to make do with the Quonset. It was a cold building, but the whites told me never to worry about fuel; they would foot the bill and they did. Thanks to this, the oil stove was going day and night, which made it pleasant enough. In the back of the Quonset there was room for a bed plus a table, which was all I needed.

I ate breakfast at the Sloan roadhouse. Mrs. Sloan would give me a couple of fried eggs with toast and coffee and would not hear of payment. My supper was usually at the house of Mr. and Mrs. John Cooksey. He was the head mechanic for the FAA and she was the best cook in town. They were well into middle age and had no children. They tried to adopt one or two but they never succeeded, so I became their unofficial adopted child.

John was a barrel of fun. At table he would start a story, laughing ahead of time, which made it contagious for me who also laughed. Poor Lou Cooksey feared that her carefully cooked meal would get cold and lose its flavor or something, so she would ask solemnly that joking be stopped and eating be renewed, which made the laughing worse, which made Lou more upset.

Once at the middle of the dinner I told a short silly joke that struck some special chord in John's heart because he burst out laughing and went down on the floor resting on his fours, almost choking with laughter.

John also could start arguments. This one, for instance: A school teacher of fifth graders wanted to use school time to write her Christmas cards . She showed the children one silver dollar and one half-dollar piece. The dollar would be for the winner of a very short story with an unexpected ending. The second prize winner would get the fifty cents.

After half an hour she asked to have the papers brought to her. The winner was a girl who wrote: "He asked her, 'Will you marry me?' She answered, 'No, never.' And they lived happily ever after."

The second prize winner was a boy who wrote about a couple back from their honeymoon:

"Hey, Bob, do you know what I am thinking?"

"What is it, honey?"

"I'm finding out that you married me not because you loved me, but because of the million dollars I inherited from my father."

"Hogwash! If you had inherited it from your mother, I would have married you the same way."

John said that the second joke should have won the first prize. The trouble was that the teacher was a woman, so she bent the rules to give the first prize to a girl, a blatant chauvinism. Lou, on the contrary, went to bat for the girl with the first prize, and I had to referee their fight.

There were other hotly contested arguments at the table. One of the loudest was about how would they raise a son if they had one. John would give him the best education in the land, but that was all. He would not leave him one penny in the will; did you hear me? Not one penny. John had had to work hard for what he had now. In America every man has to work. Lou was horrified at the thought that the poor boy would be left out in the rain penniless. She would bequeath him her last penny. And so on.

I asked them where did they meet for the first time? John beat Lou to the answer. He had gone to a restaurant and the food had been so extraordinarily tasty that he had requested to see the cook, hoping to find some Italian or Chinese chef with a high white hat and a face uglier than sin. Lo and behold there was this pretty thing . . . Here Lou broke in to say, looking at me, "He was smitten; he still is." And so they got married.

John was a Catholic, but Lou had never been baptized. Before the week was over she made it very plain that she wanted to be baptized, the sooner the better. She mentioned other people in town who were talking about joining the Catholic church. Before I knew it, she had a half a dozen white folks—well educated, articulate, and eager to take instructions. These took place in her living room.

Every evening we sat there cozily ensconced in fashionable sofas, with cake, coffee, and ice cream within reach. Every truth of the Catholic faith came under scrutiny and was put under the magnifying glass. There was free questioning. We would not advance one inch till every item had been explained and accepted by all. That gave me an opportunity to dust off my theological knowledge that had become stale for lack of usage. Four of the group had never been baptized, and asked to be baptized.

One of them wrote to her mother in the Middle West that she was about to be received in the Catholic church. The mother made a hurried trip to McGrath in the heart of Alaska to dissuade her beloved daughter from taking such a dreadful step. It did not work. The mother returned to the States unable to convince her daughter. Another family drama in the pluralistic United States. The daughter was herself a mother of three children and felt that she was both free and capable of making her own decisions. Often parents in their sixties look at their children in their thirties as little children in constant need of guidance. It has been so before and there is reason to suspect that it will continue being so.

In one of my trips to McGrath I got a little package in the mail. I kept unwrapping it till I came to the single item contained therein. It was a quart of cognac, a fine-quality liquor, according to the label on it. We were in the thick of the winter. The mail was brought to me when it was already dark. I was all alone in the Quonset. The wind was beating the snow against the window panes. It was the perfect set-up for an all-night drinking spree. I opened the bottle and must admit that the fragrance emanating from it filled the room. I took the bottle out and poured its contents in the snow at the entrance some two feet from the door. Next morning when I opened the door for Mass, I saw that there was still a yellow spot in the snow, so I covered it with fresh white snow.

A second time I received another bottle and a second time I emptied it in the snow, but this time I put the neck of the bottle in the soft snow to avoid yellow spots. The third time I received a bottle. This time it was one pint of anisette. I poured it in an empty coffee can, and threw a match to it. It was almost like gasoline. A flare erupted instantly, a beautiful multi-colored flame that consumed the liqueur quickly and totally. I thought of the "fire water" of the Indians.

My reason for not touching the stuff was double: first, for fear that I might like it and become addicted to it, and, second, to atone for the abuse of liquor. Drinking and the priesthood make a bad marriage.

McGrath had the honor of presenting me with the only perfect day I saw in Alaska, weather-wise. Alaska weather is proverbially bad. It is either cold or windy or it is rainy or the snow is falling and the skies are mostly cloudy. One soon learns to expect bad weather. But this August day in McGrath was different. I noticed after breakfast that there was something unusual all around me and I did not exactly know what it was. It was good weather, the most unusual thing.

I crossed the airport and went to the river bank to walk aimlessly and enjoy the day. It was perfect. Neither cold nor hot. Sunshine. No wind and no clouds. I sat on the river bank to watch the water flow serenely and interminably. Dear Lord what a day!

Half a dozen cranes circled and landed in a grassy swamp nearby. What beautiful birds. The daughters were as big as the mothers; I could not tell them apart. First they looked all around in all directions with their long necks stretched to see if there were enemies around. I stood motionless. Not seeing any enemies, they proceeded to look for food, but they would stretch their necks out, off and on, just in case.

A flock of ducks came crashing onto the river at the end of the bend and proceeded to dive and look for food, wiggling their feathery tails with evident joy. Such peace. Small birds of every shape and color fluttered on the trees.

This was the Garden of Eden. The skies were clear blue. The sun stood up there in his glory, filing the universe with light. This was the day that the Lord had made. I felt sorry for people somewhere else, enduring some bad storm or an earthquake or tornado or shivering or being baked in the open fields in some tropical country.

Suddenly, I heard the roar of engines in the distance. A four-engine plane came into view. The cranes took off. The big plane circled and made an impeccable landing. It taxied in front of me, moving like a giant peacock, and stopped at the terminal. Passengers came out. Freight came out. Freight went in. Passengers went in. In short order the plane roared again and taxied before me with the pride of a peacock. It made a turn and off it went to get lost in the clouds. All very beautiful—but very noisy.

God runs the cosmos in perfect silence. Man can't make even a motorcycle without filling the air with strident noises that irritate our ears. What a joy to think that our eternity is going to be spent with God in soothing silence and not with people who seem to thrive only on nerve-wracking noises.

As if to compensate me for the loss of the queenly cranes, God sent me a dozen or more Canadian geese who landed where the cranes had been. Then, as I stood motionless, a lively squirrel nervously hesitated whether to get closer to me or not. What a perfect machine for quick reflexes. If I had coughed, she would have been up a tree in a fraction of a second. I looked at her with real affection. She and I both came from the hands of the same God who fashioned us as it pleased Him and for the purpose He had intended. Had I been another Saint Francis, the squirrel would have come to my hands.

I wanted to see how close to Saint Francis I was. Gently and with a charming smile I invited her to come, not to be afraid. But sooner than instantly she disappeared up a tree. Poor me! What a long road I have to travel to be another Francis. And to think that he was only forty-four when he died! Scientists studied the bones of Saint Francis and came out with the discovery that he was very small in stature and that he suffered from malnutrition. No wonder, the way he fasted! I much prefer a skinny Saint Francis dying young to a robust well-fed Francis who lived ninety years and never made friends with birds, fish, and even wolves. When I didn't die at forty-four, I knew that I would never be another Saint Francis.

Finally I got tired of sitting on the grass. I got up and began to walk facing the north end of the runway. There ahead was the Arctic, clear to the North Pole. To the west was the Bering Sea and Siberia. To the east the mighty McKinley and the Yukon Territory and the infinite Canada. Back of me to the south was nothing less than the Pacific Ocean. Alaska was in the center of it all on that beautiful day that was neither cold nor hot nor rainy nor snowy under the shining King Sol high above.

I could appreciate the vision of Secretary of State William Seward, who in 1867 arranged for the purchase of this vast empire. He also wanted to purchase Greenland. I don't know if mother Denmark would not sell or if the cries of "Seward's Folly" prevented him from going ahead after Alaska's purchase. Who holds Alaska, holds the North Pacific. Who holds Greenland, holds the North Atlantic. Who holds the United States, holds North America. The vision of one genius is worth the prattle of the myriads of nongeniuses who will yap and yelp like curs at the heels of the genius.

It reminds me of the mule skinner who was surprised at the philosopher who needed ten hours of sleep while he, the mule skinner, needed only six. The philosopher shot back that his mind did more work in one hour while awake than the mule skinner's mind did in one month.

I kept walking back and forth on the runway all by myself. I could not see one single person. That meant that all the air, all that pure air, was for my lungs. I did not deserve that much, I knew, but I enjoyed it while I kept walking back and forth alone in that wilderness. A little plane came to land. Two or three more little planes landed at the end of the east-west runway. They were private pilots who carried freight to the miners in the creeks with the names of American states: California Creek, Colorado Creek, Montana Creek, etc. Once some miners sent a partner to town by dog team to buy some grub. As the partner was approaching the camp on his return trip, another miner yelled from a distance, wanting to know what it was that he brought. When told that it was four cases of booze and sixteen loaves of bread, the miner yelled back half angry: "What are we going to do with all that bread?" Alaskans are like that.

As I walked back and forth bathed in the beauty of that day, I recalled the story of three miners in partnership who settled in a log cabin by the creek where they had their claim. Nobody wanted to do the cooking. After a great deal of talk one agreed to do the cooking, on one condition: The first guy to complain would have to cook. Weeks went by without complaints.

The cook wanted to force the issue, so one morning he put in the coffee such ingredients as salt, pepper, onion powder, and mustard. When the first guy rolled out of his bunk like a bear coming from hibernation, he made a beeline for the coffee pot and served himself a generous cup. He took one gulp, pounded the table with his clenched fist, and bellowed: "This coffee tastes rotten."

As the cook began to crack a smile of relief, the guy at the table lowered his voice and, in a charming tone, said: "But this is the way we like it."

This was told me by Bro. Peter Wilhalm, S.J., who did his best to imitate the voice and the gestures of the beleaguered miner.

The saying of this miner has helped me in my conferences to nuns. When the sledding is tough, when all the demons from hell seem to be loose, when frustrations and contradictions pile up, when life appears like a tunnel with no light in view—instead of hitting the ceiling and going to pieces, just calm down and lower your voice and say with all the charm you can muster: "This is the way I like it, Lord." Is this a lie? To the ordinary man in the street it would appear to be a lie, but to a soul seeking evangelical perfection it would not be a lie. The heart has reasons that the head knows nothing about.

I was tired of walking, and I did not want to go home and miss the sun. I did not want to sit again on the grass. I was a bit hungry, but not enough to push me to leave that unprecedented sunshine. I found myself wondering and watching the trees, the blue sky, the horizon. Another big plane came and landed and took off. More small planes came and left.

After some time I noticed patches of white clouds forming on the east. A rustling sound from the treetops told me that a breeze was forming. Very, very slowly I headed for town, thanking God Almighty for such an unprecedented day.

In one of my trips from Bethel to McGrath and points between them I was accompanied by the new bishop, Francis Gleeson, S.J, who wanted to take a close look at each station and meet the people and listen to them. The bishop usually let me do the talking when we were alone.

I took advantage of such opportunity to tell him many things I wanted to get off my chest. This meant not only personal things but mainly things that were happening all over this vast diocese. I was fond of saying that in my humble opinion . . . or that it was my humble opinion . . . or that I could be wrong, of course, of course, but it was my humble opinion that, etc. He took an enormous amount of humble opinions of mine till he had had enough and broke in to say, "Humble, but FIRM." He said FIRM, with capital letters. From then on I either had no opinion at all, or if I had it and I expressed it, it was just an ordinary opinion, neither humble nor proud nor anything like that.

---

1. Fr. Wood became a flyer. The first Jesuit priest to fly in northern Alaska was Fr. Jules Convert, a Frenchman. Then came Fr. Wood, who was followed by several others like Frs. Saalfeld, McMeel, Kaniecki, and Sebesta. There was no doubt that flying helped to cover those enormous distances. A priest with his plane could say Masses in several places every weekend. The objection to this procedure was that the priest

passed through like rain over a roof with no time for proper instruction and consolation.

This difficulty will be obviated by the presence of married deacons who live on the spot and stay put. The Holy Spirit inspires proper solutions. Of these flying priests, Fr. Saalfeld died in the harness on the Yukon. Fr. Convert returned to France after thirty-eight years in Alaska and Fr. Wood contracted multiple sclerosis which prompted superiors to move him to Portland, Oregon, where he could get proper treatment.

16
Starting Over

In 1951 I moved again, back to the Yukon Delta. Bishop Gleeson had given the order to go ahead and move the Akulurak school to Saint Marys. The last year of Akulurak was 1951. In the spring we began the dismantling of the buildings. It was decided that I would remain in charge of the mission district and be headquartered at Alakanuk, on the other side of the Yukon; as soon as the new buildings at Saint Marys were ready, the Akulurak school would be moved lock, stock, and barrel. Fr. Francis Menager would become superior of the Saint Marys school. It was heartbreaking to see those beloved buildings tumble down, to be stripped of any material that could be reused.

On August 2, 1951, two river boats were hooked to two huge barges loaded with all the cargo they could hold plus the sisters with all the children. I stood sad on the bank with my right arm up, wishing them a happy trip. With much yelling and singing and metaphorical kisses filled with nostalgia, they took off and I was left with Steve, a big boy from Hooper Bay who chose to stay to help me. The boats returned for more loads until they had all they considered worth taking. Then Steve and I settled to a peaceful living in that immensity of nothingness and then we moved to Alakanuk.

Good Steve held out and stayed with me for four months. He hoped to get himself a wife, but no one gave him any hope. He became lonesome for his village, and we parted with a warm handshake. I also parted with what I considered adequate payment for the work he had done. He was a hunter first and foremost. He would go out with a gun and in a few hours he would be back with a couple of geese. But I had to pluck them. Wouldn't he help me pluck them? He looked at me with unbelieving eyes and answered, "But, Father, in all these years that you have been in Alaska have you ever seen one man, any man, pluck a goose? A true man would rather starve than pluck a goose. That's women's job. I would never forgive me for doing that type of work."

I retorted that he was of no help to me if he would not give me a hand plucking those geese. It was the classical clash of cultures, heritage, traditions, the genius of the race, taboos, all these things rolled in one.

As I said, we moved to the town of Alakanuk, where they had started having movies once a week. He never missed a movie. One day he asked me for money to go to the movie. I was then deep into the study of Eskimo psychology, so I began to dialogue with him by way of experimentation.

"Would you, Steve, consider not going to the movie tonight?"

"Why should I consider that?"

"Well, do you *have to* go to all the movies? All of them? Every one of them with absolutely no exception? Don't you have any will power?"

"But if there is a movie, I have to go."

"But why do you *have to* go?"

"Because there is a movie."

"But could you sit down and think that, since you are not under any obligation to go to this particular movie, you of your own accord will decide not to go to this particular movie?"

"Oh, no. I would never do that. If there is a movie, I have to go see it."

"Does that mean that you find yourself constrained, forced, coerced, irresistibly impelled to go to see every single movie that is shown in town?"

"Yes, Father."

"But, Steve, think again. Could you say no once? Only once?"

"No, I could not. If there is a movie, I have to go and see it."

There was no use continuing the dialogue. Group pressure is for them a formidable force to overcome. When the time for the movie comes, the whole town shows up. All drink; all eat candy; all smoke; all the men take to their boats and chase a seal that was sighted in the river; all . . . When I say *all,* I mean, say, 95% of the people. I looked for rugged individualism and found little. I looked for dissenters, men who disagree, men who create and keep busy by themselves regardless of what others might say—but these characters were few and far between. While *gregarious* could be synonymous with *sociable,* it also reminds you of flocks and herds. The thundering herd on the march.

Steve went back to his people and found himself a wife there. A happy man indeed who smiled a lot, and now he would smile much more since he had the lady who would pluck his geese, skin his seals and minks and muskrats and—above all—would sew and mend his hunting boots. I was glad for him when I heard he had found a wife. But soon afterward I heard that he had died, as if to prove once again that we live in a valley of tears.

That summer my next-door neighbor Fr. John Fox loaned me a boat he had, called *The Ark* because it looked exactly like the pictures we see of Noah's ark. It was a small river boat, too small even to have a cot or bunk to sleep in, but it helped me to go around and visit the fishermen in their little fish camps.

I came to a tent where Margaret Mary was dying of cancer of the throat. She had been in our school for ten years, and now she was married to Billy Buster. Billy was the happiest man in the neighborhood—one of those types who were created by God to keep everybody happy. Margaret Mary was in bed and had sent word that she wanted to see me. When I walked into the tent, everybody left. She handed me several hand-written pages and begged me to read them. It was her last confession. She could no longer talk, but she could write. When I finished reading, I was amazed. In impeccable English with perfect spelling she had analyzed her past life with the terminology of a trained theologian. You would think that she had had several courses of moral theology.

I bring this up because often at Akulurak the fathers and sisters discussed the spiritual training that the children were getting. This experience proved conclusively to me that those children were getting more than we thought. The trouble was that they were there very much against their own will. Most were orphans and had no other place to go. Others were brought in crying and kicking because they were afraid of the unknown. Others were brought in by their parents because they themselves had been in Akulurak and felt that it was good for their children to be there for a while. The priests considered it a moral obligation to bring in as many as possible so the kids would get both the three Rs and religion. It was a matter of education *and* religion.

Until 1941 ours was the only school available. On the other hand, the parents wanted their children to help at home, so they made it very difficult for the priest to get the child. The case of orphans was much worse. A ten-year-old boy or girl without parents became automatically the property of the nearest uncle who hoped to get all the cheap work he could out of the child. This uncle would rather let his teeth go than the orphaned nephew. It was a plain case of slavery. The priest had to fight royal battles to get those orphans. The result of this was that those children were not in the mission school of their own accord, with few exceptions.

At school everything was free. They were housed, fed, clothed, taught, and entertained, all for free. What comes free of charge is not appreciated. But the priest had no choice. It was either that or nothing. The benefactors of the missions kept sending alms and we kept using that money to bring in children and educate them free of charge.

And how about after the children left the mission? It all depended on how long they had been with us. In the case of Margaret Mary I could see the good effects of our school. She died with the disposition of a saint. She was a finished product of our school. She had absorbed what she was taught. Only God knows how many others benefited to a high degree. That all benefited to some degree was self-evident. Gone were the days when the medicine men ruled the land with an iron hand. Pupils from our school gradually peopled that land and raised children who, in turn, grew up better trained than their parents were.

With Akulurak school moved now many miles up river, it was up to me to hold the district single-handedly, and I did my best to hold the fort for twelve consecutive years. The first thing was to provide a chapel for every new town that was being formed as the Eskimos were leaving the flats to settle on the banks of the Yukon. These towns were Emmonak, Kwiguk, Sheldon Point, and Alakanuk.

Fortunately for me, Alakanuk had a church, a rectory, and a cabin to be used as a warehouse. Those became my headquarters. Of the many Akulurak buildings I became heir to, I made a chapel of the carpenter shop and a living room of the machine shop. The fathers' house and boys' house had to be taken down board by board to save the lumber for the other chapels in other towns.

In May of 1952 I moved back to Akulurak to start the dismantling. I traveled light, taking only my Mass-kit and my sleeping bag. Francis Lee, sixty, a very good Eskimo carpenter, helped me to do the work—until he fell off the roof and by a miracle did not get killed. He broke six ribs and hurt two vertebrae. He was hospitalized for six months. The men were all getting ready for the fishing season, so I had to do the work all by myself.

How I survived the ordeal, I still don't know. Every morning after Mass and breakfast I would put on a pair of overalls, a pair of thick gloves, a hard cap, and the work would start. With a hammer and different sizes of wrecking bars I tackled those walls one at a time. Slowly the boards were coming out whole. I took off the nails. The boards began to form big piles and the nails were filling the empty coffee cans. Those boards had been taken from an old army building in Saint Michael. They were old but precious, and had to be taken off with infinite care or they would split and become useless. Then came the two-by-twos, two-by-fours, two-by-sixes, two-by-eights, and two-by-twelves. All were neatly piled in their respective places.

Pulling nails became very tedious because of the extra care needed not to injure the board. To keep myself in good spirits I told the Lord to keep an eye on those nails and give me a sinner for every nail I pulled. Naturally, I would give Him the sinner back. It worked. As the nail came out, I would say in Spanish, "Ahi va otro"—"There goes another one." When a nail came out easily, I felt that the sinner just converted was a light-weight one. When the nail showed itself difficult, I knew that this time the Lord and I had gotten a big one. When it was not a nail but a spike clinched and twisted and rusty that made me use the crowbar and left me gasping for breath, then I rejoiced over the fact that the Lord and I had landed one of the biggest criminals walking this earth. Thus I was doing great missionary work while I was dismantling the building. When I go to heaven I have an idea that the Lord will introduce me to those former sinners, now saints, whom he and I rescued from the claws of Satan.

When I felt that the ice was about to break, I went into an eight-day retreat with a little work between meditations. The very day I finished, our Akulurak slough filled bank to bank with huge chunks of Yukon ice flowing madly in their rush to the Bering Sea. Now the real work was about to start.

My last meditation before the blessed Sacrament in the tabernacle was particularly touching to me. I had arrived at that point where Saint Ignatius encourages us to give God all we have and possess. I felt that the best I could give God was my very life. Kneeling before the altar, I died to all that was not God. I gave Him everything and immediately I got up and moved around as though I was walking on thin air. What a joy it was and what a relief to be dead, to move about without any care. This must have been around 6:00 P.M. One hour later news came that the Yukon ice had jammed just below the town of Alakanuk. The town had flooded. The current had cut a channel between the Catholic church and the rectory. The ice had pushed both buildings into the lake and both had disappeared. The cabin near the church had been totally demolished and had disappeared also.

I thought of Job of the Old Testament who got a barrage of bad news, very bad news indeed. Like Job, I said, "The Lord gave, the Lord took it away; may the name of the Lord be blessed."

Then I sat down to appraise the situation. When Akulurak school had moved away and I had been left alone, I had not minded it so much, because I had my Alakanuk buildings. From Alakanuk I had planned to build the chapels I needed in the new villages. Now I had nothing. Absolutely nothing except a skiff with a roof over it.

I left immediately for Alakanuk and I saw the disaster with my own eyes. Mine were the only buildings destroyed; the rest of the village had suffered practically nothing. Where the church and rectory had stood, there was now nothing but mud. The same with the cabin. I borrowed a rowboat and went to see where the buildings had landed. The church building, made of logs, was grounded on one of its corners and the rest was floating. Absolutely nothing could be saved. The rectory was a frame building. It had floated away two-thirds sunk in muddy water, and now it rested more than half sunk at the end of the lake. The ice chunks had forced it to take a few somersaults.

My earthly possessions were there and they were ruined. I sat in the boat by the broken windows of the house and saw the damage. There was silence all around. The night before I had died to all these possessions. The Lord in His infinite mercy had wanted to prepare me for the shock. Sitting in that borrowed rowboat all alone, I looked within myself and what I saw was this: poverty, destitution, remoteness, desolation, sadness, helplessness. Where would I eat and sleep that night? There were no restaurants or roadhouses. Providentially, I had taken with me the Mass-kit and the sleeping bag.

With the Mass-kit I could say Mass, but where? With the sleeping bag I could sleep, but where would I stretch it? I thought of the Holy Family in their flight to Egypt. They had been in a far worse situation than I was now. For one thing nobody was trying to arrest and kill me. This was the sixth day of June 1952.

The men were all fishing, that is, setting their fishing locations so they could put their nets in the water as soon as the river got rid of floating ice. Those who were not fishing were working feverishly in the cannery, putting the finishing touches on the machinery that would process the coming fish. This meant that there was no possibility for me to get workers to help me to rebuild. That year the fishing of king salmon lasted six weeks.

While I was at Alakanuk that summer, I slept in the attic of the cannery—surrounded by nets and fishing equipment. I ate in the mess hall with the workers at the invitation of my good friend John T. Emel, owner of the cannery. Then I visited the fishing camps, where I ate with the fishermen and slept in their tents.

In time I got a tent, an eight-by-ten, just large enough to crawl in with my Mass-kit and sleeping bag. The third night I was there, we got hit by a torrential rain so fierce that the raindrops pierced the canvas and fell on me as if I were out in the open; I had to abandon the tent and leave.

In the rain I ran to my skiff, tied at the river bank, and sat in the corner. The waves smashed against the boat and the rain beat on the roof above my weary head. It was shortly after midnight. I was cold, hungry, tired, a living picture of dejection. I rested my hands on my knees and closed my eyes. In that pious position and leaning against the wall I begged God Almighty to please take me to Him right then and there. I wanted to die sooner than instantly and so I kept begging God to just take my soul to Himself and never mind the body; people would eventually find me there and would give me a Christian burial, quite certainly. Then I fell asleep.

In the morning the raining was gone, so I got out of that hole reeking with the smell of gasoline and returned to the tent, which was all wet. But I had no right whatsoever to complain, because I had offered my life to God at the end of my spiritual retreat. I had given myself to Him with my past, my present, and my future. This was part of the future which now was present.

Before I go any further I want to say that toward the end of October I had finished the new church. When I was saying my first

Mass in it, after the words of consecration I sort of heard with the ears of my soul a whisper from God that said to me: "Well, my boy, aren't you grateful and happy that I did not take your soul when you asked Me to do it that stormy night inside the skiff? Look at the nice little church you have now."

I hired five Eskimos to build it. Another man made trips with me back and forth between Akulurak and Alakanuk to provide the builders with the material needed.

The rectory was floated back near the church, but it had to be lifted over the bank. We put logs under it, tied it with cables, and John T. Emel himself came with his powerful tractor to do the lifting. We tried and tried and tried. But just when it was up and should have started leaning toward land, it refused. I doubt that there had ever been in me a wish as strong as the wish I had then to have that building over the bank. When it was plain that it could not be done, I went through the motions of desperation; just then an interior grace put me at ease and taught me never, never, but never, to wish anything whatsoever with too great an anxiety. As likely as not, my wish would not be fulfilled and the reaction can be damaging to the soul. The best thing in that building was the double flooring made of the finest lumber. It had to be abandoned to rot. With left-over material I made a seven-by-sixteen living room that housed me till the next year, when it was enlarged.

The next year came along with its usual summer, the time to build, so I freighted enough material to build two chapels, one at Kwiguk and the other at Emmonak. The year after I freighted material to build another chapel at Sheldon Point. All the material came from the salvaged lumber from the Akulurak big building.

You may ask how I paid the workers. Well, God, who permits the sickness, provides the medicine. There is an antidote for every poison. The *Indian Sentinel* of Washington, D.C., sent me $1,700. A lady from Cuba sent me $1,000. When I thanked her and told her how handy her money had become, she sent me another $1,000. Money then was worth more than it is now. The wages were cheaper. The men did the building by contract, not by the hour, so they could take off seal hunting if the weather was good. There was no time limit, except that the buildings had to be finished before freeze-up.

The chapel at Sheldon Point was specially dear to me, because that part of the land is easily the most desolate. It is a piece of land that juts into the Bering Sea and is surrounded by absolutely barren flats. Because it is an ideal fishing spot, the natives congregate there.

In the summer everything is mud; in the winter everything is frozen. The place is lashed by periodic storms. If the storms come in the summer, you see nothing but water; if they come in the winter, there is no protection against the cold wind that sweeps the whole region and piles up the snow against any object sticking above the ground. The cabins get covered by the snow after those storms. The natives make steps in the snow to reach the door. There were twelve cabins, twelve families, all Catholic. The Lord loved each one of them with infinite love and wanted to live in their midst; hence the need for a chapel, which was a simple frame building sixteen by thirty with the altar, the pews, and a wood stove. Attached to it was the "rectory," that is, a room nine by twelve. It was so small because that was all we could do with the lumber we had left. In that little room I had a bed, a table with a chair, a portable kerosene heater, shelves to keep the food, and one thin bench against the wall. It was built, like the rest of the cabins, on a small hump of the ground and was surrounded by a swamp. We painted the building green and it could be seen from far away.

In that little chapel we had the most lovely Sunday Masses. Prayers were said aloud and I used to preach my sermons with all the simplicity I could muster to make the articles of faith accessible to them, using comparisons with things they knew, like dogs, geese, fish, babies, etc. Most of the songs were in Eskimo. During Mass the little children made themselves heard: a baby would get mad and throw his milk bottle with a scream; a little girl would run after the bottle; mothers nursed their babies; it was great. A real family affair. After all left, the place became silent as a grave.

In the afternoons the children were gathered for catechism and stories. In the winter we huddled around the stove; in the summer we would go out on the grass, avoiding ponds and mud. In the evenings I built a fire and sat close to the altar to transact business with the Lord. If there wasn't something specific to transact, I just sat there loving Him in silence. If I tired of sitting and kneeling, I got up and walked back and forth. That place was loved by the Lord, so it should be loved by me, too.

In my room I sat by the only window, where the table was. From there I could see the long distance to the Scammon Bay hills lost in the horizon. The only thing between those faraway hills and my window was a row of coffins by the shore of the lake. How many times I was forced to look at those coffins! Just about every time I saw them, I begged the Lord mentally to see to it that every one of those souls were taken to heaven. In my room I would sit at the typewriter and write, write, and write. Or I would read again and again certain books dear to me.

The N.C. Co. built a store in Sheldon Point and also a saltery. The store was minded by a native couple, Andrew and Olga Prince, who had fifteen children. Andrew kept Olga well provided with seals, fresh fish, and geese. Olga was an extraordinary cook. I prepared my own breakfast and lunch, but I had supper with the Prince family. Olga could roast a goose or bake a fifteen-pound fish as well, if not better, than anyone I knew. Andrew took me to many a fish camp with his outboard motor, to baptize a baby or see a sick fisherman. In the winter in his snowmobile he would take me forty miles away in a blinding snowstorm. He assured me: "Father, if I take you either by boat in big waves or by sled in a snowstorm, be not afraid. I know when we are safe and when we aren't, and I will take no chances." To me he was taking chances, but he was always right. We never had an accident.

There was in Sheldon Point an old man called Matthew. He was about eighty, almost blind. He would come to my room to chat with me. His language was so pure that I needed the help of an interpreter. He told me that in the old days all those flat lands had been peopled by natives, lots of them, living in villages so big that they had to have more than one *kazim*.

He had known many medicine men, but one of them, Katmigak by name, beat them all. He was so powerful with his medicine that he could do anything. If a woman had only girls, she would go to him and he would guarantee her that the next one would be a boy. If someone lost an object dear to him, Katmigak would tell him where to find it. If someone got sick, Katmigak would get the sickness out of him. Other medicine men were jealous of him, but they were helpless to topple him.

Once in the *kazim* he was making medicine. Another medicine man went to him to kick him out. You know what happened? Katmigak grabbed him and was holding him down. The other man made medicine fast and a man who had died a few weeks before came up from the ground and began to help him. When Katmigak saw two men against him, he made medicine fast and had two new arms born to him right under his two natural arms. So now with four arms he first made the dead man disappear under the ground and then he took after the other medicine man who was beaten unconscious. Once Katmigak had won the fight, his two artificial arms vanished and he was again himself.

If somebody was too sick to go to him, they would take the shirt of the sick man to Katmigak, who would make medicine over the shirt. Now the shirt would be returned to the sick man who would get well quickly.

Katmigak could walk any distances over the clouds. He would tell his family to go and pick berries several miles away on the other side of the river. When the family arrived there in the rowboat, Katmigak was already there and had one big can full of berries. And the same thing to go back home. When nobody was looking, he would travel over the clouds.

Several times he let people tie him with chains and strings. He was tied so hard that he could not even wiggle. Then he would tell the people to go and they went. But he followed them laughing. The chains had fallen from him. "I am telling you, Father, that Katmigak was a toughy."

I told Matthew that if Katmigak could do all those things, he would be a millionaire. He could go to the big cities in the U.S. and make a killing. Matthew could not understand. Katmigak, he said, was rich. He had house, wife, kids, traps, nets, guns, good health; what more did he need? I saw that I had asked the wrong question. It was a matter of culture, heritage, customs, tradition, way of life. Katmigak in the Eskimo culture was a millionaire. You see, Katmigak charged some small fees for his services, like a dog or a mink or a plate of seal meat or a couple of muskrat pelts, so he was sitting pretty. Every time he felt that he was losing medicinal powers, Katmigak would eat a few bones of a dead man on a moonlit night; his powers were returned to him. So very simple.

The last medicine man was John Kakortok. He got T.B. which he could not cure. He was taken to a sanatorium where it was cured. This told him that the whites had stronger medicine than the Eskimos, so he quit his native practices, or nearly so. His son took up the practice, but he was found frozen on the trail. In the sled there was a wooden pot of homemade brew. With his departure from the scene, medicine men were all but finished. The new generation knew nothing of the old practices. Now the presence of Christ in our chapel helped dispel those beliefs, as the sun dispels the fog when it shines in the sky.

Sheldon Point, small as it was, had a village council with a chief. Once in a while all the people met. I sat at one of those meetings. A man would be put on the carpet because when drunk he had disturbed the neighbors. His punishment was, say, to keep the water hole in the river open at all times by chopping the ice all around it. Another man would be charged with the same crime. This one had to bring one log to the door of the church. A third man had committed the same crime. He had to saw that log. A fourth man had been seen drunk also and the children had been scared. This man had to chop the blocks and stack the wood where Father would tell him. Once the church had been provided with some firewood, the new criminal was told to pay fifty dollars. He did not have the money. Oh, well, then he had to shovel the snow in front of the door of the church. No more criminals were brought in. Then the chief would encourage everyone to be nice and treat everybody right. With that the meeting adjourned till further notice.

The trouble with me after witnessing the proceedings was that deep inside of me I sort of hoped that someone would get drunk, so I could get another free log. I had to fight that evil desire. In those eternal nights of the winter when the snow buries the cabins and there is nothing else to do, the temptation to get drunk becomes irresistible to some folks.

I loved to spend the month of May in Sheldon Point. That was the month when all travel stopped because the river's ice begins to crack. The break-up itself was an awesome sight. It looks as though the whole Yukon comes at you with millions of tons of ice rushing madly to the sea. Before that, the big lake by the church thaws to welcome the swans. One morning I counted five hundred swans in that lake. They are protected by the law—but we know that some laws are broken occasionally.

At the end of August the natives went berry picking. There are four varieties of berries, but they prefer the blueberries which are quite abundant. These berries are kept in barrels all winter solidly frozen. When they want a taste of the sweetest morsel in Eskimoland, they thaw them a bit, mix them with tallow and seal oil, and they have what they call *akootak*. They would rather have a plate of that than of New York steaks plus lobster plus a bowl of cream and cherries.

Akootak is the sweetest word in their language and in their mouths. When I tasted it and made faces and my throat shut tight to keep it from sliding down, the natives looked at me with pity. Another case of white man's stupidity. Berries are put there by the Creator to provide the vitamin C needed to keep scurvy away. I used to pick blueberries myself. Properly washed and mixed with milk and sugar they are a delicacy.

The Creator puts many things there. I thought that God had put the muskrats to give us lovely pelts for our jackets, caps, and parkas, but the natives think differently. Once the pelt is taken, they chop off the long tail and the head with those beady eyes and fry the rest. I was sure that I would never fall for that one, but hunger is not too choosy. In the cabin of Mike Tuyak of Unuskut after a long day on the trail, I was treated to the hind legs of muskrats properly fried and sprinkled with salt and pepper. Let me tell you that I licked my fingers and so would you if caught in the same predicament.

That was also the case with frozen fish which I was positive I would never even smell. I had to eat it and it tasted exactly as if it had been fried for the simple reason that extremes do meet.

And speaking of rats, so-called Eskimo potatoes are tubers of underground stems that mice pack in nests under the grass. The Eskimo steps gently and feels with the tip of his shoe where he suspects that there may be some. If his shoe sinks, that's it. He goes down on his knees and digs. The mouse runs for his life and the Eskimo appropriates to himself the whole cache. I tasted those, too, and found them so-so. I figured that most likely they were good for some part of our anatomy like the liver or the bile or maybe the eyelashes. The ancients knew more about nature than we do with all our laboratories.

17

Alakanuk

By the summer of 1954 the flat lands between Scammon Bay and the mouth of the Yukon were abandoned. In my parish files were names of old towns that existed no longer. What an immense relief it was for me to know that I wouldn't have to cross those snow-covered lands in the winter at the mercy of paralyzing storms! The people moved to Alakanuk and Emmonak principally. These two towns need special mentioning.

Alakanuk is the spelling of white men who, being stupid, did not know how to spell the guttural sound of that village, which means "A Mistake." When I saw the village in 1936 it had seven small cabins that had no flooring. John T. Emel built a cannery that grew steadily and with the cannery grew the village. The first chapel was too small. The second was destroyed by a flood. The third soon became too small also. Finally, a fourth one was built. We built a log school that became too small. The Bureau of Indian Affairs moved in and rented a house to be used as a school and this became too small. Finally, the government rolled up its sleeves and built with an eye to more growth.

It was not only the influx from outside that made the village grow. It was the remarkable birth rate. Formerly babies had died at an incredible rate; conditions were rapidly changing. Now it was common for a pregnant woman to be flown in the mail plane to the Bethel hospital where she was delivered with medical care. The baby was also given proper clothing. A week later mother and child were flown back to the village in prime condition. To cut down expenses, the government sent teams of paramedics to show midwives how to deliver babies. At least two more talented women were equipped with tools to do an adequate job in child delivery. If any complications arose, the mail plane would fly the patient to Bethel. Suddenly, babies stopped dying.

Five years later those babies became kindergarten candidates. If you are curious to know the birth rate at that time in that part of the world, my records showed forty-eight births for one thousand population. It was a far cry from the zero growth advocated by the present enemies of mankind (as I see them when I am in a less charitable mood).

With the people now fairly well settled in a few villages, I did not see the need for me to own a dog team. Instead of being on the go as before, now I would stay at least two weeks in each place. I could hire any local team whenever needed and at the same time I had a good chance to stay longer with the people and give them a better opportunity for the reception of the Sacraments and religious instructions.

The door of my house was never locked. People then entered everywhere without knocking. The church was never locked. It was the house of the people.

I lived alone. By this I mean that I had no housekeeper. A housekeeper would have meant automatically that she was my wife. I did not have a room of my own. By this I mean that my living quarters was a room without partitions. As you came in, you could see at a glance the stove, the bed, the table with the typewriter, books, and papers, a few benches for the children who came to catechism, and that was all. I had nothing to hide.

Every school day, immediately after school, the children came in and took possession of that room. It was a good thing that the first grades let the children out earlier; thus I could have them before the bigger children came. The boys sat always apart from the girls. They all spoke English. The order of business was always more or less the same: a) questions and answers, b) memorized prayers, c) Bible stories, d) scary stories, e) a little pandemonium, f) to the church to say good-bye to the Lord.

This good-bye to the Lord was, to me at least, the most important part. We all knelt in a crescent shape around the altar with our hands pressed against our chests. I would break the ice by telling the Lord a few words. Then everyone had to say at least one sentence to the

Lord. Those who were overly timid had nothing to fear. They were told to repeat after me and so all had *their* say.

What was it they said? They would tell the Lord that they loved Him very much; that they wanted to see Him; that So-and-So was sick and wanted to be cured; that my dad went seal hunting and please give him lots of seals; that yesterday I was mean to my sister, but now I never; that So-and-So was very poor and please help him; that I want to be good; that I want to go to heaven; that I forgive Rita who was mean to me this morning; that our baby has the measles and always cries; etc., etc.

Then at a signal we all stood. At another signal we all made a very careful and reverential genuflection and stood up again. Then we looked at the tabernacle and said together: "Good-bye, dear Jesus." Some wanted to run to the door, but that was strictly against the law. They had to walk slowly, like senior citizens with rheumatism. But the minute they took one step out of the door, it was a free-for-all affair, each man to himself. The idea was to inculcate the difference between being in church and outside the church. They were trained to behave and keep silence the minute they entered the door of the church. The emphasis was on the Real Presence. As they grew up, this became a habit and it was gratifying to see how well they kept silence during Mass.

With the children of the upper grades it was different. They had more leeway in my room. Catechism was adapted to their mentality. In the church I alone would talk to the Lord to teach them how to do it when they were alone. They were too self-conscious to address the Lord before others. While they were in catechism, they were seated, but I was invariably standing and moving in their midst. I would get hold of a Bible event and dramatize it. But to do so I needed my arms, legs, and different body postures, besides the different tones of voice. The idea was to keep their eyes fixed on my motions. When I was through telling them how Cain killed Abel, they knew every detail of that macabre scene. When I told them how Joseph was sold by his brothers and how Joseph handled them afterward, they knew it never to forget it. The nativity at Bethlehem, the miracles of our Lord, the Passion, and death on the cross were scenified for them and engraved in their souls like the words on a tombstone.

Saturday nights were for confessions. People came without ringing the church bell. The idea was that Saturday nights they had all evening to come whenever they could, since I was there anyway.

Sunday Mass was something else. I would begin my sermon before the Mass. After I rang the bell, they would start coming slowly, very slowly, the men going to their place and the women to theirs. I would usher the children to open spaces around the altar, because there was no room in the pews, and all the while I was preaching, instructing, explaining the gospel, ushering children here and there till I felt in my bones that there were no more coming. Then I would put everything in a nutshell and I proceeded to vest before everybody (because there was no sacristy) and Mass followed.

Since most of them had come to confession, they came now to Communion while appropriate hymns were sung. Most of the women carried their infants in their arms. Pacifying crying babies was part of the liturgy. Standing at the altar with my arms raised I would tell the Lord that this was His family, His people, the sheep and lambs of His flock; that we sang and prayed and screamed and listened, each one according to his age; that we were all one with Him and to please bless us and love us and take the best care of us now and forever. Amen.

The idea of passing the collection baskets at Sunday Masses did not surface till around 1955, when the people were getting wages for their work in the canneries. Bishop Gleeson wrote to us priests in the bush that we should start teaching them gradually, so they would become conscious of their obligation to their church. I could not muster enough intestinal fortitude to break such horrible news.

Their idea had been always to beg, beg, beg from the church. When the first missionaries had arrived, they had had to bribe the mothers to have their babies baptized by offering them a few yards of calico, chewing tobacco, a little bag of tea, whatever. We had a supply of medicines and at times we received sacks of used clothes that we invariably gave away. Thus they grew up with the idea that the church was an agency to give things away to the natives.

When in 1959 Alaska became a sovereign state of the Union, I stood up in church and told them that now they were the masters of their own destiny (high-sounding words) and that this meant that from now on the church was theirs, absolutely theirs, and it was up to them to keep it in good shape, to build a better one if need there be, to contribute every Sunday with a donation, etc. Since there were no baskets on hand, we used an empty cigar box that had somehow landed in my room, because I never smoked. Next Sunday the cigar box was passed. It brought in twenty-nine cents. Not bad for a start.

I had to live seven days and seven nights on those twenty-nine cents—plus a few others of my own!

The all-time low was reached that fateful Sunday when the cigar box brought in twenty cents: one dime and two nickels. But things improved. The ordinary Sunday would bring in $1.25. I remember that Easter Sunday when it brought a grand total of twenty-five dollars. I was sure then that I was in business, but my joy did not last long.

A character from out of town, who had been present at the Mass and had seen such an outflow of capital, watched me leave Alakanuk for Emmonak and tried his luck. Sure enough he broke into my room that evening. Upon my return I found the money gone. I had also two bottles of altar wine that were gone. Inside by the door I saw a pair of new shoes I always kept under my bed. He had planned to take them, but at the last minute, with the money and the wine in his hands, he forgot them. He was given a ticket out of town and I never saw him again. My parishioners never stole anything from me, as far as I remember. I must say, though, that I kept the altar wine in the post office under the care of my good friend Pete Jorgensen, who kept it faithfully under his bed. Wine was a temptation too strong to overlook.

And speaking of Pete Jorgensen. He had come from Denmark as a boy. It was a complete break from the old country, because I don't think he ever wrote to Denmark after he landed in Minnesota. When the Spanish-American War broke out, he was a lanky six-footer looking for work. Not old enough to join the army, he lied about his age and was taken in with no more questions asked. His regiment, or his company or whatever it was, mutinied in the green plains of Georgia where they were drilling in preparation to go overseas. The mutiny could not have been more simple. Off limits there was a saloon where the soldiers gathered. The bartender was a tough character with the build of a weight lifter, short tempered, and with little love for human beings. One day news came to the barracks that this character had beaten unconscious two little soldiers. Immediately word was passed around that the bartender had to be suspended by the neck instantly before he would beat up other soldiers. A large group began to form. The officers heard about it. A squadron of cavalrymen with naked sabers was dispatched to avert the hanging. The soldiers ran as fast as they could to reach the saloon and hang the man, but they were overtaken by the cavalrymen and brought back to the barracks, where they were put under arrest.

Pete was not one of the runners. He was rather following the runners from a distance with his hands in his pockets, just curious to see his first hanging. But he was also rounded up and locked in the barracks. Anyway, weeks passed and the military judges could not find out who the leaders were. The men would not talk. But just at that impasse Spain surrendered. With the joy of victory, the army quit pressing charges and all were sent home honorably.

When I met Pete, he looked at me curiously and wanted to know if I was a real Spaniard, or if I was Mexican or Cuban or something else. When I told him that I was born and raised in Spain proper, he took off his cap, shook hands warmly and said: "Well, what do you know. I am getting one hundred dollars a month as a veteran of the Spanish-American War supposedly for killing Spaniards, and you are the first and only Spaniard I have ever seen."

My friendship with Pete became quite strong as time went on. He was a widower with a little son, David, who grew up and married Ruth. I married them and Papa Pete threw quite a party.

Pete was a fine cook. He had me at his table at the smallest excuse. I would get a note from him saying that he had a moose roast in the oven too big for him and he needed my help. "Be sure to be here no later than five." He baked fine cakes. When I got up to go home, he would fill my pockets with delicacies. He would say, "If it wasn't for the Spaniards, I would be starving"; he felt that I should share in what he was getting for killing Spaniards. Everybody loved Pete. On Christmas he had one present for every Alakanuker. Where did he get the money? Besides his pension as a war veteran, he had the post office. If this were not enough, he was given by Jack Emel the job of finding suitable fishing places and putting the fishermen there; this also brought in a sizable chunk of money. So he was not hurting for money, but he was most generous with it.

When he became eighty years old, we sat at table and decided that I would send to the Fairbanks newspapers an account of his many deeds in his first eighty years. But Pete in his youth had been such a roughneck that I did not have the heart to detail all that and we called it off. He had been in the Dawson gold mines at the turn of the century and then had gone back and forth in Alaska making an honest dollar in a tough environment. Although Pete was not a Catholic, the priest who succeeded me felt that he deserved an honorable funeral in the church. I heard about his death and to this day I pray for him with heartfelt devotion. I used to tell him that I was one of the few Spaniards who survived his fierce onslaught on my countrymen.

In Alakanuk, I again talked Bishop Gleeson's ear off. He had come for confirmations, and while he was there the weather turned bad. There was no flying, so he got stuck with me in my one-room so-called rectory. Two solid days, the two of us alone. Since he was a bishop, I assumed that he would prefer to talk about spiritual things, so I spoke at length of what I had garnered reading the lives of the saints. The third day I could talk only till 2:00 P.M., when the pilot came in to say that there was a break in the weather and he was about to take off. He helped carry the suitcases of the bishop, and I was left all alone in my kitchen.

Less than one hour had passed when I heard a knock at my door. I opened it and there was the bishop with his suitcases. In his quiet way he just said, "Am back for another conference." They had taken off, but a huge black cloud had come upon them threatening to engulf them; so the pilot turned back in a hurry.

Actually, it was not true that the bishop would not talk. I recall several times when the bishop did most of the talking. But as a rule he gave people a chance to say all they wanted.

With his correspondence he was also short and to the point. Seldom did his letters contain two pages. They were few and far between to start with and they usually covered half a page. A couple of times I went over them sentence by sentence to see if there were any idle words. I found none. Everything that had to be said was said in as few words as possible.

I had a friend who remarked how much time people waste saying many things that really mean very little. Suppose, he said, that you got a letter from heaven signed by God with just these words, "Dear son, you will be saved. Good-bye." What need was there to say anything about the weather and so forth? That line said all that was important to you. The fly in the ointment is that we are not God, neither can anyone reasonably expect such a letter from heaven, so in the meantime we will continue doing business as usual. Listeners will listen and talkers will talk.

Talkers have many advantages; they can talk themselves out of many a jam. There was a Frenchman who was condemned to death for his crimes. He told the French king that he would teach his horse to talk French if he were given a one-year reprieve. The king liked the idea of talking to his horse, so he granted the criminal a one-year stay of execution. A friend asked the criminal why in the world had he come up with such a crazy idea. The criminal answered that he had now a whole year of freedom, and in that year many things could happen: he could die in bed for one thing, or the king might die, or the horse could learn to speak French.

18

Emmonak

Emmonak means "Black Fish," but the spelling is very bad. The closest to the Eskimo sound of the word should be *Emangak* and that was the way it appeared on the maps for a while. But when it became a post office, a local resident who was poor in spelling furnished the present one; once the post office adopts a spelling, that is it.

When I saw Emmonak in 1935 there were five cabins. With the cannery built nearby by the N.C. Co., people began to move in. Emmonak grew by leaps and bounds. The chapel I built for fifteen families soon became totally inadequate. A bigger one was built after I left.

The whole Yukon Delta is made of alluvial soil built since past ages. It is all silt with not one pebble. The river banks cave; the river channels change; sandbars in time become river islands covered with willows; it is almost impossible to find a place for a permanent village because nothing is permanent there. Yet the only logical place for a village is on the river bank. There are no roads. Why not build roads? Because there is no gravel. How about importing gravel? That would take an act of Congress. The natives have solved this problem by moving their houses farther back as the banks continue caving.

The people of Emmonak liked that location, near the sea and with miles upon miles of brush, ponds, lakes, and swamps for the geese, the muskrats, the mink, and the rabbits, to say nothing of the black fish that gave the village its name.

The years I spent with those people were—seen in retrospect—years of peace and great satisfaction. There was a good core of solid, substantial, enlightened parishioners who made my staying in their midst quite pleasant. I was seldom alone in my room. They would come in, say hello, sit down wherever they saw fit, and I would continue typing as if my own brother or child had come in.

They knew that I loved to talk and they were great listeners. Once I was telling a married man about Spain and Spain's customs. I asked him how did he imagine Spain. He took another puff at his cigarette, looked at the ceiling, became lost in reflection, took another puff, and said: "To me Spain is a small island with little houses that have roofs made of straw." He returned to his puffing.

As I watched the smoke of his cigarette go up, I said to myself: "Gone in smoke are the buildings of the Phoenicians; the fortresses of the Carthaginians; the roads and bridges of the Romans; the *alcazars* of the Arabs; the castles of the Spaniards and their gothic cathedrals. Good-bye Granada, Barcelona, Madrid, and the rest. Poor Toledo."

I mention this to describe the level of our conversations. That gentleman was a good trapper, was raising a lovely family, knew a great deal about carpentry; he was a substantial citizen. But when it came to converse in the leisure of the evening after a day's work, I had to assume that his knowledge was limited to making a living in the surrounding environment. Period. The first missionaries faced this problem. Even after they understood the language, or after the natives learned English, the conversation had to be carried on a level so inferior to their academic training, that they had to have recourse to books where they could soar above the nitty-gritty of catching seals and skinning a muskrat.

I spoke with many white men married to native women. Many of those women had never been to school. I asked the men—if I was not intruding—which were the advantages and disadvantages of marrying native women. The general consensus was that there were many advantages. For instance, those women were hard workers who helped a great deal with their ability to snare rabbits, cut and dry fish, make their own clothes and boots, chop wood, and so on. They were meek and humble, easy to please, not a bit expensive, and when they had a baby they did not ask to go to Oklahoma to show the baby to the grandparents. These were tremendous advantages. The men saw those women as real treasures.

But then came the one and only disadvantage: They were no company. The white husband in that solitude of Alaska with the long dark winters craved for conversation. He had a radio that said that

Hitler had invaded Czechoslovakia. Mussolini had moved Italian troops to the Austrian border. Poland fell. The Germans pierced the Maginot Line. And so forth. The white husband is desperate for conversation and an exchange of views on all this. But his wife is squatting on the floor skinning a rabbit, and she cannot tell the difference between Hitler and a rowboat, between the Maginot Line and a seagull. So he walls himself behind a solid barricade of national magazines and listens to the radio in utter loneliness.

In time, though, things begin to change. For one thing, the white husband's children spoke English like their father. Schools were built. These half-breed beautiful girls married white men. Their children graduated from high school. That was the end of rabbit skinning while squatting on the floor.

The missionaries of today do not have to confront that loneliness of yore. I used to get much consolation from the thought that Jesus Christ, the Son of God, had to deal with illiterate peasants and fishermen. His desire to converse with His peers could not be satisfied; He had recourse to spending the night in prayer with His Father, who certainly was His equal as God and was greater than He was as a man. Meditating on Jesus' speaking in parables to peasants gave me much courage while telling my own stories to the children and to the grown-ups.

A priest has a fairly good academic education. His terminology in his everyday conversation could tend to be rather high-brow stuff. This goes well when he presides over a congregation of professional men. But with the Eskimos and Indians of old he was apt to feel utterly inadequate. The mystery to me is that we never had problems with priests drinking to excess in that environment of solitude, long winters, and privations. This speaks well for the mettle of such priests while God's grace has to be given the credit it deserves.

The church of Emmonak did not have a bell; instead I had a fog-horn portable box that did the trick. In the midst of winter when nights seem interminable and sunlight is negligible, I would get up at 6:30 A.M. and build a fire. When the place was warm, I would put on my fur parka, fur cap, fur mittens, skin knee-boots, and out I went carrying my fog-horn. Often enough there would be a bright moon in a starry sky. Temperature was well below zero, some days worse than others. The town was dead in its sleep. Silence prevailed all around. I felt that it was a crime to wake people up. But they had agreed that Mass in the morning during the week should be before eight, because they had to prepare breakfast for the men who had to go hunting. So I would blow the horn.

This noise precipitated a general howl from the innumerable dogs tied in the surrounding little willows. This howling was heard far better than the horn, so there was no need to invest money in a regular bronze bell.

Soon people would start coming in. They were covered with furs and invariably one heard the word *a-la-pa*, which was whispered because they were in church. *A-la-pa* means "brrrr . . . I am frozen," translated rather liberally. Watching those people coming in that cold took away from me any thought that I was a martyr. God was speaking to me through them.

If the snow was falling, as was often the case, I stood at the door first with a shovel to remove the snow piled during the night and also with a broom to sweep the snow off the boots of all comers. Otherwise the snow on those boots would melt during Mass and I would have a puddle on the floor. By the way, if in spite of my broom there was still a puddle or many little ones, I would wait till they froze during the day when there was no heat, and then I would chop them with an axe and remove them with a dustpan. So very simple! Necessity is the mother of invention.

Sometimes a woman would bring a paper bag full of homemade buns for my breakfast. They had a hard crust that I just loved to crush with my teeth and they tasted so very good. I took them as a gift that the Lord Himself was giving me.

Emmonak was then full of very interesting characters. There was one couple that had been married fifty-two years. I used to visit them partly to see if it was true what was said about them. I was told as a dogma of faith that those two people had never had a disagreement, let alone a quarrel. One day I asked them point blank if it was true. After a moment of silence she opened her mouth and said that sometimes when things went sour and difficulties piled up, she was inclined to raise her voice a little. But as she looked at him and saw him so quiet and so composed, she would lower her voice again and that was the end. I asked him if that was the case. He answered with a smile and a nod. It was true. Still only half convinced I told them the case of a couple in Nebraska who were celebrating their golden jubilee. Reporters went to their house to take their picture and to do a little piece in the local paper about their fifty years of marriage. Again in that case the woman did all the talking.

One reporter asked, "Did you ever have a fight?"

"No, never," she said.

"Never, never?"

"Never, never."

"Do you mean to tell me that you never had a disagreement?"

"We never had a disagreement."

"Do you mean to tell me that you saw eye to eye for fifty years at all times?"

"Yes, sir."

A moment of silence and incredulity followed. She broke it by resting her hand on his knee—they were sitting together—looking at his eye, and saying, "Except, of course, for those few times when each one wanted the other one to drop dead." That broke the tension and now the record was set aright.

But this was not the case with our Emmonak couple. Neither ever had wanted the other one to drop dead. No, sir.

Visiting the Emmonak homes was always an educational exercise. The man was usually away hunting, trapping, getting wood, or visiting the black fish traps. If he was at home, he was making a net or a fish trap. She was busy cooking or mending boots or clothes or skinning a seal. Small children were very much in evidence and they were liberally scolded in English and in Eskimo because they always seemed to be doing the wrong thing. But all was done in an atmosphere of general goodness and love that permeated the whole procedure.

I would sit on a gasoline box and feel at home as if I were a member of the family. The natives were very reticent with strangers. But once you belonged, they cast aside all care and opened up in a beautiful outflow of everyday happenings and concerns. They would ask me to do something about So-and-So who was doing this or that; nobody did anything about it, though something should be done soon because the wife had said this and that and he had said that and this, etc. They wanted to know why So-and-So was not going to church, as if I had to know. To them the priest was a man of God, and they generally respected him and loved him.

On Sundays when the church was filled to capacity I had a long sermon where I answered directly or indirectly many of the questions put to me in those home visits. As to the problem of drinking, I told them that if they ever saw me drunk, then they all had general permission to do likewise. We looked at each other in silence and that was that.

In that all-Eskimo population there was one white man who was a Catholic. His name was Bill O'Connor. Born in Saint Paul, Minnesota, Bill had grown up in Portland, Oregon, with two sisters who had married and moved to California. He was born—I believe—in 1869, so he was far from being a spring chicken when we met. His mother had done all she could to make a priest out of him as a teenager. But, he told me, he had had so many thousands of square miles of wild oats to sow, that the priesthood had been the last thing for him, although he was and had been and would always be a Catholic—so help me God.

He must have been extremely handsome as a boy. He said that in some great public festivity in Portland six boys had been chosen to flank and march alongside a float through the main streets; he had been one of them: trim, clean-cut, straight, and with an almost defiant look forward.

By 1897 he was already in Dawson, Canada, to dig gold and become a millionaire and then to go around the world several times. Those were the days of the budding Manifest Destiny, and he wanted to see and be seen abroad. But destiny played tricks with Bill. As a gold digger he was an absolutely total failure. But he found out that as a poker player he was near perfect. He figured that he would let the others do the digging and finding gold, and he would rake the chips at the poker table. This finding proved to be providential for him, because he never again in his life looked at a pick or a shovel other than to shovel snow off his front door.

From Dawson he moved to Nome, where gold was found and where he made a good and honest living raking chips in the casino. He showed me his hand to prove it. The outside of the little finger of his right hand together with the edge of the hand still had a hard, callous skin. I begged him almost with tears to please not shake hands with Saint Peter at the Pearly Gates, because if Peter felt the hardness of that spot in his hand, he would ask for sure how come he had such callous skin there; Bill would have to tell the truth, the whole truth, and nothing but the truth, and certainly Saint Peter would frown and wonder if there was room in heaven for hardened gamblers.

After many ramblings all over Alaska, Bill came to land—of all places—at the mouth of the Yukon in the village of Kwiguk, where he became postmaster. By then he had married Annie, half Eskimo and half Russian, who gave him a son but for a short time. The son died. To make up for the dead son, he adopted an intelligent boy who grew up in our Akulurak school and was known as Teddy. Teddy married, but both he and his wife died. Everybody was dying of consumption those days. Poor Bill was left alone with Annie and a team of three husky dogs, well fed and good pullers.

In the summer he fished and put up a good product which was advertised as Epicurean's Delight. Whether or not people knew what *Epicurean* meant did not matter to him; he knew what it meant, and that was what mattered. I tasted it and must say that it was good fish.

Bill had a chess board with him at all times, whether he was at home or fishing or traveling by dog team. His greatest joy was to find a chess player. At first I had no chance with him. As time went by, he began to lose games till the time came when he lost interest because he was losing too many games. Chess needs youth like boxing, though some chessmen are still good in their fifties. But Bill had passed that long before.

With time he also had to retire from the post office which he turned over to the Scandinavian Chris Lauridsen. I said many a Mass in Bill's cabin, between Emmonak and Kwiguk on the bank of a slough that bore his name. Bill would kneel on one knee and rest his hands on the other with the head bent down in total humility and adoration. When the chapel of Emmonak was completed, he would go there to Mass and to chat with me.

I mentioned that he had two sisters in California; they had not seen him since he had left before the turn of the century. They wrote to him often, begging him to visit them, but he refused to comply. They sent him money for the trip time and again, but he used that money for something else.

In 1952 I was sent to Mexico to attend an international mission congress. I told Bill and I added that I was planning to process my visa at the Mexican consulate of Los Angeles. His eyes beamed and he told me to be sure to locate his two sisters who were living at a certain address in Chula Vista somewhere in Pasadena. It took me one whole day to locate them, but I did find them living in a castle-like mansion. When I knocked, one of them opened the door. They had been notified by Bill that a priest from Alaska would visit them soon and to receive me as they would receive him.

What followed was hard for me to believe. Both were in their eighties. One had married a rich Canadian who had left her everything he had, and the other was still doing scripts for the movies and also was an expert in landscaping. The mansion had innumerable rooms up and down stairs. One room was a sort of a museum with antiques, valuable pieces of furniture, coffers inlaid with ivory designs, and so forth. They wanted me to see it all so I could entice Bill to come and live with them at their expense for the rest of his life. Everything would be his if he would come.

Then I had to sustain a barrage of questions. How was Bill? How was his wife? What type of a woman was she? Were they in good health? Did they have any needs? How was his house? Did he go to church? Did he have friends? Wasn't he talking about them, his sisters who loved him so much and were so anxious about him? They had even suggested to him that they would go to see him, but he would not hear of it; why did he act that way?

I don't get tongue-tied easily. But there in front of those two old ladies in their eighties who had locked the rest of the mansion and had come down to just one room near the kitchen, who walked dragging their feet (it was obvious that their days were numbered) . . . and thinking of Bill back in his one-room cabin near Emmonak living with Annie who was also old and talked to herself most of the time . . . I cleared my throat and began to give reasons, excuses, explanations all mixed up. I assured them that I was going to grab Bill by the neck and would not let go till he solemnly promised me to give all he had to the church and to leave for Pasadena the very next day. One of the sisters stood on the tips of her toes and gave me a kiss in gratitude. Anyway I assured them that Bill still had rosy cheeks. They readily believed it because he had been the most handsome boy in the neighborhood. And so we parted.

Back in Emmonak I got an outboard motor, crossed the wide river, and knocked at Bill's door. He had been told by letter that I had been in Pasadena. Poor Bill fortified himself with a clean handkerchief and sat by me almost touching my knees with his because he was a little hard of hearing and did not want to miss one solitary word. As I was describing what I'd seen, he kept wiping his eyes till his hanky was all wet. When I was through, he took the floor and explained to me what I already had suspected. He had left for Alaska telling the family that he was going to strike it rich, very rich, etc., etc. Now he was here in this tiny cabin living off his pension from the post office and social security, and beyond that he did not have one dime. He could not overcome his humiliation. Then Annie would not fit at all in his sisters' world. Very true. So he was not leaving—no and no.

Good Bill; he was so much fun! When he was in Fairbanks visiting, he called a butcher's shop by phone: "Is this the butcher?"

"Yes, sir."

"Would you by any chance have pig's feet?"

"Yes, I do."

"And cow's tongue?"

"Yes."

"And lamb's loin and rump?"

"Oh, yes, I have."

"Well, mister, you must look like a monster"; then he would hang up and feel sorry for the butcher and would apologize to heaven for the words the butcher might utter.

In time he and Annie were received into the Pioneers Home at Sitka, where the state has one of several nursing homes for its senior citizens. In my visit to Juneau I boarded an amphibious plane to Sitka where I spent one day just to visit Bill and Annie. They were in the same room with separate beds. Annie was moving around mumbling something, but Bill was confined to a wheelchair. It was going to be our last visit and we both knew it. It was hard to part.

One day I heard the news that he had died. He died in June. Had he lived till September, he would have been one hundred years old—the sturdy oak who played poker and knelt all through Mass to bribe Saint Peter. When he became ninety, I sent a story about him to the paper of Fairbanks. The paper published it and sent me fourteen dollars, which came in handy for coffee.

I heard time and again that there is no place like Alaska to build strong friendships. The one Bill and I built can be shown as proof.

19

Eskimo Life and Lore

Gradually, I became part of those villages. To avoid idleness I made a family tree of each village, or, rather, I made a forest of trees with their branches interlocking. Beginning with the grand patriarchs already dead and buried, I showed the relationship existing between those living there and then.

It was a moment of great satisfaction to me when a young man came to my room to ask what was the relationship—if any— between him and Agnes Kuspak. I closed my eyes for a few seconds and opened them to look at his bewildered face and tell him that they were second cousins.

Then I asked the question: Were they planning to get married? Well, the man was not too sure, but he might give it a serious thought. Suddenly I sank in amazement, because Agnes had been the first child I had baptized in that village. Now she could drop in anytime to be married by me in the same spot where I had baptized her. So I was getting old. Old enough to be a grandpa. The very thought sent a shock through my whole system.

In a matter of months Patrick Murphy came with his fiancée, asking me to marry them. I remembered the day when his aunt Irene had brought him wrapped up in a towel begging me to baptize him. It had been March the seventeenth, so he had to be named Patrick. I stood by him now and he was easily one inch taller than I. Yes, I said to myself, how wonderful to be young, wasn't it? It certainly was.

Patrick got his *Murphy* in a very strange way. His father Pete had gone with Bro. Murphy to Holy Cross to get potatoes. They had stopped in Marshall, where they were invited to vote in elections. When Pete had given his Eskimo name to the president of the board, a white old-timer with a temper, the man had said that he would be hanged if he could spell that name; instead he had written *Murphy*, since Pete was traveling with Bro. Murphy. Pete had returned to the village announcing that now his name was Murphy; whereupon his relatives automatically took that name.

Poor Patrick! He went with his family to work in the Alaska Railroad where he was making good wages. One day he was found dead with a bullet—or maybe bullets—in the head. When the Eskimos get booze, they get into trouble.

When I began to baptize the babies of the babies I had baptized, I realized that I had to stop kidding myself. I was getting old. But then I suddenly got used to the idea of getting old and it hardly bothered me anymore. I went merrily along, marrying couples and baptizing their babies. The State of Alaska allows first cousins to marry, but it forbids an uncle to marry his niece or an aunt to marry her nephew. This caused a trauma to the uncle and niece who came to me to marry them. The marriage between first cousins is not uncommon. Fortunately, with the mobility of people, this inbreeding is decreasing sharply.

In my visits to the homes and the visits of the people in my living room, little by little I garnered a wealth of information about their habits, beliefs, practices, and similar folklore.

Polygamy was unheard of, except in some isolated cases—very few—where a tough medicine man would have more than one wife and would defy anyone to stop him. But they had heard of cases where a man would dismiss a wife who would give him nothing but daughters. They wanted males, at least one male. Since it is not the woman, but the man, who is responsible for the sex of the children, according to medical discoveries, it was an unfair practice. But then life is not always fair either.

The worst thing that could happen to an Eskimo was to die without children. We instinctively think of the help that the son would be to his father in fishing, trapping, hunting, and getting wood for the stove, but this was not the main reason. The father's main reason was the fear that no one would feed and clothe him after death. When a man died, he passed into another world where he still needed food and clothes which could not be obtained there, but had to be supplied to him from here. Once a year, at least, the families got together in a house. They would bring their children and sit them in a circle. A man went outdoors and called the spirits of the dead relatives to hurry up and come, because everything was ready: It was assumed that the spirits were coming; indeed they were in the house already.

Then the ceremony began. A man thought of, say, his dead father or dead son and then looked at a child. The spirit of the dead man would enter into the child. The man then gave that child a small piece of fish, a teaspoon of tea, and a cracker. That food fed the spirit. Then the man gave the same child a pair of gloves or a pair of socks. This went also to the spirit and kept him warm for the next year. Every adult in the gathering would feed and clothe likewise his own dead relatives. Once the ceremony came to an end, everyone felt pious, all felt happy; they had done their duty to their ancestors.

Some people were not satisfied with this yearly ceremony. They were so exceedingly pious and generous that every time they sat to a meal, they would drop sort of casually some crumbs or small pieces of fish and likewise some tea on the floor, preferably in the cracks of the flooring, while mentally thinking of certain dead relatives who might be hungry or shivering. Considering this belief, it is easy to understand why everyone wants to have a son or sons who will take care of their otherworldly needs.

While women could also help, it is the duty of the sons to provide these needs to the dead.

Also in the old days when an Eskimo became too old to move around, a strange way was found to eliminate him "painlessly," though I can hardly think of any treatment that could bring in so much anguish. The situation was this: The family had to move to another camp—fish camp, berry-picking camp, trapping camp, whatever. The old Eskimo could not walk anymore. The family had no means of transportation. To leave him behind meant certain death. What to do? They would bring the man (or woman) to the frozen river just before the break-up with some dry fish to prolong the survival. When the ice would break, the old Eskimo would be carried away sitting on ice. Was not that certain death? Well, yes. But there was a vague hope that some fisherman might spot him and rescue him and take care of him.

I was told that every year in the months of February, March, and April there had been famine in the old days. They had lived on black fish only, with negligible nourishing value. An old man told me that when he'd been a little boy his mother had given him one half of a frozen black fish per day. That would be like one small cracker. It was the survival of the fittest. They had to struggle to find food. An invalid old man became a threat to all, since all he did was eat without bringing in food. Likewise, those days people married close relatives for this strange reason: Marriage alone caused no relationship. In other words, husband and wife were not related to each other at all, unless they were related before the marriage. So, when the famine came, the "unrelated" wife became an intruder who ate the food of the family. Therefore she was resented, frowned upon, mistreated in the hope that she would leave to go back to her own folks.

These practices were the cause of other strange practices. When a boy was born, he was immediately given the name of a deceased relative. It meant that most likely this boy had now the soul of that relative. For two reasons, this boy became automatically a king, a tyrant, an idol to be adored: a) you would not scold or spank or sadden a dead relative, and b) this child would grow and it was hoped that, when the parents became decrepit or paralyzed, he would not put them on the ice to die but would have pity on them, remembering how much he had been loved as a child.

When I began to hear confessions in Eskimo, I was startled to hear that the penitent was sorry for having scolded his child. Was it a sin to scold a child? Oh, yes, Father, we think that it is a sin. I would think back to my Spanish father, who raised me with the rod so I would not grow spoiled.

Here is an example. I was visiting a family that had a four-year-old son. The kid took a stick and began to beat the stove pipe with all his might. The noise of the blows gave him much pleasure, but the same noise made it impossible for us to talk. I told the mother to tell him to stop. She went to him and whispered in his ears. The kid laughed, said something, and renewed the noisy pounding. The mother came to me and said in a resigned voice: "He say he no want." Then, seeing my astonishment, she told me to please stop him myself. I made for the kid and there must have been fury in my eyes, because he threw away the stick and ran to Mama for shelter. Peace had been restored, but at my own risk. Now the spirit in the kid could be angry at me. So whatever might happen to me now, I had asked for it. What I asked and what I got was a bit of silence so we could talk. Never mind the spirit.

This Eskimo practice enabled me to explain to them the Catholic doctrine of purgatory. I remember the first Sunday I sprang on them this practice of feeding and clothing the dead. They were sure that I knew nothing about it and they would not dream of informing me. To their surprise I praised them for the practice. It was a most pious ceremony. Their concern for the dead was beautiful.

Fortunately for all concerned, our holy mother, the church, had better ways of feeding and clothing the dead. We have the Masses for the dead in which we beg God to apply the merits of Christ on the cross to those souls that might be still in purgatory; once the soul enters heaven, there is no longer need of any clothing and feeding. God Himself feeds and clothes them, making them share in His divine nature. God has no need in His eternity of our help. On the contrary, it is we who need His divine help, and we get it when we offer Mass for those souls who have not entered heaven because they are still detained in purgatory, where they get the "finishing touches" to become all clean and pure and beautiful and so enter heaven; nothing stained or impure in any manner can enter that heavenly city. The merits of Christ and the purifying effect of His divine blood, when applied to a soul in purgatory, help the soul and prepare her for a quicker delivery.

Perhaps you people do not quite grasp this doctrine just now, but it will sink gradually. Pray that God may illumine your minds and hearts on this. Instead of dropping pieces of fish in the cracks of your floor to feed the dead, come and ask me to say Masses for them. And teach your children to do likewise. Help the priest to spread the Catholic doctrine. We all have to be apostles. God will reward you for it; He said that he will reward a glass of water given to a thirsty person in His name.

I was constantly discovering new things. Why did some people chop wood on the ice of the river instead of on the bank where the wood was piled? They did it because of the superstitious belief that when someone dies, his spirit flutters lively in all directions, seeking a just-born baby to enter. This spirit does this for exactly three days. If in those three days he finds no baby to land in, he disappears. But the spirit cannot go over ice—only over land.

Now then, if you are chopping wood on land, you may swing your axe just as the spirit goes over that very spot and you may hit him. That, of course, would make the spirit exceedingly mad and he would get at you sooner or later. By chopping on the ice, you can't hit him.

Likewise, women do not sew for three days after someone's death. They may pinch the spirit with the needle, as those spirits are very quick in their mobility over the air.

Where do those spirits go? Here I found conflicting news. On the one hand, it is never too late to call them back when a baby is born so they may incarnate in that baby. When a baby is born, or if ten babies are born, that baby—and maybe the ten babies—will be given the name of the dead person.

On the other hand, the dead go to their reward, good or bad. Is it like heaven and hell? Well, not exactly, but it is the same doctrine of reward and punishment. Bad Eskimos, when they die, find the next life a real hell. Everything is stacked against them. Everything turns against them. They go hunting and fishing, but they return home empty handed, thus they are perennially hungry. The weather will be always bad for them. They will not find any wood to keep warm. Nobody will be friendly to them. That is sure hell.

These bad Eskimos had gone through life being mean to animals and to things. They killed their game with hatred and skinned them without care or compassion. They chopped willows when they were angry and landed the axe with anger. They kicked the grass when they were walking. Now in the hereafter, the souls of those animals and of those things are waiting to get even. Those spirits will now give such a man a very bad time.

And what will happen to a good Eskimo when he dies? Just the opposite. He goes hunting and finds more game than he can throw sticks at. His table will be always groaning with fresh food. The weather will be simply tops: no rain or snow or wind or too hot, but just right. He will hardly need any wood to keep warm and if he needs some he will find it everywhere. Then the spirits of the animals will smile at him and shake hands with him because he killed them without hatred and skinned them with a smile and carefully. So, you see, Father, it pays to be good.

A schoolgirl from Akulurak once told me that the son of Mr. Kanirtok had died. She'd been surprised at what she'd seen. The old man had spent most of the night before the body of his son lying on the floor, and he'd never tired of repeating the same thing. What was he saying? He was telling his dead son to please not come back, because he was not needed to chop wood or to bring black fish or to hunt or to trap or to fish or to feed the dogs or to bring water from the ice hole or to make nets or to fix the sled or to make a harness for the dogs or to make black fish traps or to dance in the *kazim*, etc. The old man was covering all bases. The apparition of a dead man paralyzes a person. He wanted nothing to do with a dead man, so he was telling his seventeen-year-old son to please do not ever appear to him under any excuse. You see, the son might return occasionally to ask his dad if he was needed for any of the above-mentioned occupations.

In some graveyards of old villages can be seen even today old sleds, coffee pots, old rusty guns, rusty knives, and so forth. This is proof of their belief in the immortality of the soul. When I asked why did they leave these things, they retorted by asking why do white men put flowers on the graves of their loved ones. Again the clash of cultures. I simply shut up, because I knew they were going to say that the dead do not smell flowers, if they cannot use their knives or their coffee pots.

I remember the day a man died on the other side of the river where fishermen were cutting fish. It was running time for the salmon. I brought the body in a rowboat across the river in full view of the people. My intention was to build a coffin and thus make it easier for the poor widow. But when they realized that it was a dead man I was carrying over the water, they were overcome by fear. It was obvious that the fish would not come that way anymore, but would find other rivers to come up to spawn. And fish was their main source of revenue. This priest has ruined us!

I assured them that God would take good care of them and would send them lots of fish; making coffins for dead people was an act of mercy and God rewards the acts of mercy. Sure enough, that season was one of the best; they got all the fish they wanted and then some. So in this way they found out that their superstitious fears were totally unfounded.

They also rejoiced when they heard thunder during the fishing season. Why? Because thunder scares the fish in the ocean and they run for cover by coming to the river where they can be caught in the nets.

Superstitions die hard. Hospitals skip number thirteen on their floors. Nobody wants to be a patient in room thirteen.

An old Eskimo told me that they believed that one person can kill another by thought. He mentioned a man known to us who reputedly had killed four brothers in a family. Those brothers just took sick one after the other and in time all died relatively young. But how? Very simple: When this man feels indisposed, he knows that death is trying to get him. So what does he do? He mentally places another man between him and the coming death. Thus, when death comes to kill him, she finds instead another guy and she kills that guy. Once she does the killing, death is satisfied and leaves. This man succeeded in placing in front of him the members of a family he hated, one at a time, till he killed them all. But why didn't the surviving members of that family confront this man and make sure that he stopped that grisly business? I never got the answer to that one.

I was told that a certain man was dying and died, but before he expired he told people repeatedly that he knew very well who was killing him. He did not mention anyone, yet all knew the killer. Amazing!

An Eskimo told me matter of fact that when he was a little boy his mother would strip him and smear his body with seal oil without leaving one square inch dry. Why? Because she had heard that someone had died, and that meant that death was around trying to kill a few more. Seal oil made the skin very slippery; when death hit that body, she would slide and go on seeking someone else. Medicine men were running the show those days and they constructed a whole set of tenets that people were careful to follow.

For a reason I could never understand, the first child those days had to be born in the shed of the hut, never inside the hut or cabin; the mother had to deliver the baby all alone. If it was in the dead of winter with a raging snowstorm, it made no difference. They would put some dry grass over the snow or the ice in the unheated shed and there the baby was born. The poor girl could be fourteen and might never have seen the birth of a baby. It did not matter. The law was the law.

My good friend Francis Lee told me that he was the second child. But medicine man Katmigak gave the order that this second child also had to be born in the shed though it was in the middle of January, the month of the Big Moon. When Francis was delivered over the snow covered with grass, Katmigak told the mother not to touch the child until Katmigak had made three invocations to the spirits of the netherworld.

These were the invocations: a) that this boy grow to be a good hunter, b) that he may have many sons, and c) that he may never fall. Therefore his name was to be *E-ko-yun-gi-li-nok,* which means "He Cannot Fall." When Francis was already purple and ready to quit breathing, he was taken inside where he was cleaned and clothed. So Francis grew up and a) he was a failure as a hunter and made a living as a carpenter, b) he had only daughters, and c) he fell off my roof and had to be hospitalized for months. I asked him if he still believed in medicine men. He changed the subject.

Are some of these practices still in vogue? No. They are a thing of the past. Today a decrepit old man is a real asset and every member of the family will fight tooth and nail to keep him because he is the beneficiary of a handsome welfare check. If the check is good for, say, two hundred dollars, and all he spends is, say, seventy dollars, the rest is all gravy for the family.

How about those ritual famines that plagued the land every winter? They are also a thing of the past. Now every village has one or more well-stocked stores where the people can get all they want either on a cash-and-carry basis or on credit, because everybody works at some time of the year. Babies are no longer born in frozen sheds with grass over the snow or ice. Medicine men are pretty well gone; instead there are hospitals where sick people get proper attention.

Does a husband who gets only daughters ditch his wife for another who may give him sons? Today Alaska has accepted officially legal divorces, so things are worse in this respect.

Another thing that dies hard is the widespread rumor that an Eskimo will treat a visitor by allowing him to sleep with his wife. We read stories of this sort about the natives of Greenland. We read that if a man goes hunting or trapping for a few weeks and his wife is pregnant, he leaves his pregnant wife with a neighbor and goes trapping with the neighbor's wife. The concept involved here is one of natural kindness in a pagan environment. The pregnant woman would suffer away in the wilderness, so she is given a comfortable igloo with a friendly man. On the other hand, it would be sheer inhumanity and cruelty to expect the hunting Eskimo to be all by himself for three weeks, so his neighbor accommodates him. All think that it is a humane arrangement. That is pagan thinking and a pagan arrangement and God alone will judge pagans. The same God will be harder on those civilized ladies and gentlemen of our so-called Christian cities where wife swapping is becoming a practice that brings chuckles to those who should know better. In the Alaska that I knew, husbands did not treat any visitors to such a practice, though undoubtedly it could possibly have happened when all concerned were drunk. Drunkenness and promiscuity mix quite well.

And how about igloos? Isn't it true that Eskimos live in igloos? Again, Greenland is to be blamed for this canard. In Greenland there are barren regions even close to the water where there is no wood. In the old days those Eskimos had to make do with what they had and they had all the ice they needed to make an igloo. Now the Danish government—a very rich government, indeed—provides them with housing needs if they have any.

All over Alaska I kept asking if anyone knew of people who lived in igloos. The answer was always a flat no. Alaskans live on the river banks where there is wood or on the ocean shores that are teeming with floating logs brought there by the swollen rivers in May and June. The Alaska igloos are dwellings made of timber covered with turf or soil that gives them the appearance of an igloo because they are round on the top. When the snow starts falling, they are covered completely and look exactly like igloos. But inside there is a stove with a chimney sticking out and smoking.

In early days these igloos had no stoves because the natives were too poor and lacked the means to make a stove. The temperature then was kept by body heat of the people huddled inside. There was an opening on top of the roof that was covered with "cloth" made of seal guts sewn together. This "cloth" allowed some light to filter in while it kept the heat inside. The entrance was a very low tunnel. People literally crawled in on their fours, and it had the hide of a deer or a bear for a door.

When the walls of the igloo were covered with a coat of thick frost, everybody was thrown out of the igloo; a fire was built to thaw the frost; the smoke got out through the hole on the roof; the heat coming from the glowing embers was captured by covering the roof hole and everybody crawled in again to a really warm room.

I was amused every time I passed through the heart of the city of Anchorage where an igloo was built for tourists: a clean, neat, pretty igloo made of costly materials. Tourists stood by that igloo or crawled in and out while cameras clicked and everybody smiled. Those were pictures to be mailed to the family back in San Francisco or New York to prove that they were in Alaska having the life of Riley with the Eskimos.

The Spaniards do the same thing with the bullfight industry. Tourists there are clothed like toreros (not toreadors) in front of fierce-looking bulls. The tourist from Germany or America appears terribly impressive brandishing a shining sword as if ready to kill the bull with one blow.

Is this dishonesty? Oh, no; absolutely not. This is legitimate fun. The difference between man and beast (among other differences) is that the beast neither laughs nor can laugh, while a good laugh can keep mankind away from insanity. And anything that helps sanity cannot be all bad. Alaska without igloos makes no sense. Spain without bullfights would be a dull place. New Orleans without a Mardi Gras would be inconceivable. And speaking of animals not laughing, I read that it was a good thing that animals did not laugh, because if they did, they would all die laughing watching us people, which to me seems a bit exaggerated. Some animals would die laughing, that's for sure, but some would survive to keep the species alive.

Do the Eskimos still think that white people are stupid? A good many Eskimos do resent the presence of white people, but they do not think of them as stupid. On the contrary, they think that white people are unbelievably smart. Who invented and commercialized the guns, the steel knives, the airplanes, the boats with such powerful engines, the packages of cigarettes, the good booze in beautifully corked bottles, the radios, and the movies? People who invent such things are anything but stupid.

Do the Eskimos resent the presence of white people, really? Well, yes and no. An Eskimo girl prefers to marry a white man because this means better clothes, better home, and daily breakfast of bacon and eggs. But even these amenities are beginning to be provided by native men, especially those with white blood in their veins. The white man is resented because he has the better paying jobs. The governor, the judge, the physician, the lawyer, the surgeon, the professor, the businessman, the banker, the author of books, and even the Catholic priest (to enumerate the most conspicuous occupations) are white people. The school teachers in the villages since schools began were all white, though now the Eskimos are taking over.

I was asked why was it that those jobs were invariably held by the whites. I retorted by asking how many years had the natives spent in classrooms. It was a matter of wearing out your elbows over thick books. Were their elbows sore? No. Did they love to study? No. Did they have any diplomas from well-accredited schools? No. Had they spent much personal money doing research in laboratories? No. Could they compete with the educated whites in the use of the English language which is the official language of the land? No. Did they still feel that being unable to speak the Eskimo language was a sign of stupidity? No. Did they still prefer the kayak to an outboard motor boat made of aluminum with tight compartments that made it unsinkable? No.

I was talking once with a white man living in the interior among Indians who said that if the Alaska natives were more numerous and felt that they could do it, they would mutiny against the white man just as the natives of the recently independent African republics were doing. I heard it in silence and kept silent. I was not prepared to agree or to disagree. My own gut feeling is that no such mutiny would happen. But again we are dealing with an if. *If* they were more numerous than the whites. The fact of the matter is that so many white people marry natives that the racial barriers between the two races are crumbling, if they have not crumbled already. Also it is hard for me to see all the aspects of this issue.

My own experience with the Eskimos was one of placid commingling. The twenty-two years I spent on the Yukon Delta were years of harmony—as much harmony as can be had in this valley of tears. I always felt that I had been accepted. My living quarters were open to all. Their homes were open to me. We chatted wherever we met, indoors or outdoors. They respected me and I saw them as equals.

Seeing them as equals was an imperfection for me. In my spiritual training I had been taught to approach people as an inferior to a superior, to imitate Christ who came to serve, not to be served, and washed the feet of His disciples; I had to follow His example by loving all people as Christ had and by being ready to wash anybody's feet. In some obscure or not so obscure way the natives under my pastoral care felt that I was their servant. They called me to visit sick people and to go and baptize their babies, knowing and taking for granted that I would go, indeed that I *had* to go; what was I there for if not to be at their beck and call?

One Saturday night experience will illustrate this. Next day, Sunday, I would have Mass at 11:00 A.M. in Alakanuk where I was then staying. The mail had come that day. It brought me a fine book that I wanted to read immediately, and, if possible at one session, so I stayed by the stove reading till midnight. The thermometer marked exactly forty below zero. No sooner had I tucked myself in bed, buried under heavy blankets, than heavy knocks at the door told me that I was in for something serious. The man came in and told me to get up and go with him to Emmonak because Vincent was dying and wanted to see me.

"How do you know that he is dying?"

"Because everybody is in his house around his bed."

"What is he dying of?"

"I don't know."

"Is he talking?"

"Yes, he talks."

"Well, then he is not dying."

"Sure he is."

"Did the postmaster call the hospital at Bethel?"

"Yes."

"Is a plane coming to pick him up?"

"Yes, in the morning if the weather is good."

"Well, Vincent was here last Sunday and I saw him go to holy Communion."

"Yes but father, many things can happen in one week."

Touché. He had scored a good point there. Many things can happen to a man in one week. The sagacity and clear thinking of that Eskimo floored me. Now I surely had to get up and go to Emmonak, because if Vincent would die and word spread that the priest had been called but he did not want to get out of bed—if I let him die without the Sacraments—I would have to pack and leave the country at my earliest opportunity. I told the man to wait.

Getting dressed for forty below zero under a starry sky filled with a mist that bespeaks a very low temperature is, and should be, a slow process. Proper underwear, proper woolen clothes, proper footgear, Eddie Bauer's overpants and jacket and cap and mittens. One looks like an astronaut and walks as they did on the moon. When I was ready, we went to the sled the man had ready for me. It was a small thing to be pulled by five scrawny dogs that proved to be heroes by just walking. As I sat in the sled and the dogs felt the weight, they looked back as if begging me to please get out and go back to your bed.

After a few miles over the ice of the Yukon, I thanked God for the clothing I was wearing. The outside of the clothes was frozen, but my skin kept warm from the body heat that could not escape. The stars were twinkling like mad. A mist covered the celestial vault. Not a ripple of wind, not the slightest breeze, thank God. The noise of our sled runners was echoing all over the night enveloping us.

We left the Yukon, tackled the Kwiguk River, and saw the lights of Emmonak way yonder. I was carrying the oils but not the blessed

Sacrament because I had it reserved in the Emmonak chapel. All the way in that cold night I kept in the presence of God begging Him for assistance and for so many things.

We arrived. I entered the cabin of Vincent and saw him peacefully lying in his bunk. What was the matter? His wife answered and said that he had been bleeding through the nose for three hours and they did not know how to stop it. If they could not stop it, he surely would die. Quite so. Had Vincent sent for me? No, Father, he did not. We were thinking that it was too bad that you were not here, so that man said that he would bring you. I sat by Vincent's pillow, heard his confession, and anointed him. The nose was properly plugged and the flow of blood had stopped.

Next morning (or rather that morning after daylight) a plane came and took him to the hospital. I slept on the floor near Vincent. Another team took me to Alakanuk because it was Alakanuk's turn to have Mass that Sunday and all would show up for Mass not knowing that I was not there.

When I reentered my Alakanuk quarters I went straight to the altar to thank the Lord for having sent me and having brought me back in one piece in that cold night over the Yukon ice under those trembling stars. Were the stars trembling of cold? I felt in my soul that the Lord would give me a warm place in heaven for having braved that cold.

A priest is a servant to his parishioners. I mentioned this episode to a man who remarked that now he knew why the church forbids priests to marry. Had I been in bed with my wife when that man had come knocking at the door to tell me to get up and follow him, the lady would have scratched his eyes out. Or if not the eyes, she would have scratched him anyway.

What if next night another Eskimo had shown up at the door with a similar errand? My answer is that our Lord sends us our crosses in a dosage carefully calculated. He knows the strength of our shoulders. A saint with herculean shoulders will get heavy crosses. A saint of moderate strength will get lighter crosses. The ordinary Christian battling to live in the state of grace will get still lighter ones. Leave it to God.

If next night another Eskimo shows up with a similar request, the missionary must trust God and must dress up for the weather and go. If the messenger were drunk, one would have to ask the Holy Spirit for light. If the weather is exceedingly cold, wooden runners should be attached to the natural steel runners of the sled. If the messenger has steel runners perhaps a sled with wooden runners should be borrowed to go faster. Prudence is one of the cardinal virtues. As a matter of fact, without prudence all other virtues can be out of kilter. But then we are warned that heroes and saints throw prudence to the wind; therefore, be not too much concerned with prudence. Where does prudence end and cowardice begin?

To complicate matters we are told that sinning by excess is as bad as sinning by defect. Where is the happy medium? I was talking to Fr. Lawrence Haffie, S.J., who worked on the Kuskokwim River. Christmas came along and he decided to placate the two villages of Aniak and Kalskag by saying the midnight Mass in one place and then jumping in a sled that was waiting for him and riding to the other village. The dogs were supposed to be first-class and so was the driver. But that night the temperature reached extremely low marks. It could have been close to fifty below zero. The dogs were not pulling properly for whatever reason. After hours in the open, frigid air he became quite numb.

When he reached his destination much later than expected and with the consequent grumbling of the people tired of waiting, he walked into a heated church and lost consciousness or something akin to it. Jumping from an ice box to a heated oven can be traumatic. He had meant well. The calculations had seemed well made. All concerned felt that it could be done. But was he in a position to celebrate this second Mass with the fervor, jubilation, and concentration expected in a Christmas Day Mass? Did he risk his life? Did those parishioners have a right to have Mass under such circumstances? The missionary weighs all these reasons pro and con and takes the plunge.

Pain itself should not be even considered. Pain is the inseparable companion of life. There is much redeeming power in pain suffered supernaturally. The folly of the cross is what makes martyrs and big saints. The soldiers on Calvary wanted to give Christ a tranquilizer by offering Him a mixture of wine and myrrh, but He did not swallow it. It was through accepted pain that redemption would be accomplished. The trouble with us today is that we are very much confused about pain and sedatives, prudence and heroism and laziness.

Personally, if I were accused of sinning, I wish it would be of sinning by excess. When in doubt, take the plunge. Burn out, don't rust out. If the next night another messenger comes saying that the

son of Vincent fell from the roof and wants to see the priest, dress up
and go, of course.

20

Kwiguk and Saint Marys

Between Alakanuk and Emmonak is Kwiguk. These names on the Yukon Delta are like San Francisco and Los Angeles to Californians. *Kwiguk* means "Two Rivers," although you can actually see four rivers from its banks. The village had undergone many changes, but it actually settled into being a good fish camp with long rows of tents and innumerable sled dogs tied to the surrounding willows. I had a little church in its midst with a living room that gave me all I wanted: a stove, a chair, a table, and a bed. Eventually, the chapel at Kwiguk had to be abandoned when the river banks began to cave in.

My door was never locked. People came in and out at will. Children played on the floor while adults talked business with me. I simply was one more in the family, or so I felt.

June and July were the fishing months. The N.C. Co. had a cannery there. The manager of the company and John T. Emel of Alakanuk had made a gentlemen's agreement to divide the lower Yukon's fishing grounds so as to avoid the natural bitterness that comes when someone else plants his tent and nets just so many feet ahead of you. Jack Emel had the southern part and the company had the northern. It worked quite well until other private enterprises came on the scene and somewhat complicated matters, but all was legal.

Ninety-five percent of all those fishermen were Catholic and they were scattered in all directions. I was extremely fortunate to enjoy the friendship and good will of all the powers concerned, so I availed myself of their boats to visit my scattered faithful. Sometimes it was the *Mildred* run by Edgar Kalland and other times it was the *Agulleit* run by Richard Kosevnikoff.

Richard would take off with his crew headed for the north. I sat on deck with a book or magazine in my hands for those long distances between fishing sites. It was just great. Coming to a tent, I would jump off and see the family while the men threw the salmon into the hatch. Every fish was checked and the fisherman would get a carbon copy receipt. The round could take the greater part of the day. If there was a baby to be baptized, we did it right there.

When I wanted to visit the fishermen on the south, I would board Jack's fish tender, which was usually piloted by his father-in-law, Eric Johnson—a sturdy Swede who had migrated to America as a youngster and had been a navigator of many waters. He was now a grandpa, but he looked solid, well put together, with ruddy cheeks and blue eyes. He made me feel that Eric the Red's sailors must have been like this healthy specimen. With sailors like this, it was no wonder that he did what he is credited with having done all over the North Atlantic.

This latter-day Eric had been a U.S. marshal on the lower Yukon for a number of years. He had a famous dog team with a sled that could take several prisoners in one trip. One sure thing was that no drunkard ever dared to tackle Eric, and if he did, he knew better the second time he attempted. He was always at the steering wheel, while I sat by him chatting about many things. The shores of the Bering Sea can become very foggy when the sun is low on the horizon. Eric knew every channel and went about like those blind people who move and work totally unaided. Thus I managed to keep in touch with the parishioners in those faraway areas. Back in Alakanuk or Kwiguk I felt that I kept close touch with them all.

Before I built the chapel in Kwiguk, I used to say Mass in the N.C. store run by Axel Johnson, who had Eskimo and Russian blood. He would get me a bed from the attic and put it by the stove where I slept like a log. Mass was said on the counter with the Eskimos crowding all around it. All very democratic, very simple, very humble, and very beautiful—but we could not then keep the blessed Sacrament.

With the chapel, came the altar and the tabernacle and the pews, and we were then in business. Once in a while strange voices would be heard. It was a guy who drank too much and could not keep still. I would tell the Lord that this was the way we were and to please have mercy on us and do not give up on us; understand that in our hearts we did love Him and wanted to do better. Praying for others helps also the one who prays. Many times I thought of Moses in the desert, how he succeeded in obtaining God's mercy for the chosen people when these people betrayed the Lord. Moses himself was punished not to enter into the land flowing with milk and honey. Most likely his faith was not as pure as God wanted it to be.

Axel's wife, Pearl Johnson, gave me many a meal, first in Kwiguk and then in Emmonak. I baptized their baby Mae in Kwiguk. Then, before I knew it, I blessed Mae's marriage in Emmonak to Martin Moore. Axel and Pearl threw a party for the wedding with cakes and everything. We were all happy in an atmosphere of neighborliness and simplicity.

To break the monotony of that perennial commuting between Emmonak and Alakanuk, I made some visits to our Saint Marys school, as the old Akulurak school was now called. Fr. Menager, its first superior, would call me to his room to converse—just to talk. A Frenchman and a Spaniard should by definition be talkers. Like a good Frenchman he enjoyed a glass of wine.

I recall the day when we were in his room talking about spiritual things. He filled two glasses and gave me one. Since we needed the right arms to talk, we held the glasses with the left hands and there we were locked in a heated discussion as to whether it was more perfect to beg the Lord for crosses and suffering or if it was better to let the Lord Himself send us what He considered best and accept it. I held the latter. Fr. Menager kept arguing that we should be brave, that we should aim at the very best, and we should not be satisfied with those tiny everyday crosses we were called to embrace; rather, we should try to be other Christs by begging for a life of suffering and real crosses, etc., etc.

I, in my timidity, argued that the Lord knows very well what we can bear and that is what He sends us; it behooves us to accept with joy, if possible, absolutely everything God sends us, etc. And there we were, holding a glass of red wine with one hand and philosophizing with the other.

When I told this to Fr Paul Deschout, S.J., I feared that he might get a stroke laughing. He bent over screaming and twisted his body in every manner of contortion, yelling and almost unable to breathe as he kept repeating: "And there you two were, both drunk and talking about asking God for sufferings . . . " It was too much for him as he was wiping the tears out of his eyes with new outbursts of uncontrolled laughter.

Fr. Deschout was something else. Born in Flanders on January 4, 1900, he used to say that all he had to do to remember his age was to look at the calendar on the wall. In 1930 he had landed in Akulurak where he'd spent four years, and where he'd acquired a commendable knowledge of the Eskimo language. From there he'd gone to Nelson Island, where he spent twenty-nine years with the same congregation. In theory it was a beautiful arrangement. He spoke their language and they loved him and the congregation had the reputation of being perhaps the most religious in northern Alaska.

In practice, though, those arrangements in the long run cause many difficulties. For one thing, the parishioners identify the church with the pastor. Then the pastor gets so wedded to that congregation that he finds it impossible psychologically to function anywhere else. The superiors tried to correct this by sending him to Hooper Bay and to Saint Marys, but it was too late. He made it plain that it had to be Nelson Island. The day he became fifty, he looked at the ceiling in utter disbelief. Fifty years! Half a century! How could he continue living and working at so advanced an age? Then he became sixty. That was much too much and he began to give signs of incipient senility. To make it worse, he got hit in the head by the propeller of a snowmobile and had to be hospitalized. Those of us who saw him in 1936 when he was in his prime, and then in 1963, found it hard to believe that he was the same man. He died in Portland on February 12, 1966.

Fr. Menager was replaced by Fr. O'Connor as superior of Saint Marys. He was soon in the habit of sending word to me to come and visit. He had many excuses. I had to give a retreat to the sisters and to the brothers, or I needed a break and should come, and of course four times a year I had to replace him for a long week. For fourteen consecutive years he was the chairman of the Alaska Housing Authority and had to go to Anchorage or some other city to meet with the board.

These visits to Saint Marys were a good break for me who lived all alone in Alakanuk. In the afternoons if the weather was good I would take a "walk" on the Andreafski River in front of the school—on foot over the ice in the winter or in a rowboat in the summer. I kept harking back to that day when Bro. Murphy and I navigated those waters looking for a suitable spot to build the school. And here was the school with its imposing buildings, an accredited high school and grade school with some 150 children, including those from the village adjacent to the school. God does it slowly but surely. First we crawl, then we walk. A soaring swan comes from an egg. The three little boats of Columbus brought about the present American continent. Slowly but surely.

Those imposing buildings came about through the expertise and hard work of Fr. James Spils, S.J., a native of Colton, Washington, who had come to Alaska in 1938. He was the right arm of Bishop Gleeson, who had obtained the building material and became the cook of the little crew of native workers under Fr. Spils. Yes, the bishop was the cook, and a good cook. He was also the cook for the small crew who helped Fr. Spils build the Copper Valley High School near the confluence of the Copper and Tazlina Rivers.

I heard it said that the bishop could get a job as chef-de-cuisine in the best American hotels. When he cooked, he used just about everything in the kitchen. When the meal was over, he sat back satisfied in his favorite chair and watched with amusement the diners as they struggled with the mountain of dishes to be washed and dried and put back in their places. This exercise probably helped digest the tasty meals. And nobody complained as it was obvious that the work should be about equally divided between the cook and the diners.

Fr. Spils built also the magnificent cathedral of Fairbanks. Then he built the rectory. The short time that he was pastor of Ruby on the Yukon was enough for him to build a decent church to replace the one that was inadequate. Those curious people who want to know how much money Fr. Spils saved the bishop of Fairbanks will have to wait to the last judgment and ask the supreme Judge.

Fr. Spils was built like a rhino. I always hated to shake hands with him. His right hand was not an ordinary hand as we know hands. He told me casually that once he wanted to finish a wall before going to bed. He would give a little blow to the spike to keep it in place and then with a heavy blow he would drive it in clear to its head. That night he feared that he might get bursitis. But Saint Joseph, the patron of all carpenters (and specially of holy carpenters), came to the rescue and saved him from any pain in the arm.

Saint Joseph also helped him save his life when he was replacing the pastor of Talkeetna, along the Alaska Railroad. At midnight when Fr.Spils was sound asleep, the burner blew up and in very short order the mobile home went up in smoke. He ran out in his pajamas and walked on the snow to the church building nearby.

Just to prove that he is not an ordinary Alaskan, he was one of the first to shake hands with Pope John Paul II when he landed in Anchorage in February of 1981. I am sure the Holy Father had a sore hand for some time.

In Saint Marys School I gave retreats also to the newly formed community of Eskimo sisters. Bishop Fitzgerald had disbanded the remnant of the old Sisters of the Snow, as I previously explained. But the idea of native sisters was kept very much alive. Six fine school girls took the habit of novices. This time it was thought that the Ursuline nuns who were teaching in the school should train those novices. The experiment failed again. The Ursuline nuns were all white, with a white mentality. Furthermore, they had the Ursuline mentality and subconsciously they felt that that mentality, which was excellent for them, should be good also for the native sisters. The old clash of cultures.

To the Ursulines, regimentation was necessary to religious life. Regimentation worked well for centuries. Then the crisis that followed the misrepresentations of Vatican II did away with all regimentation. Near chaos followed. I suggested that one Eskimo novice who gave signs of being talented above the ordinary should be sent to the Lower 48 to live in a religious community of nuns where a measure of sanity was still kept. And there she would get the foundations of religious life plus a thorough indoctrination in basic theological doctrine. She would return to Alaska with that knowledge and start a community of native sisters right from scratch.

The rules would be adapted to the environment and to the native character. They could chew tobacco and have cuspidors for their black spittle. (The first Eskimo woman who came to me for a favor did not ask for money, clothes, or food. The word she uttered was *chu-ya-yur-pa:* "I am desperate for chewing tobacco.") There would have to be flexibility about getting up in the morning and going to bed at night. In visiting the Eskimo houses those sisters would have to be free to stay as many hours as they saw fit and never mind the wrist watch. Eskimos feel uncomfortable with tight schedules. (I still remember the way they looked at me when I visited them and asked what time did they eat. They ate when they were hungry if they were hungry, and never all at the same time. This does not go well with the whites, accustomed to keeping hours.)

This plan of mine was seen as one more utopian dream and died on the vine. And so did the Eskimo sisterhood. Perhaps too much was made of those sisters. Dressed in their cute religious garb they looked very pretty. Pictures of them appeared everywhere in religious magazines and papers. They were paraded a great deal in the hope of stirring dormant vocations. It went a bit to their heads.

Then white volunteers came on the scene and told them that they did not have to be sisters; instead they should become teachers to teach in the villages or nurses to cure the sick or counselors to give advice to their people. With this sort of fare they got fed up with religious vows and left to get lost in the anonymity of raising children like the rest of the women in the neighborhood. No new attempt has been made—to date—to revive them.

With regard to Eskimo priests, I gave a retreat to two full-blooded boys who had finished high school and felt that they had a vocation for the priesthood. The bishop sent them to Boston to a seminary for special vocations—as far as I recall—but it did not take long for them to return. They could not hack it. It was felt that what we needed was a seminary in Alaska where they could study in their own environment. Coming to the continental United States put them at a disadvantage, as it would be too hard for them to march abreast with the sophisticated Americans of our big cities. This idea has caught on and Fr. Charles Peterson, S.J., has been appointed to draw a plan and get it airborne. To date the plan is still grounded. Time will tell.

To those who wonder that Alaska has not produced Eskimo priests or Indian priests (because there are more Indians in Alaska than there are Eskimos), my answer is that the actual number of Catholic natives is very limited. Half of them are women. Of the other half you have to delete married men and children. There are relatively few teenagers left. Of these, 90 percent would be expected to get married. How many have you left? Precious few! Look at the number of priests coming out of our thickly populated Catholic communities. Perhaps one in one thousand.

In my estimation we should look in Alaska for vocations for the priesthood in every nook and corner without any discrimination: whites with red hair and blue eyes, husky half-breeds with Scandinavian fathers and Irish mothers, mulattos walking the streets of the cities, quarter-breeds, and also full-blooded natives. They are all Alaskans. Anyone who thinks that he could produce a desirable number of Eskimo seminarians is doomed to fail. The numbers are not there. What is flourishing now in northern Alaska is the practice of ordained deacons—married deacons, that is. Once the Eskimo is married he can do anything in this respect. There is the rub. This matter has been the subject of interminable discussions, which is a very good thing. As long as the matter is discussed, there is hope. If and when the matter is no longer discussed, pessimism and fears will take over and the very idea of an indigenous clergy could fade and die, and nobody wants this to happen.

Saint Marys boasted of a good-sized cannery, thanks to the talents of Fr. Edmund Anable, S.J., from upper New York. He brought along with him many of the sophistications of New Yorkers and perhaps the greatest one is his penchant for efficiency. Wherever he shows up, things begin to move and no nonsense is tolerated. Armed with paper pads and an array of ballpoint pens, he delineates the shape of a huge river boat, a floating platform, a building, whatever is contemplated or needed. With a shade over his eyes, he can work under a bright bulb for hours till he is satisfied that the plan is flawless and so will be its execution. His ideal short vacation is to go fishing with the finest fish tackle on the market.

His power of concentration is truly remarkable. Before we knew it, he had the cannery in Saint Marys operating smoothly and efficiently. This gave work to the villagers and initiated the big boys and girls of the mission school in this truly Alaskan work. Once the natives learned to run it, the bishop began to pass it on to them gradually. But it is one thing to know the *how* and another quite different to know the *why*. It is said that anyone who knows *how*, will have a job; the one who knows *why*, will be his boss. Fr. Anable is a born boss in this respect.

Fortunately, there are natives who also learn the *why*. These will run western Alaska. What do I mean? I mean that the area west of the Alaska Railroad will eventually be run by half-breeds: canneries, stores, post offices, and aviation. Fairbanks, Anchorage, and the Panhandle will continue in the hands of the whites principally. Anchorage alone has almost half the population of the whole state, and Anchorage is firmly in white hands.

21

The Alaska State Legislature

Alaska was organized as a territory in 1912. From then until 1959 when she became a state, Alaska was represented in the U.S. Congress by an elected delegate who had the right to speak on the floor but could not vote. Alaska then had its own legislature, but the laws she passed were subject to approval by Washington. The governor of Alaska was also appointed by the president.

All this changed abruptly when on January 3, 1959, she became the forty-ninth state of the Union. The great land was divided into districts and was dotted with voting precincts where every native in the bush was told to come and vote. The whites and some natives were already familiar with the voting mechanism, but the natives at large were not.

Eager-beaver Democrats were quick to tell the natives that the welfare checks they were getting were the work of Democratic administrations in Washington, under Roosevelt and Truman. A vote for a Democratic candidate meant more checks, whereas a vote for a Republican meant fewer checks or no checks at all.

It worked. It was amazing to listen to the results on election night. Village after village in the bush was coming out with something like this: for the Democrats, seventy-nine; for the Republicans, two. These two lonely votes were cast by the teachers, a white couple from Kansas or Illinois.

In the fall of 1960 Alaskans were preparing to vote for candidates to the second state legislature. I was still at Alakanuk on the Lower Yukon, a voting district of easily sixteen thousand square miles (twice the size of Massachusetts) with only about 3,200 people (mostly children) and at least 90 percent Eskimos. One of the voters, a Caucasian, asked me if I would serve in the Alaska State House of Representatives if I were elected on a write-in vote. He knew that I would not run myself. My answer was in the affirmative, provided the bishop of Fairbanks—my bishop—approved of it and allowed me to take my seat if elected.

A week later this man came to tell me that he had contacted Bishop Gleeson in Bethel, where he was visiting with Fr. Hargreaves, S.J. The bishop had said that if the majority of the voters elected me, he would not oppose it. This was interpreted as the green light to go ahead. The man spoke to voters here and there and the snowball began to roll. In light of what followed, it is my belief that the bishop gave the green light because he felt in his heart that my chances of being elected on a write-in vote were very slim, indeed.

Father Paul O'Connor, S.J., had presented his candidacy for the state's constitutional convention a few years back. He had not made it, so there was no reason to believe that the same voters would go now for a priest.

On election night the Nome radio announced that the voters of my district had elected Segundo Llorente on a write-in vote. It further clarified that Segundo Llorente was a Jesuit Catholic priest. Now everything broke loose. Since Kennedy had been elected president that very night, people here and there began to ask what the wily old Vatican had up its sleeve. The Associated Press was quick to broadcast the news.

My bishop contacted the Office of the Apostolic Delegate in Washington and was told that it was up to him—the bishop—to allow it or not to allow it—but the feelings at that office were against it. Other contacts brought the same results. People had not heard of a Catholic priest ever elected to such office and there were mixed feelings about it. There was fear that now priests would be running and perhaps stampeding for elected offices. My bishop wrote to me asking that I submit my resignation.

I wrote a letter to the governor resigning, but instead of sending the letter directly to him, I sent it to Bishop Gleeson, asking him to send it to the governor himself. That way the governor would be more convinced that the resignation was altogether proper. I added to Bishop Gleeson that I wanted to be reassigned to another post in

Alaska. I did not have the heart to confront my people and tell them that all had been a mistake; they would not understand.

I am sure that the poor bishop agonized over all this. In a few days I got a letter from him and—for the first time—the letter was a very long one, explaining to me the mess we were in. In view of the fact that it was now too late to resign, he had not sent the governor my resignation. He told me to go ahead and take part in the first session of the legislature, but to be sure to resign after it was over and let someone else take my seat for the second session. Putting myself in the bishop's shoes, I wondered if Solomon could have done better. But I spent sleepless nights.

Time magazine instructed its head representative on the West Coast to fly immediately to Alaska and hold an interview with that priest no matter what it took. It took quite a bit. The gentleman flew to Fairbanks and asked where Alakanuk might be. Those asked did not know, but someone told him that in Nome he could find out. He flew to Nome, where those asked did not know, but someone told him that surely in Bethel he could find out. He flew to Bethel, where he was told exactly where Alakanuk was.

He instantly chartered a plane. The pilot told him that he was a personal friend of Fr. Llorente and he would find me immediately if not sooner. We were getting close to Christmas and the weather was not too good and the reporter wanted to be back in San Francisco to spend Christmas with his family—hence the hurry.

I was having a cup of coffee with Pete Jorgensen in his kitchen when a plane landed. It was not mail day. Probably a fur buyer is coming, Pete said. Suddenly, in came the pilot with the reporter, asking if Fr. Llorente was around. We shook hands. The reporter breathed a sigh of relief; he had chased me all over and now he had me.

When I told him that my priest brother had been a teacher of Fidel Castro in Havana (La Habana to be exact), he exclaimed, "Heavens, I hit pay dirt here." It was in the afternoon. A thick fog settled over us. The pilot announced that we had to spend the night in Alakanuk. The reporter filled a high stack of sheets with rapidly scribbled lines where he took down all he wanted to know. Next morning the weather was good and he left. My Christmas mail brought me a letter from his wife in San Francisco, thanking me for the pleasant evening I had given her husband and telling me to spend on myself the fifty dollar check she enclosed.

With the article *Time* magazine published about my election, mail began to pour in. People in Indiana or Nebraska wanted to know the chances of farming in Alaska. James A. Farley, former postmaster general and a political leader in America, wrote to thank me and to assure me that politics was a highly commendable profession. He was also sure that the presence of a Catholic priest in politics would tell Americans that politicians were not a bunch of crooks. (Polish Pope John Paul II was not around yet!)

Someone wrote philosophizing over the American way of life. While in other countries missionaries are either persecuted or ignored, American Alaska had elected one to its legislature. Furthermore, the first priest elected to be a legislator with active and passive voice was a naturalized foreigner, and the electors were Eskimos. This, he pondered, was America. Where else could this happen? he wanted to know. To my surprise the mail was unanimously favorable.

The second week of January 1961, I left for Juneau, the capital. I visited the Catholic rectory and was presented with a copy of the letter the bishop of Juneau, Dermot O'Flanagan, had written to the pastor concerning my status in Juneau. When I finished reading it, I did not faint. To this day I wonder how I managed not to faint. The bishop of Juneau—who was not my bishop—had made his own contacts regarding the presence in Juneau of a priest who was there as a legislator. The answers he received had been negative. As a result, he panicked and took appropriate measures to make it clear to me what my status in Juneau was as long as I was there as a legislator. He and I had been friends for many years. He had welcomed me into the Anchorage rectory on my first trip to the Yukon. Now, suddenly, he felt that he had to defend his own position. He feared that my vote on the floor of the House would be construed by the people as reflecting his own vote. He wanted in no way to be identified with me as a legislator. This is what he wrote in the letter.

I was not to be seen in the cathedral, which was the only Catholic church in town. I was not to be seen in the rectory with the other priests nor could I eat in the rectory. I had no faculties to hear confessions. I could not use the facilities of the parochial school to give talks. Perhaps I could come to an agreement with the sister in charge of the Catholic hospital as to the hour when I could say a private Mass with nobody attending it except the altar boy or a sister in a pew.

The thrust of the whole thing was that nobody would see me in any way affiliated with the Catholic machinery of the city. The letter added that since I was making forty dollars per diem (it was later cut down to a mere thirty-five dollars!), it was up to me to find proper lodging in some hotel and eat in the public restaurants with the rest of the legislators. The letter ended hoping that these injunctions would be followed literally.

I learned lately that the letter had been written by Bishop O'Flanagan and his chancellor together. A copy was given to the pastor and copies had been sent to the sister superior of the hospital and to the chaplain of the same hospital.

It was a letter written in panic. History was being made. The bishop of Juneau did not want to go down in history as giving aid and comfort to a priest politician. That was clear. But I saw myself as a leper. If I could not function visibly as a priest, what was I good for? I saw no reason for my existence. I had been a priest for twenty-six years, preaching and giving spiritual talks to people, and now I was told to hide if I wanted to say Mass.

I went to the hospital to see sister superior and arrange for my private Mass. She was in tears. She had read the letter to the sisters of her community and they were all grieved. Two of them had made an eight-day retreat under my guidance at Holy Cross on the Yukon and had hoped that I would give them spiritual talks in some spare time. Their chapel was free at 7:00 A.M. every morning, so that was my opportunity to say Mass.

I found the Baranof Hotel much too noisy for me. In my Eskimo villages I always slept like a log because of the beautiful silence surrounding me. Here at the hotel people came and went all night. I was saved from that infernal noise by Frank Duggan, who told me to use his duplex, where I slept in peace. He was a local lawyer and befriended me during the first session, just when I needed him.

Nobody looking at me could possibly suspect the enormity of the tension working inside of me. I was to be there only for the first session and then resign. I was to say Mass in an almost clandestine way and with no faculties to hear confessions or preach. That was a very poor state of mind to be in as I tackled for the first time the very difficult task of taking full active part in the conduct of the legislature.

I saw much irony in the fact that newspapermen from everywhere flocked to interview me and take my picture. The movie makers came with all the paraphernalia to take me in their film, answering questions and moving around. I never told anybody how I was feeling: Inside I was plagued with migraine headaches that threatened to split my cranium in two any minute.

Then the local political leaders wanted to know if I would join the Democrats or the Republicans, because I was elected on a write-in vote and I had not promised allegiance to any party. Frank Duggan was of some help. He pointed out to me that the administration both in Washington and in Juneau was Democratic. Of the forty members of the House in Juneau, eighteen were solid Republicans. Among the Democrats one member at heart was Republican and was expected to vote Republican. That made nineteen Republicans. If I sided with the Republicans, the House would be split into twenty-twenty. This would be a disaster; it would paralyze all meaningful legislation.

So I joined the Democrats. Those days it was hard to tell them apart. Now things have changed. With me as a Democrat, there were many bills that passed by one vote. To make it harder for me, since the committees had to have a majority of Democrats, one representative had to be a member of three committees; the rest were members of only two. I was chosen to take on the third committee on the grounds that my education enabled me to handle any committee. So I was a member of the judiciary committee, the state affairs committee, and the health, welfare, and education committee. I am writing from memory. I hope I am stating the facts as they were.

If anyone thinks that legislators have a good time with little work, he is sadly mistaken. The work load is hard to believe and it weighs very heavily on everyone's shoulders. You just have to be there after breakfast, one hour out to lunch, back either in committees or on the floor till suppertime and back for more work after supper till late at night quite often, and thus six days a week.

On Sundays the legislators are given time to go to the church of their choice if they so wish. But very often they are doing work on impending tough bills that demand much study.

One soon learns the terminology peculiar to legislation. Verbs like *implement, preclude, enact, rescind, undertake,* and others become very familiar. Words like *procedural, contingency funds, defunct,* and others are soon common parlance. One colleague asked me what *retroactive* meant.

Then there were the caucuses, where arms were twisted to the snapping point. I saw one man bury his head in his hands and weep openly. He had promised his constituents that he would oppose a certain thing; now he was told by the party to vote for it, and he felt that he could not do it in conscience. Party loyalty. Keeping your word to your constituents. Then the ever-present pressure from labor groups demanding this and that and threatening with reprisals those who did not come across. Then the ubiquitous lobbyists coming to you like flies to honey. The long-distance telephone calls requesting that you kill this or that bill, or that you vote for it. The daily telegrams.

There I was, with my black suit and my white collar turned backwards, milling daily in that circle of legislators, lobbyists, witnesses, and pressure groups. From sun up to sun down. Grin and bear it. Day after day keeping the nose to the grindstone. The grindstone was bills and more bills covering the daily social and political life of the citizens. Schools, hospitals, airports, roads, harbors, jails, policemen, crimes, the marriage code, trade, labor, unemployment compensation, faulty dentists' chairs, welfare to unwed mothers, divorce, redistricting, and finally the budget. Was I ordained a priest to give my time to these matters? I will come to this later.

I said Mass every morning in the empty chapel of the hospital. As I left the chapel after Mass, I found in a tiny room a table with breakfast ready: two fried eggs, toast, cream, and coffee. I blessed the table, sat down, ate in silence, and left. I did not see anybody. It was there, so I ate it.

On Sundays I would attend the beautiful ceremony of benediction with the blessed Sacrament in another very little chapel of the hospital. I knelt with the faithful. When it was all over, everybody left, but I remained there till there was silence all around.

Just then I would walk out into a corridor, stepping hard on the wooden floor. A door would open. A sister would invite me to come in. It was their recreation room and they were all there, about one dozen, eager to ask me questions about my work with the Eskimos. On the table there were cookies and tea. The curtains were drawn to make it look more like the Upper Room where the Lord chatted with the twelve apostles.

The letter of the bishop did not make it clear at all whether I may or may not speak to the sisters when nobody would know, so we took it that we could do it, and I did it. That was God's way of keeping me from going insane. For one hour and a half I spoke to the sisters about the doctrine of Saint Teresa of Avila and about the writings of the great mystic Saint John of the Cross. It did me more good than it did them. Now I was a priest again and I was in my element like a fish in a wide lake.

As the legislative session went on, I was getting carbon copies of letters sent to Bishop Gleeson in Fairbanks signed by this or that legislator who wanted to express his gratitude for the bishop having allowed me to take my seat on the floor. They started by saying that when they had heard that a priest had been elected, they had cringed, fearing that the priest would be the preachy type who would harangue the House on morality at every chance he had. The reality was quite different. This priest has proved to be a very cooperating partner both in committee meetings and on the floor, etc.

When I told the governor privately that I would not be back for the second session, he sent me the carbon copy of a two-page letter he sent to the bishop requesting that I be allowed to come back. I knew right then and there that I would be back.

When the first session ended, I flew to Fairbanks to report to the bishop and to ask him if I should resign. He waved his hand signifying no at the same time that he shook his head meaning also no, and without even opening his mouth he let out a hardly audible no. We changed the subject. With that we put an end to that vexatious affair.

When the time came to return for the second session next January, I wrote a letter to the bishop of Juneau requesting to know if his letter would still be in force. O'Flanagan answered through the chancellor in the affirmative.

But this time I was a seasoned warrior. No sooner had I landed in Juneau than I called him on the phone to invite him to dinner anywhere he chose to eat. He chose Mike's, at Douglas across the bridge, and he would pick me up at a certain place. Throwing aside any remembrance of the letter, I met him with that cordiality that had been mutual between us for years. That broke the ice and from then on everything was beautiful. I realized how very lonesome he was and how he craved company. I invited him several times and he always accepted with pleasure. Mind you, technically I could not be seen fraternizing with the priests nor could I be seen officiating in the cathedral since I was in Juneau as a legislator, but he did not mind being seen with me at Mike's, which was the best restaurant.

Once at table he almost choked with laughter when I told him that I knew how long it took the Lord to get to heaven on Ascension Day. It took Him exactly five days. It was in the Bible: Jesus told the apostles that when He got to heaven, He would send the Holy Spirit. The Holy Spirit came ten days later: five days up, five days down, since both travel at the same speed and the law of gravity would have no effect on them.

On another occasion he laughed loudly when I pointed out to him how fat that lady was who sat across from our table. Should I address myself to her? But what would I tell her?—the bishop wanted to know. I said that I would tell her to eat less, because the gate of heaven was narrow. After all, a priest should know something about the gate of heaven or any other thing related to heaven. Wasn't his job to pack people for heaven?

When I left Juneau for good I visited Bishop O'Flanagan in his office and we had a two-hour visit. I told him that, upon reconsideration, his letter had been proper. Thus the church was innocent of any misdeed I had perpetrated. Here he broke in to assure me that he had agonized over that letter, but that he had no precedent to go by, so he had deemed it proper to build a barrier between the legislature and the cathedral. Now he was pleased to tell me that everything had ended in a highly commendable way. He always had loved me as a priest; now he complimented me as a legislator. With that we embarked on a thousand and one things about the church in Alaska. At the end I knelt down and asked for his blessing, which he gave me resting his episcopal hands on my balding head.

I have been asked many times if, in my opinion, a priest should run for a political office. We have now the authority of the Vicar of Christ who has ruled against it, so my answer has no longer any bearing on the matter. But to judge by my own experience, my answer is an unequivocal no for many reasons.

While I served in Juneau as a legislator, my district on the lower Yukon was left without a resident priest. The more pious Eskimos said that it had been a mistake to have sent me to Juneau without having been assured that I would be replaced by another priest. The bishop had no spare priests.

But suppose there are lots of priests available, then what? If the priest who wants to go into politics is not a saint, he can do more harm than good by his presence among politicians. Soon he will be worldly; his language will deteriorate; his very mien will carry a certain arrogance; he will go from party to party, mixed parties, noisy parties that end after midnight; he will be poorly prepared for Mass and the breviary and the rosary, assuming that he still believes in these things. He owes loyalty to these and those interests and he sees himself walking a tightrope, afraid to antagonize some and determined to help crush opposition to what is dear to him, which may be something objectively good. People are soon scandalized that he, a priest, should vote for such an abominable thing, etc., etc. If he is not saintly, if he is blind to the teachings of the church, then he does much damage to the faithful with his performance.

But what if the priest is a saintly one? Then the priest himself will refuse the political job. He is not at home spending the evenings with politicians and away from the altar where he belongs.

Saint John of the Cross wrote that the gift of thought is so precious that God alone should be the object of our thoughts—thoughts that we squander on superficial, ridiculous, and even sinful things. I used to regret that I was spending so many hours contemplating bills. This would be proper for lay people, but not for me.

Then the political alliances. A priest should be above parties. He should be like the sun who is high above and sends his light to everybody regardless of his political leanings. God is the God of the Republicans and of the Democrats and of the Independents. All are His children. The priest should imitate God in this. But the minute a priest takes his seat in the Congress, he is tagged and he carries that tag wherever he goes. That is unfair to the priesthood as such.

The history of the church is full of sad cases. Thomas Wolsey, cardinal archbishop of York and chancellor of England, has been severely castigated by historians for his performance as "the would-be reformer who did not reform himself first." Richelieu, cardinal, minister, and head of the royal council of Louis XIII of France, allied himself with Gustavus II Adolphus of Sweden to defeat the Catholic Ferdinand II of Germany, thus putting an end to all hopes of Catholic restoration in central Europe.

If we look for examples outside the church, we all know the performance of the Ayatollah Khomeini, who came in supposedly to undo the work of the autocratic Shah of Iran. Seldom does a religious leader fit as a politician.

22

Nome

After leaving the legislature I moved north, where I pastored in Nome for two years.

Nome is about 110 miles south of the Arctic Circle, which is north enough. Nome is also technically a port, though ships have to anchor way out. Until recently Nome was the metropolis of northwestern Alaska; of late she has seen Barrow surpass her in population. Everything about Nome is involved in a sort of mystery, beginning with the very name. When gold was discovered in 1898 in Anvil Creek nearby, the man who drew its location on the map found that the place had no name; he was at a loss and simply scribbled *Name?* Someone mistook the *a* for an *o* and removed the question mark. Thus the location began to be known as Nome, which means nothing.

The discovery of gold in rich quantities brought in motley throngs of mustached men with greed in their hearts and total disregard for laws. By 1900 there were probably twenty-five thousand people, mostly men ready to defend their claim at gun point. Law and order was established in due course. Gold became scarce and, by 1910, Nome seemed to be destined to become the proverbial ghost town. Then came devastating storms from the sea which threatened to wipe it out. To all this we must add devastating fires. Yet Nome like an unsinkable boat kept afloat.

When I first saw it in 1939 I could not figure what kept it going. There was no arable land or even land for home gardens. There was no timber in its vicinity. There were no fisheries. There was no trapping to speak of. There were no industries. Mining had ceased to be of any importance. Just what is it that kept Nome alive? The answer is to be found in the federal building located in the center of the city. Bear in mind that in Alaska a town of five hundred people is a city. In fact, every locality is more or less a city. Places that would be totally unknown in the continental United States are cities in Alaska.

To put order in Nome when the miners were living in a state of lawlessness, the U.S. government had sent a judge. He needed a house to live in and he needed a clerk. A jail was built. This meant marshals and people to guard the prisoners plus clerks to help the marshals and deputy marshals. A post office had to be built. This meant a post master with clerks. All these officials were married people with children who needed schools with teachers, naturally. So schools were built. A fish and wild life office had to be built and agents had to be hired to man it. An immigration office. The district attorney. The tax collector. Now, mind you, all these people have to eat, so in came the baker, the storekeeper, and the restaurants. They had to drink, so in came the saloon keepers. And they needed a haircut. Everything started with the arrival of the judge and the post office.

Where did the money come from? The money came in the form of federal and then state checks to pay the officials who pay the storekeepers and the baker and the barber. It is all artificial. Why don't people leave? Simply because towns, like people, hang on to sweet life till that life is forcibly taken away from them. The devastating storms from the sea were about to take that life from Nome forcibly, but here came the sagacity and determination of the people to save and prolong Nome's life.

Politicians in Washington, D.C., were approached and were told that government property was in jeopardy, imminent jeopardy, if something was not done very soon. Federal property in Nome had to be protected by building a sea wall to contain the periodic rage of the sea. And sure enough, a gigantic sea wall was built. Dynamite went to work in a nearby quarry and huge piles of enormous rocks were transported in barges and lined up on the beach the whole length of the town. As I walked over that imposing wall of solid rocks, I had to admit that once again mind had beat matter hands down. Now Nome can sleep with ease when the sea breaks loose and threatens to engulf it.

With the coming of World War II, Nome became a military base. After the war it looked as though Nome was going to go back to its littleness, but aviation became of age. An airport was built. Offices were built to handle flights and tickets. Then tourism came. The natives discovered a new gold mine in their ancestral dances that became the delight of people from Rhode Island, Illinois, and California. Nome kept afloat with a business-as-usual attitude. When I was pastor of Nome in 1965 there were eighty natives to twenty whites; I mean eighty Eskimos to twenty whites, because many of those whites are natives of Nome. The total population was about 2,400. Nome is a legend. No Alaska town can compare with Nome when it comes to history. I hold a personal affection for Nome for two reasons: I became an American citizen in Nome in 1956 and I joined the Pioneers of Alaska there in 1965.

In 1956 it cost me $150 to buy a round-trip ticket to Nome from the mouth of the Yukon. The immigration agent was satisfied that all my papers were in order, so the only thing between me and my citizenship was an examination that I was expected to have ninety days hence. I winced at the thought of having to buy another $150 round-trip ticket, so I told the officer that I was ready right then and there to have the examination.

He was about to hand me a pamphlet with questions and answers to learn the whole matter in ninety days. When I insisted that I was ready for the examination, he was visibly annoyed, but he took the challenge and told me to sit down. It was a grilling ordeal. The gentleman covered the whole gamut of the American political fabric. Toward the end he caved in and asked me how I had learned all that. I told him that I had read the *Congressional Record* for some time plus the national magazines for years plus the papers—plus I had an inborn penchant for politics that I carried in the marrow of my bones.

When I told him that I knew the names of the nine members of the U.S. Supreme Court and how they voted, he put an end to it by telling me that "the day after tomorrow" I should appear in court to get my citizenship.

When the moment came to swear allegiance to the American flag and to the Constitution for which it stands, something went through me which I cannot explain. After all, my early education, my folks, my language, my very soul were rooted in faraway sunny Spain. The judge made a short speech to say that he welcomed me in the name of all Americans and that our nation was glad to accept a new substantial citizen and so on and so forth. I asked if I could say a few words. He told me to go ahead, by all means. I stood up and said that I had pronounced the oath of allegiance without any mental reservation; that I was ready to defend America with arms. But I was sorry to say that I had never fired a gun; therefore, if the defense of the United States depended on my marksmanship, our country had better surrender before real war began. This brought the roof down.

Mr. Mike Walsh (known all over Alaska as "Mr. Democrat") came to shake my hand and to congratulate himself because another Democrat had been added to Alaska voters. I told him that I intended to vote "for the best candidates," to which he said, "Who are always the Democrats, of course."

The Pioneers of Alaska were started as early as 1905 as an organization or club to help early miners in distress. At first only those who had been in Alaska in 1899 could belong to the club. As they were dying out, the rules were changed to embrace any white man (*Caucasian* was the word) who had been in Alaska since a later date and finally the rule was passed that any Caucasian male who had spent thirty years in Alaska could belong. Then their wives (if they were Caucasian also) who had been thirty years in Alaska were admitted as auxiliaries. It was obvious that the accent was on being a white man. This exclusion was the cause of royal battles as the years went by, but whiteness prevailed; the reason given was that if anybody who had been thirty years in the land could be a candidate, then every man and woman Eskimo or Indian or Aleut could come in the day they became thirty, and that was not the original purpose of the organization.

There were some conditions attached. Not every white man could join and many were turned down repeatedly. The white man in question had to be of "good moral character." This infuriated some people. What do you mean by a good moral character? The unofficial answer was that if you drink to excess or tamper with your neighbor's wife, it is your own business and the Pioneers of Alaska do not go into that. But if it is known that you ever passed a bad check, then, mister, you are a rat and will not be admitted in the company of honorable men. No, sir.

I was admitted in Nome, where the club started. It spread to all the towns with enough people to assure continued membership. We met regularly. As far as I knew, no other priest had ever bothered to join. Maybe I was a maverick. It gave me a chance to meet gentlemen whom I could not possibly meet otherwise and it gave me a feeling of belonging.

The Catholic church moved into Nome with a great deal of strength from the very beginning. Fr. Jacquet, S.J., a Belgian, and Fr. van der Pol, S.J., a Hollander, had arrived in Nome in 1901. Next year the Sisters of Providence had arrived. The priests had begun building an imposing church with an adjacent rectory in the very heart of the town and next to them the sisters had built a yet more imposing hospital. There were giants in those days in the land.

When I first saw those buildings I was greatly impressed. Considering the fact that every bit of material had had to be imported, it must have been a very expensive enterprise. Yet they accomplished it and probably did not think much of it. Fr. Jacquet must have found it too difficult, though, because he had shown signs of mental disturbance and had been adjudicated to be insane. He had been sent first to Holy Cross and from there to Canada, where he had died in 1922. Fr. Camille, S.J., had filled in his shoes and also Fr. Cataldo, S.J. The hospital did a superb job till 1918, when it was abandoned. Nome by then had dwindled to a small town.

Unfortunately, no sooner had the hospital closed than the Spanish flu broke out all over the Seward Peninsula and many died for lack of medical care.

In 1903 Fr. Bellarmine Lafortune, S.J., a French Canadian, had arrived in Nome, where he was going to remain for the next forty-four years until his death. He outshone all others. We might say that the history of this priest became the history of that region. Fr. Louis Renner, S.J., published recently the history of this admirable missionary in a neatly bound book that is a delight to read. All those imposing buildings were dismantled in time. When the war was over, Fr. Edmund Anable, S.J., acquired two army buildings and converted them into church and rectory. Fr. Lawrence Nevue, S.J., added a spacious hall and bought two buildings near the church. Finally, Fr. James Poole, S.J., built a radio station, KNOM, that went on the air on July 14, 1971.

The church has been doing all she could for Nome from the very beginning. We must add to these accomplishments the establishment of three Little Sisters of Jesus, who built a permanent residence in the heart of the Eskimo quarters one mile south of Nome, where they live with the natives in poverty and simplicity and thus give a living testimony of evangelical perfection. These sisters also spend time in Little Diomede Island.

As pastor of Nome I had to take care also of Teller, of Diomede

Island, and of a couple of military installations in the vicinity. My work was made easy by the presence of Fr. Francis P. Ready, a fine Bostonian priest who had volunteered to work in Alaska. He was a former captain of the marines in the Pacific theater of war. Well, he was actually from Cambridge, Massachusetts, but I could never tell the difference between Cambridge and Boston. He minded the store at Nome while I traveled.

Teller, north of Nome, had a small congregation that was worth cultivating because they had maintained themselves loyal during times when they had not been cultivated at all for lack of personnel. There was always a good attendance. There were also white Catholics who mixed very nicely with the natives and loved to invite the priest to a hot supper.

A priest on the road always welcomes these invitations. Our Lord in the Gospel told His disciples to remain in whatever house received them. He also said that those who take care of the apostle, or invite him to a hot supper in the evening and give him a comfortable cot to spend the night, will receive the reward of the apostle—or words to this effect. The amazing thing to me has been how the Lord touches the hearts of the good people to invite the traveling priest to a hot supper.

God has been doing this for a very long time. In the Second Book of Kings we read about the lady of Shunem who prevailed upon her husband to make a room in their house for the prophet Elisha—a very simple room with a bed, a table, a chair, and a lamp, so the prophet could spend a comfortable night every time he visited the town. For doing this, God blessed the lady first by making her fertile, for she was barren, and giving her a beautiful son. But, alas! The child died. Elisha then made a special trip to the house to resuscitate the child. When the mother took back the baby in perfect health, we can well imagine that she felt that she had received good dividends for the meals she had cooked for the prophet. God also took care of Elijah (or Elias) during a famine by sending him to a Sidonian widow who miraculously kept him alive. And when the Lord runs short of tender-hearted women, He sends ravens as he did to Elias. Those admirable ravens brought Elias bread and meat every morning and evening. And when He runs out of abstemious ravens, He sends an angel as He did to the same Elias. Elias was sound asleep in the wilderness where he found himself running away from the queen who had vowed to cut off his head. The angel of the Lord woke Elias and told him to sit up and eat the bread and drink the glass of water that he had brought him by God's command.

We may not be as holy as Elias and his disciple Elisha, but in God's eyes we are holy enough to prompt Him to come to our rescue every time we feel the pangs of hunger in our insatiable stomachs.

It is worth noting that it is through food that we keep alive. Life is the most precious thing to us, so actually, when someone invites us to dinner, he intends to prolong our life; hence our great appreciation when we are invited to a hot supper in the evening after a hard day's work.

Besides Teller, I had to visit Little Diomede Island which lies half way between Alaska and Siberia. When America bought Alaska from the Russians, the demarcation line between the two nations was drawn between the two Diomede Islands which are separated by only two miles. Their island is almost five times bigger than ours. This line of demarcation is also called the Date Line. They are one day ahead of us.

For a long time after the purchase of Alaska these two islands continued living in harmony like one family. In fact, they were related by blood and commingled as if nothing had happened. Then Stalin came along and passed the word that any resident of Little Diomede caught in Big Diomede would be treated as an American spy. To prove his point, the Russian authorities in Big Diomede gave a bad time to a crew of Little Diomedans who landed there innocently unaware of the new Russian policy. That was the end of all commerce between the islanders. It seems that the Russians also removed the Big Diomedans to the mainland in Siberia and their places were taken by other people who knew nothing of the past between the two.

When the mail plane landed me on the ice surrounding Little Diomede, the island had exactly seventy-nine people, all Eskimos except the school teacher, who was a good-natured gentleman from the Middle West. Seventy of them were Catholic, and the rest were only half convinced that the Catholic church was for real.

My heart sank to my feet when I took a glance at the village. Every house was hanging precariously over long poles stuck between huge rocks. As I walked or rather hopped like a goat between rocks, I noticed that I could not possibly rest my foot flat on any spot. People walk on uneven, steep paths and in lopsided postures balancing themselves the best they can. At first it is very irritating. Then one adjusts.

Other houses cannot be seen and probably should not even be called houses, but huts hidden under the rocks. The entrance is through a tunnel, not an artificial tunnel but a natural one between enormous rocks. As you crawl through the tunnel you come to an opening. By resting your hands on the rock, you climb up and come to an open space where you see bunks, clothes, boots, people, etc.

You discover things gradually as you sit there. The heat is provided by burning oil from the fat of seals. To go outdoors you simply retrace your steps and you find yourself at the mouth of the tunnel. One wonders whether this is America or Tibet. The only flat spot is in front of the school building and very limited. Another flat spot is a small piece of rocky ground by the water where the Eskimos drag in their seals and walruses.

As I looked west, I saw in front of me (I could hit it with a rifle shot) the Big Diomede. I could see the island only, not the town which is built on the opposite side facing Siberia. But our village faces their island, so they built a look-out with glass all around and from there they keep a close eye on everything going on in our village. At times a pair of Russian soldiers with rifles can be seen walking on the ice around their island. Also Russian planes circle around and land on the other side. There is no way for us to see what goes on on that side. One gets the spooky feeling of being in the firing line with no defense other than the might of the United States—an abstraction, that is.

My first question was what on earth were those Eskimos doing in Diomede Island, a veritable mountain of rocks in a rubble formation, when there is so much open space on mainland Alaska. The answer is always the same. Their ancestors settled there to live off the ocean and now their descendants continue living off the same ocean by that law of inertia that keeps things put.

The source of income of those Eskimos was the ivory of the tusks of walruses. This brought them money which they used to buy things in a store they had in their midst, run by themselves. One good-sized walrus alone gave them one ton of food or close to it, and there were herds of walruses. Then the varieties of seals plus an occasional polar bear. Then in June the island crawled with birds, diving birds that nested on the rocks and produced all the eggs the people needed. Then their independence.

Wherever they went on the mainland, they were known immediately as Diomedans. For some reason or other they did not fit too well on land. So back to the island fortress they returned in their skin boats propelled by outboard motors. If the weather was good, a rarity, they got mail by plane once a week. Besides mail, the plane brought in cases of booze that disappeared in a hurry, because they did not stop drinking till the last drop was gone. The night after the plane landed, one heard crying, screaming, wailing, and all sorts of strange noises. When the last drop of booze was gone, the town settled to a most peaceful and amiable state. Life then became a joy.

The chapel of Diomede was built by Fr. Thomas Cunningham, S.J., a native of New Zealand who had grown up in Australia and became a Jesuit in Ireland. He had studied two years of philosophy in Belgium and had come to Spokane, Washington, to study philosophy one more year. From Spokane he'd gone to Holy Cross, Alaska, to teach one year. Then to Montreal, Canada, for his theology. He had returned to Alaska after finishing his studies and settled in Nome, where he had spent three full years studying the Eskimo language which he mastered.

Thence he'd gone to Diomede Island, where he'd built the chapel and converted almost all the Eskimos living there. He'd had a first-class rifle and joined the natives in their hunting expeditions over the ice as well as by boat in the summer. During the war he'd become a chaplain in the armed forces. This gave him a chance to see the other half of the world he had not seen yet. In a navy ship he went from Alaska all over the Pacific, including his native New Zealand, the Philippines, Japan, and back to Alaska, where he returned to his "civilian" status and went clear to Barrow at the northernmost tip of Alaska; there he built a chapel and living quarters.

While he was there he accepted a contract with the government to help spot suitable places on the ice between Alaska and the North Pole to build stations for the Department of Defense—that is, prefabricated buildings resting on floating ice, nine-foot-thick ice, revolving around the Pole. In those stations carefully chosen crews would do research work on weather, the ice, the aurora, plus God knows what other things important to the government. For this he was getting forty dollars a day, which he turned over to the bishop of Fairbanks. He was known as Tom only.

He told me that he was also given the job of screening candidates for those floating stations. This screening was necessary because living conditions on that ice were so difficult that only men with good nerves and well-controlled emotions could stand it. Men with marriage problems, for instance, or idealists or insecure, etc., were automatically eliminated. This is where the sun does not set in six months and does not come out in the other six months, leaving the men in total obscurity. At times the ice breaks into wide cracks right under the buildings or between them. Quick decisions need to be made to move those buildings and where to move them. Special pilots are needed to fly to those spots which are very hard to find. Tom moved in that world as a fish moves in water.

He was a cool man, spoke in a low voice, smoked uninterruptedly, and was generous to excess. He would give away anything he had. That was a virtue carried to excess or so I felt when he came to Nome and gave away a bundle of salmon strips I had just bought from the store at a high price. While he was pastor, he would take up a collection only when he was absolutely broke, so people knew right away his financial status by the collection being taken or not taken. He died of a heart attack at Barrow on September 3, 1959, after having been in Alaska twenty-five years.

We were born the same year, joined the Jesuits the same year, were ordained the same year, and came to Alaska the same year. The Lord kept me here a little longer. Tom was fond of telling stories and it got to the point where one never knew whether he was telling the truth or just spinning a yarn. He was buried in Fairbanks with military honors.

The chapel Tom built in Diomede served its purpose for many years. I spent part of a summer in that chapel, living practically all alone with the Lord. I could not walk outdoors. Periodically, I visited the homes. The people came to Mass where I taught them and explained over and again the articles of our faith. Thanks to the Bureau of Indian Affairs school, they spoke English.

During the day I used to sit in the chapel by a window. With my right eye I was watching the tabernacle on the altar. With the left one I watched Big Diomede. There was Russia with its nearby Siberia and the rest clear to Moscow.

From my window I was also watching the national guard unit of our Eskimos performing over the ice right there where the border line lies—an imaginary line with no visible marks.

The Russians watching over there must have been amused at the performance of those few Eskimos. Someone said that all the Russians had to do to take them all prisoners without firing a shot was to drop several cases of vodka from a helicopter and wait a few hours. Then they could come and handcuff every male without any opposition as all would be flat on the ground talking to themselves. But that would be an act of war and Russia's leaders never tire yelling that Russia is a peace-loving nation dedicated to improving social relations all over the earth.

One day the ice began to crack and next day the ice disappeared, carried by a swift current northward. That was the signal for the Eskimos to get their skin boats and go hunting. One of their biggest boats with eight Eskimos and two outboard motors was getting ready to go to the mainland, specifically to the village of Wales, which is the closest. Would they take me along? Oh, yes, Father, of course. I was anxious to return to Nome, so I went along. To Wales it would be only a little over two hours.

When we were in open water I noticed that they were constantly looking all over the horizon with their binoculars to spot walruses resting over the big ice floes moving north by the strong sea current. I begged heaven from the bottom of my heart to please hide from those Eskimos every walrus on the sea; otherwise our trip would be delayed. Either my faith was deficient or God had other plans of His own. One of the Eskimos yelled and our boat turned north and took up the chase at full speed. Sure enough, as we were approaching I could see big yellow spots over the traveling ice. The engines slowed down. Every man took his rifle.

At least two dozen enormous walruses were sound asleep on the ice or so they seemed to me. But one of them must have been on guard duty, because a grunt was heard and the herd stirred. Just then a barrage of fire was directed at them. They slid into the water quickly, snorting with fury, but half a dozen did not make it.

The men rammed the skin boat over the ice and we all got out. I thought I was dreaming. The men sat on the animals and lit cigarettes in a detached and cold manner. It was obvious that that was their life inherited from their ancestors, and they were merely continuing it and passing it to their progeny in an endless chain.

Those six walruses meant a mountain of meat, but the men wanted only the tusks for the ivory. They also wanted one liver. They chose one of the biggest animals and took off a liver so big and heavy that two men could not lift it; they dragged it and dumped it in the boat. Then with sharp axes they took every tusk to be divided evenly afterward.

I had always assumed that God had given the walruses those beautiful tusks to dig up the clams from the bottom of the sea. An officer of the fish and wildlife service told me that, while it could be so, scientists have come to the conclusion that the walruses pick up the clams with the tough, sharp bristles they have all around their lips.

In one way those tusks turned out to be the walruses' natural enemy. With those valuable ivory tusks, walruses like elephants would have man as their natural enemy. As it is, man is so deadly an enemy that governments have to put limits to man's greed. The yearly harvest of walruses in Alaskan waters is very carefully watched by the fish and wildlife agencies to make sure that a determined number of walruses is permanently kept riding those ice floes.

Those tusks are also used to fight. I was amazed to see walruses hit each other on the neck with such anger. The skin of the old males is covered with self-cured wounds that protrude as nodes the size of big walnuts. To realize how heavy their skins are, it takes eight or ten men to drag one skin. These skins are used to make boats. Only the skins of females are used because they are thinner; even these skins are cleared of half their tissue with careful and patient work.

A full-grown walrus in water is an awesome monster. The men told me about a polar bear crouching on floating ice. He could see nearby on another ice floe a baby walrus that was visited every ten minutes by its mother. The bear figured that he had a good meal ready for him. When the mother nursed the baby and returned to the swimming herd, the bear plunged into the water, grabbed the baby walrus, and plunged in the water again, making for the safety of the ice floe.

But he was seen by mama who yelled and brought the whole herd to her defense. The hapless bear saw himself surrounded by those monsters, who hit him with their tusks and beat him unconscious with their heads. That was the end of that bear. It was also the end of the baby.

Later on our trip to the mainland, more walruses were spotted. We made for them to repeat the operation. Again more walruses showed up yonder in Russian waters. Altogether twenty-nine walruses were killed. The whole operation took a long time. Suffice it to say that the crossing took us exactly thirteen-and-one-half hours.

I said that we were in Russian waters. It was so patent that we could see the western side of Big Diomede. I was expecting a Russian coast guard ship to come out of nowhere and neatly invite all of us to be their guests. This thought did not cross the minds of the Eskimos with me. They had seen the walruses and they followed them, guided solely by their inborn instinct. They were on what they would call open sea and that was that. But the trouble was that that was not open sea, though no one could convince them. I expressed my concern over this but they exchanged a few words in Eskimo and gave me a look of half pity and half annoyance. To them this was another instance of white man's stupidity. The walruses were there for the first man who saw them, and they had seen them first, so, there!

In my imagination I saw the headlines in the papers giving their own account of what had happened. I, being the only white man and a priest to boot, would be assumed to be their leader, so I would be put on the carpet as a prime witness. Of course, the Eskimos could give numerous instances of Russian natives crossing over to our side, and all got away with murder. What is sauce for the goose should be sauce for the gander.

What God and I knew very well was that I had prayed that no walrus be seen in our crossing to the mainland, so I was as innocent as a newly born baby. Right then and there I saw how it could happen that innocent men were put to death as lawbreakers. Fortunately, no Russian boat showed up. I felt in my bones that God had answered my prayer in a different way: Walruses would be seen since they were there already anyway and the Eskimos would not care about imaginary borders; but then no Russian ship would be there at that time quite providentially to enable me to return to the Alaska mainland safe and sound and with a new experience about life in those waters so cold, so lonely, so remote, so filled with ice floes covered with walruses, so dangerous, yet so thrilling, with Siberia on one side and Alaska on the other. Was I the first Spaniard ever on that unseemly spot? And when it was all over, I was glad God had not answered my prayer as I had intended it. God seems to delight in giving me surprises.

Epilogue:
More Missionaries

The Alaska Missions deserve a historian familiar with conditions as they were before the turn of the century and as they are at the present time. Unfortunately, there seems to be no such person. Anyone attempting such history will have to depend on the writings of the early ones, the missionaries. They lived and worked under conditions that exist no longer. Some measure of the conditions under which they had to work can be gathered by learning that in the 1880 U.S. census of Alaska only 33,426 people were counted with 430 of them being whites; all the rest were Eskimo, Indian and Aleut aborigines. This in a land equal to one-fifth of the continental U.S. Every person in Alaska had then almost 17 square miles to himself, so he could wing his arms and breathe with very little interference. Those were the days when Alaska was still very much as she was when she came out of the hands of the Creator. Wild animals were roaming at will: caribou herds followed by packs of ravenous wolves; the moose, the wolverines, the various families of bears; the small and beautiful fur-bearing cuties like the ermine, the mink, the marten, the otter and the red, white, blue and mixed foxes. Any man who ventured into that wilderness had to have a stout heart, the health of a polar bear and the stubbornness and determination needed to meet head-on the brutal forces of nature unleashed on him in season and out of season. The adventurers who did it and came out the victors became thereby fiercely independent, assertive, arrogant, and hard to handle. They came, they saw, and they conquered; that was their badge of honor; no other proof was needed and they demanded a wide berth as they walked. They had arrived at port through uncharted seas; they had blazed trails for others to follow; they had made history, and they had set the pace. They had done all this unaided, so they considered themselves second to none and they would not take orders easily. A new breed of man had come on the scene. It was called the "sourdough," a pioneer or prospector who guided himself by the stars and carried the law in his own pocket.

Against this background we can now see what was in store for the first Jesuits who began to arrive on the Yukon as early as 1887. To Bishop Seghers, who had arrived in Alaska earlier, it meant being shot to death on November 28, 1886.

Frs. Tosi and Robaut had spent that winter in Harper, Canada, living in a log cabin that began to sink. They didn't have enough altar wine for both to say Mass daily. If Fr. Tosi's temper got short, who is there to cast the first stone? When they entered Alaska in the spring of 1887 and saw that the bishop had been murdered, the two Jesuits found themselves cast away in an endless wilderness, adrift in a sea of uncertainty—all alone on the banks of the Yukon, whose muddy waters were flowing totally unconcerned with their worries.

Fr. Tosi was fifty-two, hardly the right age to adapt himself to the new environment. But he did and he was the man who set the foundations on which the Alaska missions were built. He died ten years later in Juneau, a worn-out man.

Fr. Robaut by contrast was only thirty-two. He did not know it, but he had ahead of him forty-three consecutive Alaska winters, commuting between the Yukon and the Kuskokwim rivers.

In 1897, after gold had been discovered at Dawson on the Canadian side of the border, it was estimated that one hundred thousand North Americans made for the gold-bearing creeks, but only one-third of them actually arrived in Dawson. The others either perished in the attempt or turned back or settled somewhere on the way. Those who arrived were the toughies.

When gold was discovered in Nome two years later, many men left Dawson for Nome, crossing Alaska from east to west by dog team in the winter or by boat to Saint Michael in the summer. Some made it; others settled somewhere in Alaska. These men woke up every morning ready to slug it out against man, beast, or the fury of the elements. The survivors showed, in their very eyes, a haughtiness that was considered well deserved.

In 1889 Fr. Ragaru was given twenty dollars to start a mission on virgin soil. As late as 1948 Fr. George Endal was given also twenty dollars to start a parish in Dillingham. He built a school that soon burned to the ground. He rebuilt it, but it soon went up likewise in smoke. The third building he raised remains alive and well to this day. This is easier said than done.

By 1900 there were twenty-four Jesuits in Alaska. All but two were foreigners: hardy people, pious people, priests and lay brothers doing their part to help plant the church in a soil called later by Pope Pius XI "the most difficult in the world." One can't but shudder at the sight of that handful of foreigners keeping their sanity in such a hostile environment.

Not all succeeded. Fr. Parodi was forty-six when he came to Alaska. He found the solitude of Nelson Island too hard to bear for his nervous system, which cracked under the pressure. He was taken to the States where he bounded back so well that he lived to be eighty-three, working all the while with his fellow Italian immigrants in Detroit, Michigan. Fr. Jacquet, a Belgian, also lost his mind for a while and had to be taken out after only one year in Alaska. He was only thirty. He died in Montreal, Quebec, twenty-one years later.

Suffering in many forms was the order of the day. Mail was slow in coming. A cartoon circulated at that time depicted what happened when the expected mail finally did arrive at a mining camp. The crowd in a frenzy attacked the post office and broke the door to pieces. Men fought each other, grappling indiscriminately at beards, throats, hair, or pants and landing clenched fists at random. On the side, two stretchers were carrying dead men. The caption was: "The mail came." The thirst for mail in that isolation became unquenchable. But mail from Europe did not always bring the missionaries good news. They were in their middle age and began to lose their fathers, mothers, older brothers, sisters, or friends whom they had not seen for many years and now would not see again in this valley of tears.

Fr. Francis Menager, a former professor of cosmology and a voracious reader of big books, found himself in Kashunak in 1927 with only one magazine. I believe it was called *General Mechanix*, a thick pulpy magazine full of tools and engines. He told me that he learned it by heart to keep from "going bugs." The winters were long and cold and fuel was hard to get. The buildings were poorly insulated against those abominable blizzards. The winter nights were long, but blazo gasoline or coal oil for the lamps was scarce and expensive.

In those small and faraway villages the missionary trained in logic and theology had no one with whom to converse on a high level. The white man running the local store could very well be an agnostic, or worse yet, an active anti-Catholic who poisoned the natives against the church. Or he could be a pious Catholic who invited the priest for breakfast every Sunday. One never knew what to expect. This constant swimming against the current demanded from the priest a character with as few and small flaws as possible. If he didn't have that, he ran the risk of going under. But when all is told, those few early men, fighting against such tremendous odds, succeeded in planting and nourishing the seeds of what has become the Ecclesiastical Province of Alaska, with one archdiocese and two dioceses. The Lord, who started His church with twelve men, started it in Alaska with a handful of foreign priests and brothers and sisters.

Some of those priests were extraordinary men by any standards and their names will remain in the annals of the Alaska missions forever.

By 1950, of the thirty-seven Jesuits working in Alaska, twenty-six were American born. The church in the American northwest had come of age and had taken over. One feels relief. By 1968, of the fifty-four Jesuit missionaries in Alaska, forty-six were Americans. Alaska was depending no longer on foreign-born missionaries. There is an impressive list of missionaries who have spent thirty years and more in Alaska, and some who went over the forty-year mark. At the same time there is a much longer list of men who spent less than five years there. Actually, twenty-seven of them were in Alaska only one year. Why this great difference?

Some found Alaska unbearable from the very beginning. Everything repelled them. Others had heard and read a great deal about Alaska and they thought that it was worth giving it a try. But the Alaska they found was quite different and they maneuvered themselves out of it rather early.

Others were simply sent to Alaska. They had never asked to be sent. When the sledding became rough, they fell back on the excuse that they had no vocation for it, if that was an excuse. It could be a valid reason, yet the genuine spirit of the Jesuits sees a vocation in the act of being sent. But, again, when the sledding gets tough, the distinction between an excuse and a reason can become very much blurred in the mind. Superiors are apt to remove from the field a man who says that he does not like what he is doing.

Others said that they did have a vocation and went. But in time they developed doubts and began to say that they could do better work somewhere else. By better work they meant that they could give more glory to God and do more for the salvation of souls somewhere else. This could be a purely subjective appreciation, but the man sooner or later found himself working somewhere else.

Others found themselves in Alaska and in their very hearts they did not like it, but they pulled themselves up by their boot straps and worked like Trojans till they died in the harness. It was a revelation to hear Fr. Lafortune say on his deathbed that he had hated every minute he had spent with the Eskimos committed to his care for forty-four years. Someone had asked him if he missed them. This type of answer is not without mystery. Here was an exceptional missionary who was considered highly successful and could be presented as a model to all. His people loved him. He moved in their midst like a venerable patriarch. Why, then, did he utter those words? As I see it, he wanted to imitate Christ who washed the feet of the apostles. So he made himself the servant of those Eskimos. He loves to do it to imitate Christ. He also wanted to be used by God as an instrument to save their souls. He saw these goals as worthwhile and he went all out to attain them.

But he found most distasteful to have to do it the way it was cut out for him to do it. He had to live with them day and night; listen to them in their own language; eat their food, put up with their mentality, their reactions, their ancestral habits, and to do so day after day with no respite. When he came to dying and was asked if he missed them, his answer could be construed as meaning: "Thank God it is all over." One is glad that hardships are over.

But wasn't Fr. Lafortune overflowing with internal joy at the thought that he had done a *good* job? Not necessarily. When Saint John of the Cross was on his deathbed, a monk told him: "How happy must you feel, Padre Juan, at this moment. You have spent most of your life doing so much penance and practicing such high virtues, keeping so much silence and praying so much . . . "

Here the saint broke in to rebuke the monk, telling him to stop that nonsense. He added, "I want you to know that everything I ever did is accusing me at this moment." The saint felt in his aching bones that he had done quite imperfectly everything he ever undertook for the glory of God; everything was now accusing him. Great souls see things under a different light. Or at least certain temperaments react in a way that is disconcerting to the rest of us.

One Jesuit missionary told me that he asked to be sent to Alaska simply because he wanted to stay out of hell. He hoped that doing missionary work for life under such severe conditions would win him those extraordinary graces the soul craves in order to keep on the right path. I must admit that this manner of looking at it left me speechless, but I also bowed to the promptings of the Holy Spirit. He inspires souls and guides them as He sees it, and He is God.

Fr. Gaspar Genna had arrived in Alaska in 1888. Very shortly after arrival he sent a wire to his provincial superior that left no alternatives. It said. "Genna leaves or Genna dies." No superior wants to see a young priest die, so he told Genna to leave for Spokane, where he lived twenty-two more years. Come to think of it, that superior should have known better than to send to the Yukon a priest who was in his forty-sixth year and had come from the sunny skies of Sicily. Superiors have learned many things since 1888.

In 1925 there was the case of Fr. Julius La Motta, S.J. He was forty. He was a linguist. He spoke Latin, Italian, English, Spanish, and French as fluently as anybody. He could make himself understood in German. For pastime he used to read Greek with a dictionary. His provincial superior felt that a man who had such talent for languages would pick up Eskimo in a short time, so he sent La Motta to the Yukon to learn it and then teach it to the newcomers; the word from Alaska was that the Eskimo language was a lulu. Probably La Motta himself welcomed the opportunity to sink his teeth in a language that had no connections with any other known to man. This I don't know.

But what we all know is that he arrived at the port of Saint Michael in the last boat well into the month of October. The mouth of the big river froze early that year, so he had to wait at Saint Michael till the ice was thick enough to travel by dog team. He did not like Saint Michael. One of the best dog team drivers was chosen to take him to Akulurak, where there was a boarding school.

Father was tucked into the sled like a sick person wrapped in blankets. The first day—a very long day for him—was over the ice and through portages covered with soft snow over a flat landscape under a gray sky threatening snow. They reached Hamilton in the dark. There they spent the night. After an early breakfast they took off for Kwiguk, following frozen sloughs and cutting through portages in thick brush covered with soft snow that made it hard for the dogs to make good time. Not one soul was seen all day. The driver told me that every half an hour or so Father would shake his head and say in a low voice, "My, what a country!" There was no conversation between thembecause that Eskimo was the silent type.

After spending the night in Kwiguk, they had an early breakfast and took off for Akulurak after a long diagonal crossing of the mighty Yukon plus portages and lakes and the long Kanelik River and finally they arrived at Akulurak, located on a flat area nowhere on the map. Father got out of the sled and walked into the house in a stupor, like a man who walks into a cemetery where he sees a gaping grave waiting to be occupied.

The local superior, Fr. Lonneux, tried to revive him with thunderous laughter and much patting on the well-padded shoulder, but La Motta had arrived already at the conclusion that that was not for him. He wore skin boots outside of the chapel to keep his feet warm, but he considered it irreverent to say Mass in such footgear. He lived practically in his room. Yet the sisters told me that he was the most courteous man, most delicate, soft-spoken, a true gentleman, extremely neat and the soul of kindness. Had his provincial superior been acquainted with conditions in northern Alaska, most likely he would not have sent such a man to such a place. Fr. La Motta left Alaska in the first boat, late next June, and taught languages at Gonzaga University in Spokane. He died in Seattle in 1952.

Fr. Charles O'Brien, S.J., formerly of the British navy, arrived in Akulurak in 1921. Next year in the spring he made the month-long trip to Nelson Island with eight dogs and with Mike Tuyak as guide. On the return trip the weather got warmer, so he followed the sled with his coat over one shoulder at first and then with no coat at all to walk lighter. He got a cold. When he arrived in Akulurak his whole body began to suffer from rheumatism. It got worse as the weeks went by. He sensed that he would die soon, but insisted that he be taken to California. He wanted to feel the heat of the sun and—above all—he definitely did not want to be buried at Akulurak. On the fifteenth of June Bro. Murphy took him out in the mission's river boat to meet the N.C. boat that would take him to Saint Michael, where he could take the *Victoria* on her way to Seattle from Nome. All very carefully planned. On reaching the Yukon they were invited aboard the government boat run by Cal Townsend, the official inspector of fisheries in that area. Mrs. Townsend prepared a delicious dinner. Fr. O'Brien ate to his heart's content and went back to Brother's boat to continue the trip. Within half an hour he was dead. Just like that.

So Bro. Murphy turned around and went back to Akulurak, where Fr. O'Brien did not want to be buried, but where God had decided—or permitted—that he be buried. He was the first missionary buried there. Five years later he was joined by Fr. Jette. And in 1940 they were joined by Bro. Keogh. The bodies of those three Jesuits are there, totally abandoned now that the school has closed and moved to Saint Marys and the spot is the domain of mice, weasels, rabbits, and land otters. In the summer the numberless ponds surrounding the place are the oasis of geese and ducks of all varieties. Red foxes also roam those flats.

Fr. O'Connor and I were commenting once on the apparently little progress we were making with our missionary efforts. There was a lull in the conversation. He broke it by saying, "All right, you take the present missionaries out of Alaska overnight and have us replaced by an equal number of priests, brothers, and sisters brought in from anywhere on earth and see if they do a better job." It was well said; at least we both felt better.

Weren't there some saints among those missionaries? Sanctity can be an elusive thing. We are dealing here with many imponderables.

I was told repeatedly that Fr. Treca was never seen angry. Never? That's right. I made it a point to clarify this. No one ever saw him angry. And he was a Frenchman. Aren't Latins known for getting easily excited? The first question asked when a cause for beautification is presented at the Vatican is whether the person controlled his temper. If the answer is no, the process ends right there. If the answer is that yes, he did control it, there is this further question: How often did he fail? It is assumed that sanctity in an adult cannot be attained without a temper. It is through a well-controlled temper that the saint goes to battle against the three enemies of the soul. A person without temper is a spineless eel. If a person *habitually*

controlled his temper, that person won the first round for his canon-
ization. *Occasional* loss of temper is more or less taken for granted. So.
Fr. Treca would breeze through the first requisite for sainthood. Saint
Jerome had a hard time controlling his temper. The poor doctor of the
church had to live surrounded by Eastern monks who made fun of
Rome just to get Jerome's goat. He had enemies in Rome, too, who
made it a point to anger him, so he dished it back in kind.

Fr. Treca made the month-long trip to Nelson Island when he
was seventy-two, a real record in the annals of the Akulurak mission.
One month on the frozen trail sleeping in Eskimo dugouts and baptizing babies all along. He spent thirty-seven years in Alaska. Bro.
Keogh told me that one morning Fr. Treca came for breakfast with a
sort of halo, his face flushed with reverential awe and his eyes ardent
with indescribable joy. The two of them were alone in the kitchen.
They looked at each other as if they had never met. Fr. Treca lowered
his voice to a whisper and said, "Brother, this morning at the moment
of consecration as I held the Host, I saw the face of our Lord smiling
at me. It wasn't the only time." That was that. Take it or leave it.

Father William Judge, S.J., was only forty-eight when he died in
Dawson. After six years with the Eskimos and Indians of Alaska, he
crossed into Canada following the miners of the Yukon gold rush so
he could be of spiritual help to them. He built a church and a hospital.
It is my understanding that the hospital building was damaged by a
fire and that he rebuilt it in a hurry. The miners needed a hospital, so
he had one ready for them. Those miners were not saints, but they
could tell a saint when they saw one, and every miner referred to Fr.
Judge as "the saint."

They knew very well what *they* were after. They had come to
Dawson to get gold and get rich and have a good time. They also
knew what it was that *he* was after. He had come to Dawson for
purely supernatural reasons. He was working harder to save their
souls than they were to dig gold. With *them* it was a mixture of greed
and adventure and they were wallowing in riotous living, whereas
he was solely dedicated to do good to them by preaching with word
and example.

When the hospital he built ran out of beds for so many sick
miners, he gave his own bed to one of them and slept on the floor
where he caught the pneumonia that killed him. His funeral was the
loudest sermon on Christian charity ever preached that far north in

our hemisphere. The history of Dawson cannot be written without mentioning Fr. Judge, "the Saint."

Sanctity is soon recognized, but its degree is known to God alone, and in the Last Judgment mankind will be treated to some mighty big surprises. The church canonizes men and women not to prove that they are the holiest people of their time, but to put before our eyes, as examples to imitate, men and women who excelled in virtue to a heroic degree. Perhaps there were others more perfect yet in God's eyes. The church does not go into that. Other missionaries left Europe for the Far East in the time of Francis Xavier. Other priests worked with blacks in the time of Peter Claver. Many Carmelite nuns struggled to keep the Rule of Saint Teresa of Avila in the past century just like the Little Flower did. But these three were the persons canonized among their peers. Others, to my knowledge, were not. I am talking about so-called "confessor" saints, that is, saints who died quietly (or not so quietly) at home without shedding their blood for Christ.

Sanctity could be compared to a selected group of Olympic runners or swimmers. All perform extremely well, but there is always one who tries a little harder; drives himself a bit faster; puts more of himself into what he is doing and so he comes out the victor. Even in a horse race, one horse may win by "a nose." So it is with holiness. This particular person concentrates a little more in the presence of God; loves God with a little more intensity; shows more loyalty and delicacy and finesse in his dealings with the Lord; says or hears Mass with more attention and devotion; rejects temptations faster and with more vehemence; prays for his enemies more sincerely; throws himself more wholeheartedly into the service of others. Others do all these things and quite well but not as well as the saint does them. It is a question of coming out the victor by a nose or even by a hair.

God alone has seen the interior trials and ordeals of those early missionaries and how and for how long they sustained them. Each one was given a cross to carry. We all have our individual crosses. There is no doubt in my mind that those early missionaries, who blazed the trails for us, carried their respective crosses following quite close in the footsteps of the Master.

Segundo Llorente, 1906–1989